NOT COUNTING TOMORROW

The Unlikely Life of Jeff Ruby

By Jeff Ruby and Robert Windeler

Printed in the United States of America

ISBN 978-1-4675-9348-9

Front Cover Photo by
Ross Van Pelt
Back Cover Photo by
Jeff Swinger, Cincinnati Enquirer. Used with permission.

Dust Jacket Design by
Mike Meiners
Copy Editing by
Saundra Sheffer

Published by Black Tie Press,
A Division of Black Tie Productions, Inc.
P. O. Box 14527
Cincinnati, OH 45250

www.blacktieinc.com
www.jeffruby.com

FOREWORD

By Cris Collinsworth

I'm still mad. The name of this book should be *Runaway Success*. Not since Huckleberry Finn has a runaway kid told a story of adventure like this. The "book people" thought that *Runaway Success* sounded like another one of those "get rich quick" books. But, anybody who knows Jeff Ruby knows that this is one of the most unlikely stories of a runaway who succeeded imaginable.

Fresh material on Jeff is not hard to find. Jeff asked me to be a celebrity roaster at one of his charitable events. Usually, those roasts are filled with boring recycled jokes and canned material. This one was televised with national celebrities like Michael Douglas, Brent Musburger, and Nick Lachey doing the roasting. Every story was about a zany first-hand personal experience with Jeff, and each was more incredible and entertaining than the one before. As you listen to Jeff Ruby stories, you have to remind your brain not to think, "There is no way that really happened!" It did! Most Jeff Ruby stories start with the line, "You're not going to believe this, but…."

For example, I once jumped into perhaps the most shark-infested waters in the United States to save Jeff's burgeoning butt. We were in Florida to check out a restaurant named Yesterdays as a possible model for The Waterfront, and had stopped into a nice waterfront bar for a drink. Jeff asked the waiter where Yesterdays was, and he said, "Heck, you could swim there. It's just across the Inter-coastal." He pointed across the water. After a few jokes about Shamu the killer whale and Jeff's inability to swim (despite growing up at the Jersey Shore), we moved on to other subjects. Next thing I remember was hearing this huge "SPLASH!" Jeff had not even bothered to remove the jacket of his $2,500 suit. He made it about twenty-five feet before he started to struggle. He was swimming with only one arm, having dislocated his shoulder on the dive in. I threw a plastic garbage can at him, thinking it might act as a life preserver. It sank to the bottom. Jeff started to yell for help. The restaurant and bar emptied out to watch. One guy jumped in and I followed. I had already decided that if this was a joke, I was going to drown him my-self. It wasn't.

We somehow got this former Cornell defensive lineman back up on the five-foot-high dock. It was exhausting for everyone. As we sat there trying to catch our breath, the bar owner came by to tell us we were all kicked out. He also took great joy in telling us that we had been swimming in the most shark-infested waters in the United States, because each night at closing time the restaurants dumped all of their leftover food into the water. Whenever something splashed in the water, it didn't take long for the feeding frenzy to be-gin. I punched Jeff on his dislocated shoulder. He almost got us all killed!

When we finally got back to the hotel, Jeff started hyperven-tilating. We thought he was having a heart attack. We called 911 and the paramedics arrived. Jeff was breathing into a bag when a paramedic asked him what was wrong. Without removing the bag, he yelled, "IT IS MY TOE!" What???? Jeff had a splinter in his toe from the boat dock. I punched him again.

Or how about this one? I was twenty-five years old when I first met my future wife, Holly. Jeff had told me Holly was thirty years old and had two kids. Jeff also had said that Holly's ex-husband was a friend of his. I almost cancelled our pending date. In reality, Holly was twenty years old, had just graduated from college, was on her way to law school, had never been married, and had no kids. But I didn't know all that. As we drove to dinner on our first date, I told Holly that Jeff Ruby had mentioned that he knew her ex-husband. Holly responded to that absurdity with a look of disbelief. Not picking up on her astonishment, I innocently proceeded to ask about her advanced age and her non-existent children. Luckily, Holly wasn't driving. I kept thinking I really should have let those sharks have their Ruby snack that night in Florida. The fact that Holly eventually married me was the single greatest come-from-behind victory of my life.

Most lives produce a handful of stories that you remember. Jeff generates one per week. Don't believe me? Start reading.

INTRODUCTION

I'm Still Standing

Elton John, 1983

I have a habit of asking some of the employees in my restaurants, "How long have you been working for me? … Not counting tomorrow."

When I ask this I'm kind of kidding. No one's job is in jeopardy, at least not at that moment. My more serious underlying message is that tomorrow is not promised to anyone—certainly it hasn't been to me.

In 1987, I leaped out of a moving car after an argument with my wife, who was driving. I was declared brain dead and not expected to live. It was only the most serious of six decades' worth of setbacks that have required me to constantly reinvent myself and to succeed in spite of whatever fate handed me.

I've been in two comas, three deadly fires, and was a key figure in two race riots. I lost 20 percent of my brain in Cincinnati and 20 percent of my blood in Louisville. I nearly drowned in shark-infested Florida waters when I was drunk. When I was eight, it took 250 stitches to sew me up after a close call in the ocean at Miami Beach. I survived a private airplane crash in Chicago, had a Colt 45 put to my head in an armed robbery (and I still refused to open the safe). I suffered a brain seizure while driving alone on the I-75 bridge crossing the Ohio River, collapsed in the car and woke up in the hospital. For good measure, I've had five angioplasties and a heart attack. If a cat has nine lives, I'm one lucky cat because I'm sixty-five years old… not counting tomorrow.

Boomer Esiason, my friend for almost thirty years, calls me

"unique and unexplainable" and says that I have a way of "landing in situations that defy logic."

To say that I grew up poor and rootless is an understatement. I never knew my real father, and my four stepfathers were sorry substitutes. My mother was both problematic and alcoholic, so I left home at age fifteen. Nonetheless, as the owner of a succession of eateries, she was my inspiration to own my own restaurant. (She never got to see even my first one, having died at the age of fifty-eight.)

Neither of us ever could have imagined back in Asbury Park, New Jersey, that I would get more money to put my name on a restaurant than anyone in America. Why shouldn't I be able to negotiate better deals than celebrity chefs? They're better chefs than I am, but they are busy selling salsas and salad dressings, and their time is consumed on television. I have better restaurants.

My eateries and my employees are the best. Zagat voters rank two of my steakhouses the best two in America.

I know how fortunate I am to be alive, and I know whom to thank for that. I'm grateful to be successful, and I know who is responsible. I believe God played a part in saving my life–as did two brilliant neurosurgeons and one equally skilled cardiologist. My success in the restaurant business is, without question, the work of the team I have always considered my family–our employees. For me to be the best I could be, they had to be the best they could be. Collectively they are the reason I'm still standing and our restaurants are still standing.

Every steakhouse, five-star gourmet restaurant or river restaurant that has attempted to compete with us has closed its doors. When Morton's came to town, they had brand recognition and big money behind them for marketing and buying power. They were Goliath and we were David. Goliath had size but David had balls. It's the same as in sports: balls beat size every time.

I don't know what's next for me. Hardly a day goes by that I'm not asked, occasionally with much earnestness, to open a Jeff Ruby's Steakhouse in some city. I sit and listen to the developer, landlord or investor, and then I tell them the same thing I tell my advisers: I have no game plan. God is my tour manager. He will let me know when I'm ready, rested and good to go—and where.

Music has always been an important part of my life, as a listener, performer and restaurateur, from the 1950s forward. That's why I've chosen song titles from the soundtrack of my life as chapter titles.

CHAPTER ONE

BORN TO RUN

Bruce Springsteen, 1975

Funny, this song was written by another kid from Asbury Park, who once worked a block from where I did. In different ways, we both escaped.

When I was born in Newark, New Jersey, on April 19, 1948, I was named Brian Jeffrey Kranz. It was a normal birth. I was a healthy ten-pound, six-ounce, blue-eyed baby. There was one serious complication: neither of my parents had blue eyes.

I suppose I came as a surprise to my mother's first husband, Lou Kranz. For the first seventeen years of my life I believed he was my dad, although he and my mother lived apart. I didn't understand why he didn't stay in touch with me and never came to see me, even though he lived only forty-five minutes away.

My brother Wayne Kranz, being six and a half years older, remembers my beginnings better than I do: He told my co-author, Robert Windeler, "My father and mother and I lived in a five-story walkup apartment building in a Jewish ghetto neighborhood in Newark, New Jersey, when Jeff was born. My parents fought so much my mother kept a separate apartment in Newark and would go there with baby Jeff when things got bad. Three years after he was born, my parents divorced. I stayed with my father. Our mother took little Jeff and moved to Florida, where she opened a restaurant. She married a Floridian who had restaurant expertise, Walter Ruby, and they came back to Jersey. They opened a luncheonette in Newark, and both worked very hard at it."

My working mother was lucky I wasn't murdered on the streets of Newark by the time I was six. She didn't pay much attention to where I was or what I was doing.

She had four husbands. America has its forefathers, and I have my four fathers. I don't think of any of them as stepfathers, because none of them ever stepped up to be a father to me. I guess since I wasn't really their son, they chose not to be my dad. Wayne finally told me, when I was a senior in high school, that his father, Lou Kranz, was not my real father. Now I didn't even have an older brother, only an older half-brother.

Whenever my mother remarried or was between husbands, we moved from town to town in New Jersey. I recall riding with her to Miami Beach in her search for Walter Ruby, in an attempt to bring him back to Jersey. Like detectives, we drove up and down the streets off Collins Avenue, looking for the place where "Grandma Ruby" lived.

Living with my mother, I could see why she went through so many husbands and countless boyfriends in between. The former Miss Newark was beautiful, glamorous and flamboyant. My ex-wife Rickelle told Robert, "When I first met her, I thought she looked like Jayne Mansfield."

My longtime girlfriend, Susan Brown, also met my mother later in her life and described her to Robert, as "great-looking, with big chocolate-brown eyes and the clear, smooth skin that Jeff has. When Leanore walked into a room, she owned it. Just like Jeff does."

Mother was extremely argumentative and had a drinking problem. By the time I got home from school in the afternoon, she had already had too much to drink. All she wanted to do was argue with me. It was never about my grades or anything substantive. She also argued over nothing with her husband of the moment. Many nights,

My mother, the former Miss Newark

before I went to sleep, I would pray to God for Mommy and Daddy to stop fighting. I tried to tell my mother that she could get along with "Dad" if she didn't let so many things make her mad. I badly wanted for my parents not to fight. I would beg them to stop, crying the whole time. My childhood and how I grew up may have caused issues with commitment for me, allowing someone to love me, or even feeling I deserved to be loved.

One day, when she had been through her third husband and her fourth Seagram's VO on the rocks, she started in on me. (Her marriages and her VO were always on the rocks.) She began ranting about the Neptune High School football game, which she had heard on the radio. (Mother never bothered to show up to our games in person. Even when I was co-captain of our undefeated team in my senior year and became first-team all-state, she didn't come to one single game.) Listening to the game on WJLK, she hadn't liked the way Neptune had played, and she blamed it all on our coach, "Jeep" Bednarik. I was only a sophomore at the time and hadn't even played in the game!

That day became the first day of the rest of my life. I was only fifteen years old. After the argument, which ended with me throwing a jar of spaghetti sauce against a wall, I went to my bedroom, locked the door and packed whatever would fit into a small white suitcase. I jumped out of the window. I saw a Good Humor ice cream truck, and I ran until I caught up to it. I climbed aboard—despite the powder-blue sticker on the side of the truck that read "No Riders." I peeled the sticker off and stuck it onto my little white suitcase. I kept that suitcase with its sticker for more than twenty years to commemorate that day I broke free—until it burned up in a house fire.

The ice cream truck took me as far as Route 33. As I walked along that highway, I sang, to myself, "Bye, Bye, Blackbird": "No one here can love or understand me…."

The only thing I would only miss was "Oxford," the stray dog I had found on Oxford Way and kept.

(Nearly thirty years later, a kid named Jack Armstrong came to Cincinnati as a rookie pitcher for the Reds. He was from Neptune and was married to my friend Dick Davis's sister. Jack told me that the Davis family had found and kept Oxford. That kid from Neptune was the first rookie to become a starting pitcher for the National League All-Star team, and Manager Lou Piniella used me to get inside my friend Jack's head. Jack Armstrong was different, like me. He was a Jersey boy.)

I walked a few miles from Neptune to the Asbury Park YMCA, where I checked in. On my way I had walked past Brockton Avenue. I decided to call myself Larry Brockton, because I didn't want my mother to find me. I needn't have bothered. She never came looking for me.

For my final three years of high school, I lived alone and supported myself. Although I didn't have anywhere else to go, I didn't want to stay at the "Y" longer than one night. The only other place I could think of was the beach. I walked from Main Street to the Asbury Park Boardwalk and checked in "Under the Boardwalk," recalling the lyrics to the Drifters' hit: "You can almost taste the hot dogs and the French fries they sell." How many of those dogs and fries had I sold at Syd Goldstein's place, not so far away? I thought to myself that I could have inspired that damn song.

For a few weeks, I slept—blanket-less—on the sand under the boardwalk in Asbury Park, each day walking the five miles to Neptune High School. A scene in *The Sopranos* shows Tony and his soldiers walking directly over my "bedroom." *The Sopranos* series rang true to life for me: it was filmed in four Jersey cities or towns where I had lived.

I slept right on the sand and used my little white suitcase as a pillow. It was hard, but it beat the sand. I didn't have many clothes, but I did have $600 I had saved from working at the Perkins Pancake House on Asbury Circle.

Eventually, I rented rooms in various rooming houses where elderly folks lived. We all shared a bathroom down the hall. I graduated from Neptune High, went on to Cornell, and came to Cincinnati and became JEFF RUBY. (My last name is my only legacy from my mother's second husband).

When I came out of my mother's womb with blue eyes, my fate was determined. I was born to run and I never looked back—until now.

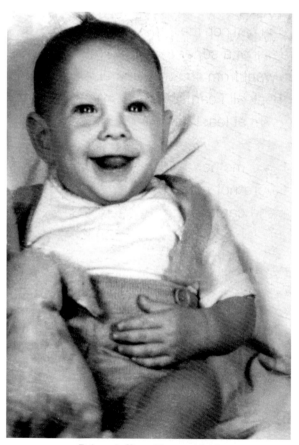

Brian Jeffrey Kranz,1948

CHAPTER TWO

NO SON OF MINE

Genesis, 1992

In 1999, "He Didn't Have to Be" was a number-one country hit for Brad Paisley, from his critically acclaimed platinum debut album, "Who Needs Pictures." The lyrics tell the story of a boy who gained a stepfather and everything the man had done for him.

> "I met the man I call my dad when I was five years old.
> He took my mom out to a movie and for once I got to go
> A few months later I remember lying there in bed
> I overheard him pop the question and I prayed that she'd say yes
> And then all of a sudden it seemed so strange to me
> How we went from something's missing to a family
> Lookin' back all I can say about all the things he did for me
> Is I hope I'm at least half the dad he didn't have to be."

None of my mother's four husbands treated me like a son. The first three were not married to my mother long enough. When her fourth husband came along, I was already in college and it was too late.

Lou Kranz looked at my baby blue eyes and knew I wasn't his son. He divorced my mother when I was three, and I never heard from him again until I was seventeen. My brother Wayne told me that Kranz (his father) owed a lot of money to bookies in North Jersey. I knew little else about him.

One night he showed up at my rooming house in Ocean Grove. It blew my mind when I saw him walking up the stairs to my floor. The only thing he had come to say was that I should move back with my mother. He didn't want to go out and get something to eat. He didn't even want to see my room. He just ordered me to go home. I ordered him to get the hell out of my house. I told him, "For fourteen years you haven't called me once, come to one of my games, taken me to a Yankee game, asked how my grades were or sent me a birthday card. Get out of here!"

It was a week or so later that Wayne told me that Lou Kranz was not my father. "We felt it would be better for you if you didn't know this growing up," Wayne said. He told me that my biological father was Louis Weiss, a prominent Newark attorney my mother had once worked for as a secretary.

I remembered Lou Weiss. He came to my bar mitzvah with his wife. I never contacted him and never told my mother I knew he was my father. I wanted nothing from a father who wanted nothing to do with a son he had brought into this world. I also wanted to remain self-reliant. But at least now I knew why my mother called me a "bastard" whenever she lost her temper and yelled at me. It was true.

I never felt any resentment toward my real father, any of my stepfathers, or my mom. I just kept looking forward to the future. The Bible said, "He is the fool that looks behind." Ann Landers said, "Hanging onto resentment is letting someone you despise live rent-free in your head."

My best friend in high school, Bruce (Boopy) Hoffman, told Robert that he didn't recall ever hearing me "complain about not having a father, or resenting those of us who did. In fact, he never seemed to envy anyone who had anything more than he did."

My mother's second husband was Walter Ruby, who owned a "greasy spoon" luncheonette on Raymond Boulevard in downtown

Newark. I was about six or seven years old and hung out there every night while he worked behind the soda fountain. He was the only person I can remember working there. I don't know what my mother was doing at the time or why I wasn't with her. My brother Wayne was living with his dad.

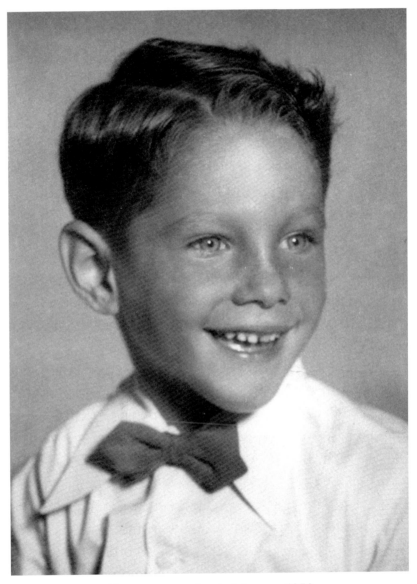

My grammar school picture, c. 1956

Most of the time I hung around outside the joint by myself. My only positive memory of that time is of Steve the cop and his horse.

Steve kept me company and talked to me when he saw me alone at night. Steve told me about the scary guy known as The Bogeyman. He pointed out the big building where the Bogeyman lurked and said I should stay away from there. For a long time I thought the Bogeyman was from New Jersey.

My strongest memory of Walter Ruby is of the braided metal belt he used when he put me over his knee to spank me. He never used his hand. He always took off his belt, took off my pants, and whipped my butt with whatever belt he was wearing. I dreaded the days when he was wearing that braided metal belt.

Walter Ruby gave me the name I carry to this day, and not much else.

My mother sent me to a summer camp for Jewish kids for a few years. One summer she called me at camp to tell me that she had divorced Walter Ruby in Mexico. The next summer she called to tell me that she had married Syd Goldstein, the Hot Dog King of New Jersey. My first words to her were, "What, didja feel like a hot dog, so you married him?"

Wayne recalls that "Syd's in Newark was across from Weequahic High School, in the upscale Jewish section of the city. The author Philip Roth lived there, and he later wrote about it. Syd was famous for his boiled kosher hot dogs. He also had a hot dog place in Bradley Beach, known then as Bagel Beach, across from the Boardwalk, in the Lorraine Hotel. It was open only in the summer, when the Newark store across from the high school was closed."

I went to work for Syd at his stand in Bradley Beach when I was twelve. He had three custom, stainless, water-bath pots: one boiled the franks, another held them, and the third gave him the option to do either. He speared each frank out of a pot with a fork and onto the bun. He used the same fork to apply mustard, sweet or hot relish and sauerkraut. No one else worked his station. He was fast. The faster he was, the more hot dogs he sold. He also took the money and rang the cash register.

When things slowed down I got to work "the pot," and it was the thrill of my life. In Syd's lingo an MK meant mustard and kraut; an MO was mustard only. "Hot works" meant everything with hot relish; "sweet works" was everything with sweet relish. Few patrons ordered their hot dogs "naked."

When someone ordered fries we yelled "drop one," meaning into the French fryer. The fries were served in a small brown paper bag. They were the best of all time. Jersey Boardwalk Fries are still on my restaurant menus today, prepared just the way Syd made them. I peeled, cut and blanched the potatoes in the back room with a few other guys, all of them black, every day. It was hot back there. Syd was a nice man who worked very hard. He liked professional sports and classic cars. He had a 1957 Chrysler 300F and an old black 1940-something Cadillac with running boards. Like all my stepdads, Syd never had kids of his own.

I got the scare of my life one night when I was still living at home with Mom and Syd. At around three or four in the morning, a policeman woke me up. Police had come in the past to break up fights between my parents, but this was different. Syd had been attacked just outside our front door, and his face and white hair were covered with blood. Someone had taken the cash from his restaurant sales that he had been carrying in his bank bag. When the cops asked if I had done it, I got into my first cop fight. Someone had watched Syd's routine after he closed and followed him home. He survived the mugging, but every dollar he had worked for that day had been stolen.

When it came time for my bar mitzvah, Mom was still married

to Syd and she wanted me to use their last name, instead of Ruby. So, by day, at grammar school in Ocean Grove, I was Jeff Ruby. After 4 p.m., when I attended Hebrew school in Asbury Park, I was Jeffrey Goldstein. I was twelve and already had an alias.

Dancing with Mom at my bar mitzvah, 1961

Since I was a "runaway" during my last three years at Neptune High School, they wanted me to see a school psychologist. He said to me, "We have to find the real you." By then I had been using four names, so I said, "You're not kidding. Under what name do you wanna start looking for me?"

Having been born Brian Jeffrey Kranz, then becoming Jeff Ruby and Jeffrey Goldstein (for a time, simultaneously)—and later Larry Brockton when I was hiding from my mother—I wasn't too sure myself about where to start looking. But I graduated from high school as Jeffrey Brian Ruby--and I've been Jeff Ruby ever since.

Dancing alone, a metaphor for what was to come?

13

By the time my mother married Lieutenant Leon Wurzel, at the Alameda Naval Base in California, I was at Cornell. Leon was a wonderful man, and my mother had finally found her soul mate. I wish she had met him thirty or forty years sooner, because she was so happy with him. I wish he could have been my stepfather when I was a kid. They moved to Sea Bright, New Jersey, where an episode of *The Sopranos* was filmed. I stayed with them when I visited from Cincinnati.

Mom was dying of ovarian cancer at Riverview Hospital in Red Bank, when she was only fifty-eight years old. I flew to New Jersey to see her one last time. I took Rickelle with me. She remembers the circumstances better than I do and told Robert this story:

"I had flown home to Cincinnati for the weekend, from touring on the road with my musician fiancé. Jeff and I were just getting to know one another. He asked me to do the craziest thing—to fly to Jersey with him that same weekend, because his mother was dying. He wanted to assure her that he had settled down with a nice lady. I said, 'You want me get on a plane tomorrow, to go there and pretend to this woman that I am your fiancée?' He said, 'Yes. I'm asking you to do this because she's dying.'

"I protested that I hadn't brought any clothes home with me suitable for meeting a mother. I said I would want my own room and that we would not be sleeping in the same bed. He promised to get me my own room, and he bought me an outfit to wear to the hospital. The first night we stayed in New York, and the hotel had only one room for us. I hit the ceiling and said, 'This was not the agreement. This was supposed to be a quick in, meet your mother, and then I'm going back home.' He said, 'I'll sleep on the floor'—which he did. The next morning we got up and drove to Sea Bright, where we stayed with Jeff's stepfather, Leon. Jeff and I pretended to be a couple, but we slept in separate bedrooms.

"When I met Jeff's mother, I just adored her and decided to spend the whole weekend. She was so excited and happy that Jeff and I were 'engaged' and her son was settled and she could let go. That was probably the weekend I fell in love with Jeff, because when I saw how moved and sensitive he was and how much effort he put into making his mother happy just before she died, I saw another side of Jeff Ruby and came back feeling completely different about him. I broke off my engagement and immediately starting dating Jeff."

* * * * *

When I got to the hospital, not only did Mom not have a private room, her bed did not have a view of the Raritan River. That bothered me. I walked around her floor and saw an empty room with a beautiful river view. I returned to her room and pulled a Michael Corleone. I pushed her bed into the empty room and told the nurse I would pay for the upgrade. I was then making $18,000 a year. I didn't know if the nurse had seen *The Godfather*, but she watched me with her eyes and mouth wide open in amazement as I maneuvered the bed through the hallway with my mother still in it.

Mom was so happy she had a river view. But she had it for only two days.

I left my mother when I was just fifteen years old, and now she was leaving me for good. My mom was there the day my life began, and I needed to be there for her the day her life ended. Like the 1967 Beatles film, my life had become a *Magical Mystery Tour* of sorts. And from the soundtrack of my life, nothing was more important to both of us than for her to know before she died that I still loved her, and always had. "Your mother should know, your mother should know."

CHAPTER THREE

GREETINGS FROM ASBURY PARK

Bruce Springsteen, 1973

Whenever I answer the question, "Where are you from?" with "Asbury Park," the inevitable response is "Bruce Springsteen!" It's unlikely that any other city or hometown would immediately trigger a person's name in that way. I was working at a joint called The Wonder Bar, down the street from The Stone Pony, when I first saw Bruce perform in the late 1960s. I have always had a good ear for music, and I knew back then that this guy was special.

The Wonder Bar, which had the longest bar I have ever seen, is where the late, great tenor sax player Clarence "Big Man" Clemons played before he decided to take a look at Springsteen at a club called The Student Prince. The Wonder Bar's owner was John Stamos, a man in his thirties, who took a liking to me. He was a man's man, a Greek with olive skin and big forearms. I looked up to him, and he treated me the way I treat kids today—with respect.

When I was seventeen, I often went to a bar called The Orchid Lounge, an R&B joint where a black guy played a Hammond B-3 organ and sang soul music. I didn't drink. I just liked the music. The place catered to middle-aged blacks, and the only time I saw a white person in the place was when I looked at myself in the men's room mirror. The Orchid Lounge was on Springwood Avenue, which was then considered America's most dangerous street, even though it was the main road connecting Asbury Park to Neptune. Most whites were afraid to drive it, never mind walk it. I walked it often and was the only white person on the street, all the way to Neptune. It was the shortest way between my two towns, and I liked the fear factor, living on the edge. Even when I went to The Orchid Lounge one New Year's Eve wearing my bathrobe, the blacks didn't give me a hard time. The blacks never gave me a hard time. The whites thought I was living dangerously. I guess I was.

I also hung out at Freddie's on Asbury Avenue. Freddie's served the best pizza I have ever had. Right down the street was Carvel, my favorite soft ice cream. Danny DeVito was always there. Farther down, on Asbury Circle, was the Perkins Pancake House, where I worked all through high school. I was a master "eggologist." I could crack four eggs at a time, two in each hand. The owner of the New York Jets, a Mr. Hess, was a Perkins regular.

I revisit our Asbury Park apartment building

Starting when I was eight, we lived in an apartment building called the Miramar. It's still there and doesn't look any better now than it did in 1956. My mother, who was still married to Walter Ruby, owned a restaurant at the Kingsley Arms Hotel, where I hung out all day. There was no Pop Warner football or Little League baseball in my childhood.

When that restaurant didn't work out, Mom took over a closed dress shop in downtown Asbury Park and turned it into a coffee shop. She named it The Press Box, since it was right across the street from the daily newspaper, *The Asbury Park Press*. My mother designed all her restaurants, and for this one she lined the walls with black and white murals of journalists at their desks. Her slogan was "Where Food is News." The Press Box became one of Asbury Park's longest-running restaurants, woven into the fabric of the city's downtown business district. Even after Mom sold it, it remained successful—until all of Asbury Park became a ghost town in the 1970s.

In the 1950s and '60s, casual restaurants like Mom's were known as coffee shops. They didn't serve alcoholic beverages; none of my mother's restaurants did. But The Press Box was known for its ice cream: parfaits, milkshakes, malts and sundaes. Every ice cream company wanted the account. Now, instead of just hanging around Mom's restaurant, I had a job—tasting ice cream from the various purveyors. Dolly Madison was usually the best. Forty years later, I told my lender, Carl Lindner, that story. He turned to his wife, Edith, and asked, "Honey, didn't we used to own Dolly Madison?" They did.

One day I got the idea to walk across the street to *The Asbury Park Press*, buy a stack of papers at wholesale, and sell them in the bars of Asbury Park at the newsstand price. I didn't have a bicycle then, but most of the bars were close by. I made very good money for my age, a lot more than the kids who were selling lemonade. I had no competition, whereas our neighborhood had lots of lemonade stands.

From the time I was eight, I was never a "me-too" kid. I have always been a nonconformist. My childhood is why I became an advocate for the underdog. I was the only Jew in my school or my neighborhood from fifth grade through high school, and the only Jew on the Neptune High football and wrestling teams. I was proud of that; it made me unique, it made me tough, it made me who I am today.

In Jersey all the kids were Yankee fans; their hero was Mickey Mantle. I was a Cincinnati Reds fan; my hero was Frank Robinson. When the Reds traded him to Baltimore, the Orioles became my favorite team in the American League. In 1999, Frank Robinson came to the opening of Jeff Ruby's. When I gave him one of our baseball caps with the Jeff Ruby logo, he asked me to autograph it. It would never have crossed my mind when I was ten years old and the biggest fan Frank had in New Jersey, that he would one day ask for my autograph.

My favorite basketball player when I was growing up was Oscar Robertson. Now he eats at my restaurants and we smoke cigars together.

* * * * *

On February 3, 1959, when I was still ten years old, I was standing outside The Press Box on Cookman Avenue, when I heard about "the day the music died," as Don McLean wrote in "American Pie." An airplane carrying Buddy Holly, the Big Bopper, and Ritchie Valens had crashed in a snowstorm at Clear Lake, Iowa, killing all three singers. Ritchie Valens was my favorite for a number of reasons: he was underrated, as I realized even then; he had achieved success when he was only seventeen; as a Mexican-American he was a member of a minority; his big hit "Donna" was my favorite

19

song; and, unlike Elvis Presley, he wrote his own music. He wasn't very good-looking, but he had talent, unlike the manufactured pretty teen idols of the day. I cried like a baby when I heard about that plane crash.

I remember saying a horrible thing to my stepfather, Walter Ruby, at the time. I told him that I wished it had been he and not Ritchie Valens who was on the plane. I guess it was my way of telling Ruby what I thought of him as a father. He left us about a year later, anyway.

One of Ritchie's other big hits, "La Bamba" (actually the flip side of "Donna"), was covered much later by Los Lobos for the movie of the same name, in which Valens finally got the credit he deserved. Rick Dees was in that movie. Today Rick is a friend of mine who introduced me to Robert Windeler, my co-author.

The Press Box was a few doors down from The Upstage, which became the headquarters for the musicians who formed Springsteen's E Street Band. Bruce really got the ball rolling at The Upstage because the musicians could jam there until 5 a.m. Danny Gallagher, all 300 pounds of him, always had my back when I was little and other kids tried to beat me up. Once at The Upstage he was playing Monopoly, and Bruce joined him at the table and sang. It still seems odd to think of Danny Gallagher playing Monopoly.

When I was eleven, my mother married Syd Goldstein, who was established as the Hot Dog King in nearby Bradley Beach for the summer. Besides his frankfurters and French fries, Syd served up the best cheeseburgers and onion rings in the business. Quality food, I learned at that young age, does not have to be gourmet or expensive; quality food just has to be done the best way it can be done. Nobody else makes hamburgers the way they were made back then, but my restaurants still do.

That year I was eleven, I found a friend in a thirty-three-year-old man from the Bronx named Ray Franco. He was the one who gave me my penchant for street fighting. He was short but stocky—and fearless. He was the toughest guy I ever met. One day, some six foot five guy walked by Ray and me in front of Syd's. He was in his twenties and was either a college football lineman or a weightlifter. He weighed about 240 pounds and it was all muscle. Ray was about five foot nine and weighed about 170 pounds.

Ray, for some reason, picked a fight with the big guy; I think it was over a girl. I begged Ray not to fight this huge jock because I figured this guy might kill my hero right before my eyes. When it was all over, I called an ambulance. They carried that giant away, and Ray and I each had one of Syd's hot dogs. I thought that was pretty cool. It was Jersey Shore decades before *Jersey Shore*.

We moved out of Asbury Park the next year, but only one town over, so I still considered Asbury Park one of my two hometowns, and it continued to be part of my life for another ten years.

The summer I was twenty and home from Cornell, an Asbury Park cop who liked me, Billy Cello, approached me at The Wonder Bar. Billy was a short Italian right out of Central Casting, and a terrific guy. He was also a wrestling promoter. Billy and The Wonder Bar's owner, John Stamos, thought that I, having been both a football and wrestling star in high school, would be a big draw on the card at an upcoming event at the Asbury Park Convention Center on the Boardwalk. The bouts would take place before I had to return to Cornell for football practice. I told Billy I was interested. It would be exciting to be a pro wrestler, even for one night. It paid good money, and I was broke.

However, Billy then told me that the winner of the match was always predetermined. Competing at the time were Haystacks

Calhoun, who weighed about 500 pounds; Bruno Sammartino, who could throw me into the Atlantic Ocean; and such other bruisers as Argentina Rocco, Arnold Skolin and The Sheik. Billy told me I would definitely be the loser. My opponent and the money, we would discuss later. I told him I would think about it.

I had taken one dive in a wrestling match in high school, in order to get into Cornell. Was I now going to take another dive as a wrestler, just to be a big shot and make some money? What if my Cornell football coach found out? I turned down Billy's offer to be a professional wrestler.

In 1970, race riots in Asbury Park portended the death of the city. Springwood Avenue was virtually burned to the ground, and our seashore resort quickly deteriorated and emptied out. Springsteen left for New York City and I took a job in Cincinnati. Although Asbury Park has been making a comeback in recent years, at least until Hurricane Sandy hit in 2012, nobody has received a "Greetings from Asbury Park" postcard from me—or from much of anybody else—since.

CHAPTER FOUR

VALLEYS OF NEPTUNE

Jimi Hendrix, 2010

From the ages of twelve to fifteen, I lived with my mother and Syd Goldstein in a red-shingled house in Neptune, the small town just west of Asbury Park. Neptune was the Roman god of the sea, but the town wasn't by the ocean. We did have the Shark River, a tributary to the Atlantic, where we went crabbing. I observed something when I was crabbing in sixth grade that stayed with me forever. When our peach basket was full of crabs, every time a crab was just about to make it out of the basket, the other crabs pulled it back in. The crab at the top was never allowed to escape. It must be tough being at the top, I thought, even if you're a damn crab.

I also remember that a fellow sixth grader killed himself by slitting his wrists in the boys' room. I didn't know him and I couldn't understand why he would do such a thing. We students had no grief counseling sessions, nor even a moment of silence for Mike Christie. No one in authority—no teacher or principal—told us students about his death, We heard about it by word of mouth, almost as if it were a secret and had never really happened.

My seventh and eighth grade classes were held at an old building in Ocean Grove, another town adjacent to Asbury Park. My two best friends there were what we still called "colored" kids: Gus "Pops" Lane and Ricky Freeman. I would take them home to our house in the all-white neighborhood of Asbury Gables, right behind Fitkin Hospital, where Jack Nicholson was born. I was the only resident who ever brought colored kids into one of those houses. Pops and Ricky helped me finish off my bar mitzvah cake. I often heard the other kids call me a "nigger lover."

At temple, during receptions every Saturday, I drank wine in the basement and was getting drunk when I was only twelve.

Ocean Grove Elementary, where I spent grades 7 and 8

At about that age, I started working as a cook at my mother's restaurant. I also worked at my stepfather Syd's hot dog place in Bradley Beach on the same days, about a ten-mile bicycle ride away. Jack Nicholson was a lifeguard on that beach. Neither parent paid me, but I had room and board and ate for free at both restaurants.

After she sold The Press Box, my mother rented an empty corner building on Main Street just outside of Asbury Park, in Allenhurst, and gave it her inimitable touch. She created the most elegant coffee shop anyone had ever seen. She called it The Grapevine. Her décor was built around grapes and the color purple. One wall was covered entirely in purple velvet, bordered with braided gold rope and tassels.

Standing outside the building that housed my mother's restaurant, The Grapevine

All of her triple-decker sandwiches were named for grapes: The Tokay, The Concord, The Gamay, and The Muscatel. The cover of her menu opened upwards, and on the front were three illustrations. At the top was a ringing telephone, in the middle was a Western Union envelope, and on the bottom two women were depicted sitting at a table and gabbing away. These pictures represented the three ways that news back then was "heard through the grapevine": telephone, telegraph, and tell-a-woman.

Mom went through chefs the way Imelda Marcos went through shoes. I studied under each of those chefs. I was so young, impressionable and cocky that I figured if I took the best from each of them I would be a better chef than any one of them individually. I learned one thing that has stuck with me. A waitress once asked one of our cooks if he would prepare something a customer had requested that was different from the menu. The chef responded, "I'll put this hamburger in a malted milk shaker can and throw it on the blender and make a hamburger malt if that's what the guy wants." I have known chefs who wouldn't steam Alaskan king crab legs because they were offered on the menu only as a cold appetizer. I learned, at age thirteen, from that Grapevine cook, to give the customer what he wants the way he wants it. That philosophy, "Guest First," became our Jeff Ruby Culinary Entertainment company policy.

I loved cooking at The Grapevine, and I loved all the waitresses, especially Connie. The Grapevine employees were really the only family I ever had. Now I understand why the employees at my restaurants are my family today, and why I love them so much. Maybe that also explains why I was the first—and maybe the only—restaurateur to provide 100 percent free medical insurance for every employee, even the dishwashers, at a cost of hundreds of thousands of dollars a year.

From The Grapevine's Cuban dishwashers I learned "kitchen Spanish," so I could tell my seventh-grade classmates where to go and what to do with themselves in Spanish. To this day I have a special relationship with our Hispanic employees, who are in every department of the company and include our corporate executive pastry chef. They are terrific people to work with. I love cutting up with them in Spanish the way I did back in Jersey.

I opened my own first "restaurant" when I was twelve. The food at our elementary school cafeteria was so-so at best. Some of us kids would sneak out to a deli to buy submarine sandwiches, but we usually got caught. I got caught so often I ran out of chances. So, I decided to make myself an Italian sub at The Grapevine and take it to school. I put Genoa salami, prosciutto and gabagole (cappicola) on a baguette, added lettuce, onion and tomato, and topped it with oregano, red vinegar, and olive oil. The "sub," also known as a hoagie, was, in my view, perfected in New Jersey. It was torpedoed somewhere west of the Delaware River and is now sold across America at Subway sandwich shops. However, Jimmy John Liataud replicates "Jersey Jeff's Subs" pretty well and delivers the sandwich faster than I could.

My fellow seventh and eighth graders saw me eating my sub every day; more important, they could smell it. They all wanted one, too. The cafeteria lunch was 35 cents, so I priced my submarine sandwich at 65 cents. My philosophy hasn't changed in 53 years: price yourself higher than the competition and provide a much better product. It works just as well today as it worked for kids in 1961. As my friend Joe Deters told Robert, "Jeff's not afraid to charge."

I was selling so many subs I was called into the principal's office. He said I was hurting the school's food income and I would no longer be allowed to conduct business at Ocean Grove Elementary. Only twelve and I was already having problems with my "landlord." I still regard most landlords as school principals. However, no one can negotiate with an adult like a kid. I reminded the principal that he was still getting the side dish, soup, milk and ice cream sales. He agreed to allow me to stay "open."

One morning when I was thirteen, I had an intuition during first period that something was wrong at The Grapevine, so I asked permission to go to the restroom. Instead, I headed to the pay phone in the hallway. Connie answered my call and said that the chef hadn't shown up. My mother wasn't at the restaurant, and they didn't know how they could be ready for lunch. I hung up and did not return to class.

It was about a five-mile run down Main Street from Ocean Grove to Allenhurst, with Asbury Park and Loch Arbour in between. I had to get to The Grapevine fast, so I could bring up lunch by 11:30. My biggest challenge would be making soup from scratch, something I had never done before. It would also take the longest preparation time. I looked at a cookbook and decided my first soup would be split pea. I got it going and walked into the cooler to find some meat to toss into the pot for flavor; I settled for a leftover hunk of pastrami. Then, in our larger front kitchen, I had to peel skirt steak off its membrane and cut it into steaks for London broil. Onions and tomatoes had to be peeled and sliced, and egg salad made.

When I returned to the tiny prep kitchen to check on my soup, I saw a new chef walking around. He had been sent by the New Jersey State Employment Department. My mother had called the employment office from home. I was relieved, and I hoped to learn from him just as I had from our other chefs. But when I looked at my simmering soup pot I couldn't believe my eyes. My soup had changed color from pea green to chartreuse, and I couldn't figure out why. When I asked the new chef how that happened, he said he had added milk, as he always did to pea soup. I told him this was my pea soup, not his. I took off down the street to the grocery store and returned with green food coloring. When he wasn't looking, I doctored his doctoring and got the putrid color back to a reasonably close pea green. When I asked him why he had put milk in my soup, he answered, "Because I'm the chef."

"You're not any more," I retorted. I had fired my first chef, at the age of thirteen. More than fifty years later, I'm still firing chefs. They still don't get it.

Gui Bordeaux was a French-Canadian chef who worked at The Grapevine. We all felt he was the best chef we'd ever had, and we'd been through plenty of them. Gui told us he was a former NHL hockey player with the Montreal Canadiens. He stood six foot three and weighed about 220 pounds, had silver-gray hair, broad shoulders and a face marked by distinctive scars along his chiseled chin. He was the kind of man a fatherless boy like me looked up to. I idolized him, and he became my first real father figure.

When Gui and my mother began having an affair, I pretended I didn't know. I prayed that they would get married so he would be my dad. Mom was still married to Syd Goldstein, and Syd knew about the affair. I saw him confront her about it, and it was ugly. I couldn't understand why my mother had married Syd. She was gorgeous and flamboyant. He was much older, short and heavy, with white hair. He cooked hot dogs for a living, maybe the best in America, but still hot dogs. Gui was handsome, and both he and my mother were real culinarians. They also looked good together.

But this restaurant romance turned into a "reduction" of Bordeaux. The Grapevine lost its chef and I lost my father figure.

About a year later, Gui called me at The Grapevine. He and two friends had opened a new club in North Bergen, New Jersey, and he wanted me to come visit him. Buddy Hackett, one of America's most famous comedians, would be performing at their club that night.

I took the next train to Jersey City. I was thirteen years old. Changing trains, I walked past a *Jersey Journal* newspaper rack. The main headline read something like "Three Mobsters Arrested." But what really caught my attention was the mug shot. It was my father figure, "Gui," but the name under his photograph was different. My hero was one of those mobsters. He had been using an alias.

When I got to the club in North Bergen, there they were, "Gui" and his partners, Frankie and Jimmy, both Italian. My first words to my hero were, "I read about you in today's paper." The three of them began laughing. They acted like it was no big deal.

"You hungry? What do you want to eat, Jeff? "Gui" asked me. I ate five or six steaks that afternoon. Their chef was terrific. He cooked my steaks directly on an open burner, without a frying pan. I couldn't believe it. They tasted like they had been charcoal-broiled. That night I sat in the club and saw Buddy Hackett.

The scars on my father figure's face were not from playing hockey; they were a byproduct of his time in the North Jersey mob. I would never again see the only man I had ever looked up to, or who had invited me to spend time with him. Years later, "Unanswered Prayers," a number one hit for Garth Brooks, got me thinking: What if my prayer that Gui and my mother would get married had been answered? She would have married into the Mob!

In the 1960s, the Mafia was rampant in New Jersey, especially North Jersey. The mob dealt mostly in gambling, loan sharking and extortion. Police and politicians were paid off, so they caused the Mafia no problems. Gui and his guys were real-life Jersey "Sopranos." Decades later, David Chase masterfully portrayed them and their milieu in his HBO series, which was filmed in towns I lived in: Newark, Long Branch, Sea Bright and Asbury Park. Three of the series' stars visited our restaurants. Lorraine Bracco (Dr. Melfi, Tony Soprano's psychiatrist) had dinner with me at our Cincinnati steakhouse. Jamie-Lynn Sigler (Tony's daughter Melanie) ate at The Waterfront. Dominic Chianese (Junior Soprano) came to Jeff Ruby's Steakhouse in Louisville for two nights during our first Kentucky Derby Week. When he arrived at the restaurant, he asked to meet me—by name. This often happens with celebrities coming through Louisville and Cincinnati.

One afternoon in 1961 I took my mother's '57 Caddy and drove from Neptune to New York City. I was thirteen at the time. Somewhere along the Garden State Parkway, over the sounds of Newark's own Frankie Valli and the Four Seasons (the original "Jersey Boys"), I heard a siren. In the rearview mirror I saw a state trooper and I pulled over. I wasn't speeding, so I figured my mother had reported her car stolen. I got out of the car and met the trooper face to face on the edge of the Parkway. He informed me that New Jersey law required that the left lane was to be used only for passing. I apologized and he let me go, without asking to see my license.

In Manhattan I passed by Gallagher's steakhouse on West 52nd Street. From the sidewalk I could see their beef sitting on shelves behind large glass windows. I thought that was so cool and vowed that if I ever owned my own restaurant I would do the same thing. Thirty-nine years later, I did open my own place and returned to Gallagher's to find out how they dry-aged their beef. Their assistant general manager was also named Jeff. He took me inside their dry-aging room and answered all my questions. I offered him the position of general manager at my first Jeff Ruby's Steakhouse. He was ready to come to Cincinnati, but his wife didn't want to leave New Jersey. I could relate to that. (Gallagher's is still on 52nd St. in New York in 2013, and it still has steaks displayed in the window.)

When I was fourteen, I quit working at Syd's hot dog stand and took a job at a restaurant down the block for 65 cents an hour. To get there, I rode my bicycle ten miles from home. After work, at around two o'clock in the morning, I rode back.

I entered ninth grade at Neptune High School while I was still living with my mother in the Asbury Gables subdivision. It was a middleclass all-white subdivision then, but it has since become all black. I visited the neighborhood recently. The lady who lives in our old house was kind enough to allow me to come inside. It still has the same deep red shingles it had in 1961. In fact, every house in the Gables was the same color it had been in 1961. But everyone living in those houses was a different color from the 1961 inhabitants.

My freshman year at Neptune, an interracial school with sixteen hundred students, was a disaster. I had no direction, ambition or goals, and you can't reach a goal you haven't set. I was a loser and

Our red-shingled house in Neptune, unchanged in 50 years

at a time when Jews were no more popular than colored people. My algebra grade was 50 percent, a solid F. I was dropped down to a basic arithmetic class. Since I was the only white in that class, I was therefore the dumbest white kid at Neptune High School.

My best friend all through high school was Bruce "Boopy" Hoffman. He told Robert how we had first bonded in middle school in Ocean Grove, as sports fans, and later spent way too much time at Monmouth Raceway:

"We just connected, right from the start. We were both interested in horses and liked to go to the track, although he was much bigger at the track than I was. He was taking book on the Kentucky Derby in 1963, when he had just turned fifteen. In high school, every morning he'd hand me the sports page of *The Newark Star-Ledger* as we passed each other on my way to study hall."

I went out for the baseball team and didn't make it. So then I went out for freshman football. Everyone who went out for that team made it, but forty-four kids were picked ahead of me. There were two of us left, but only one jersey. I don't remember the story, but my former teammate, Doug Irvin, does. He told Robert:

"In September of 1962, we freshman practiced in an empty lot with no grass, across the street from the high school. The freshman coach, George Washington, was a tall, burly black man. He was a former Army colonel and a talented, polished, well-groomed gentle-man. The varsity coach, Jeep Bednarik, was in a class by himself. He raised football at Neptune to a new level, but Washington gave us all the basics as freshmen and didn't get enough credit for it.

"I remember vividly that Jeff was one of two guys left at the end of tryouts, and that there was just one jersey left. He and the other boy were both defensive linemen, and Coach Washington was trying to be fair, like you do. He set them up on opposing sides of the line and asked them to try to block each other. The player who pushed the other one back the hardest, in three out of five tries, would make the team and get the jersey.

"Jeff was a roly-poly kid at the time, not fully matured the way some of us were, but he showed his determination on that dirt field. He pushed the other kid back into the dust three times, until Coach said, 'OK, Jeff, you've got it.' Jeff had something in him, even then, like a reserve tank that allowed him to come through in the end. I don't think Jeff really cared about making the team. He just wanted to win the fight."

At our forty-fifth high school reunion, Doug re-told the story of how I'd just barely made that freshman team and said to me, "Look how far you've come, from the last kid to make the freshman football team to the best player in our senior year and all-state, then on to Cornell and where you are now."

I was the worst player on that freshman team, a second-string center, and I seldom got into a game. Boopy remembers one time I did. "Either our center got hurt or we were winning by so much that it didn't matter, so Jeff went in at center," he told Robert. "I was the quarterback, and in those days we were usually just about right underneath the center in "T" formation—except when we were kicking for an extra point. We'd just scored and now we're going for the extra point. I'm not under the center, I'm the holder, and I'm six or seven yards back, waiting for Jeff to hike me the ball. He just hiked it to me as if I was under center. I saw the ball go right under his butt, with him thinking my hands were going to be right there to get it. Walking off the field, I asked him what had happened; we were going for the extra point, and I wasn't right under center. He said, 'You sounded like you were a little far away.'"

Boopy told Robert that "the maturation that Jeff made between our freshman and senior years in high school was just astounding. Everybody changes and grows in those four years, but it was astonishing just how far he went. Jeff made a much greater leap than anyone else. He went from sitting on the bench when he was a freshman to making all-state when he was a senior. I think that was the harbinger of a lot of things that were to come. He made up his mind that he was going to be a good football player. He had a great drive to succeed. The seed was planted for his going to Cornell and into the restaurant business, and succeeding. He got a lot more serious about his grades between his freshman and senior years. He improved dramatically every single year. By the time he was seventeen, Jeff was a changed person. His being one of the hardest workers ever started back in high school, but little did I know where it was going to take him."

Today, I'm in Neptune High School's Sports Hall of Fame. I tell my kids, the kids I mentor, my employees, and anyone else who wants to listen to my advice: "If you want to be a winner I can help you. If you want to be a loser I can't stop you."

CHAPTER FIVE

RUNAWAY

Jon Bon Jovi, 1984

Jon Bon Jovi is from Sayreville, New Jersey, minutes away from West Long Branch, where my brother Wayne attended Monmouth College and where I learned who my real father was and wasn't. Bon Jovi's first hit was "Runaway," which hit the charts on my 36th birthday, in 1984. Five years later, Bon Jovi had dinner with me at my first restaurant, The Precinct, as a guest of Q102 Radio, which was promoting his tour. And when my house band's hand-picked keyboard player, Jeff Kazee, left town who did he go play for? Bon Jovi, of course.

Before I left my mother's house for good, when I was fifteen, I had already run away from home a few times and slept in the woods. One night when the ground was wet I slept in a discarded shopping cart. Another time I got so mad I punched a framed picture and cut my finger on the broken glass. I took myself to the Fitkin Hospital in Neptune, where they stitched up my finger. They also left the glass in my finger.

I don't recall my mother ever discussing my running away or any of our problems. I suppose she felt it was a waste of time.

Word inevitably got out at Neptune High that I was living under the Asbury Park Boardwalk. Gale Catley was one of my friends who found out about my "home" situation. She was one of the most popular kids in school and a very good student. Gale's father, Haddy, owned some rooming houses for the elderly in Ocean Grove and wanted to help me out with a place to live. He gave me a helluva deal on the room. I paid him eight dollars a week. The room was about 8'x10' and was furnished with only a bed. The bathroom was down the hall and all the tenants shared it.

Haddy Catley was a wonderful man. He didn't have a son but he supported Neptune's athletic teams. He bused every football player from the school's ninth through twelfth grades to Philadelphia's Franklin Field to see my final game for Cornell University, a victory over the University of Pennsylvania. He even treated the kids to a filet mignon dinner after the game.

Ocean Grove was and is a Methodist community. Thousands of Methodists come from all over to an annual worship retreat in its outdoor pavilion. As probably Ocean Grove's only Jewish resident ever, I was again in the minority. Eventually I bought myself a small motor scooter. No motor vehicles were permitted in Ocean Grove after midnight Saturday, as Sunday was sacred. So, when I got off work at two in the morning, I parked my scooter in Asbury Park and walked across the bridge over the lake that separates Ocean Grove and Asbury Park.

Ocean Grove is still advertised in 2013 as "God's one square mile of happiness," and for me it was. I ate many of my meals at Nagle's, the drugstore across the street from the rooming house. They had a soda fountain with stools at the counter. On Thanksgiving Day the drugstore was closed, so I walked to the intersection of Routes 35 and 33 and had the turkey dinner special at The Neptune Diner. Nagle's drugstore is still there, and I took my kids to see it, and where I had lived.

People were very nice to me those three years in high school, but I worked hard, too. I cooked breakfast at Perkins Pancake House and also worked there after school, on Saturdays after our games, and on Sundays. The barber wouldn't take my money for haircuts, and one day when I got to my "winter apartment" (after the summer tourists had left), which did have a kitchen, it was stocked with food. My classmates had put together enough to feed me for weeks.

Mary Anne Valente, who taught English at Neptune High, lived in the same rooming house as I did during my junior year. So did Jerry Carroll, our JV coach. He drove me to school. Mary Anne was in her early twenties and had an apartment with a kitchen, next door to my room. I spent a lot of time in Mary Anne's apartment watching TV with her, since I didn't have a television. Rumors, all false, swirled about Mary Anne and me, decades before teachers "home schooled" their students in sex education.

My home alone, the rooming house in Ocean Grove

"Jeff wasn't in any of my classes, but he was a football player and I kind of knew who he was before he moved in next door to me," Mary Anne told Robert. "We became friendly, and he'd come to my apartment most nights. We'd cook together, because I had a kitchen. We'd make mac and cheese or scrambled eggs, and sometimes we'd cook a chicken and potatoes. He would study while I graded papers. I helped him with his English, and he became an "A" student in his senior year.

"One day I came home from school, and there was this woman standing outside my door. She was gorgeous, with black hair and eyelashes out to here. She was a big, imposing woman, dressed to kill, with a wonderful figure, thin legs and wearing high, high-heeled shoes. She asked me, 'Are you Mary Anne Valente?' When I said 'yes,' she said, 'I'm Jeff Ruby's mother and I'm going to sue you for alienation of affections.' I was stunned at first, and then I invited her in to talk about it. I assured her I was not taking away her son or doing anything with him that I shouldn't be doing. By the time she left, we were the best of friends, and we remained that way. We'd go out to dinner often for the next couple of years, and she came to my wedding. That was the last time I saw her, because I moved away, and then she got sick and passed.

"All I had known about her before I met her was what Jeff used to joke about her: 'She has a wash-and-wear wedding gown' or 'Her marriage certificate is made out "to whom it may concern," ' because she was married so many times. That was his humor.

"His mother, Lee, was like a female Jeff, very demanding, a drama queen who needed a lot of attention. She was also a very smart woman who was concerned about her son and loved him. There was still a bit of friction between her and Jeff, but that eased as my friend Betty Sieburg and I got to know them both. Betty, who taught French at Neptune, and I acted as buffers between Jeff and Lee."

Betty recalled to Robert, "Once we even drove up to Cornell in my little red Volkswagen with Lee and Syd Goldstein, all four of us stuffed into that tiny car, to spend the day with Jeff.

"We called Jeff 'Mr. Big Time,' but not always to his face. It was more an affectionate nickname we used when we were talking about him. He was always in the middle of things. I co-signed the loan for Jeff's motor scooter, which annoyed my fiancé, but Jeff paid me back."

Those two young women drove me to Ithaca, New York, to visit Cornell for the first time. Betty and Mary Anne were great to me and great for me. We stayed in touch. They came to my sixty-fifth birthday party in Cincinnati, almost fifty years after we'd met.

My senior year in high school, I moved to a room in a house in Asbury Park owned by the mother of Bernie Milmoe, who had been a star football player at Asbury Park High, Neptune's archrival. Bernie was a linebacker and a real animal. He was a senior when I was a junior—the year we beat Asbury Park. He was still living at his mom's after graduation, and I was concerned that he would report to the authorities that I was living down the street from Asbury Park High School and should be going to their school and playing for them. (I rode my motorbike past Asbury Park High every morning on my way to Neptune High.) Bernie never said anything to anyone. I was paying his mother rent.

By then I had made quite a name for myself along the Jersey Shore. I had made many friends by then, too. It was only after I left home that my high school friendships began to take shape. I was even voted King of the Senior Ball. My date, Cindy Herbst, was the Queen. (I had never even been to a prom before.) Most important, I co-captained our undefeated Group IV football team in our senior year with my best friend, Bruce "Boopy" Hoffman. He was our quarterback and a point guard on the school's basketball team. Doug Irvin was another close friend. He was my teammate on both the football and wrestling teams. His dad was a former Methodist minister, who also mentored me. None of my high school friends smoked cigarettes. None of them ever got into trouble, and all of them had good grades. Drugs? Forget about it! When you raise yourself like I did, you can raise hell. I did raise hell, but I did it all without drugs, cigarettes or alcohol.

Although the newspaper was unaware of my unique living

King and Queen (Cindy Herbst) of the Senior Ball

arrangements, *The Asbury Park Press* couldn't write enough stories about me. One article was captioned "Student, Gentleman and Athlete." I was proud of that one in particular. In football I made first team all-shore which covered three counties (Monmouth, Ocean and Atlantic), and I made first team all-county and The *Newark Star Ledger's* first team all-state Group IV, which included New Jersey's largest high schools. I made second team all-state in the *Newark News*, which didn't break down the groups by school size.

I didn't know it, but my friend Bill Findler's mother was keeping a scrapbook of my articles and photos. She gave it to me for graduation. I hadn't seen most of them, and those I had seen I hadn't kept. (The book was destroyed when our house caught fire decades later. So was my little white suitcase with the "No Riders" sticker. In fact, I lost just about every memento and keepsake I had, but I got the kids and Rickelle out, then went back and got Tucker, my Rottweiler.)

Neptune High School's undefeated football team, 1965. Doug Irvin, standing top left in glasses; Bruce Hoffman, standing third from right; me, bottom, sitting second from right

By 1966, since I was the most publicized athlete in the three-county area, my mother decided she wanted me to move back home. She accused the school system and the team's Boosters of paying me. My mother said I was a "paid athlete" in high school, and she may have been the first person to bring this subject to the public forum. She was ahead of her time. Mom couldn't believe I had able to support myself all those years by working at Perkins. She never did know that I had saved $600 before I even left home.

When I was seventeen, Sonny Herbert, the school's truant officer, drove me to Freehold to see if a judge was going to make me move back to Neptune and live with my mother. Sonny would be making his recommendation to the judge on behalf of the school. I had no idea what he was going to say.

My mother's attorney was the first to speak, having been coached by my mother: "Jeff Ruby is a paid football player and wrestler at Neptune High School who is living in Asbury Park." That wasn't a bad opening, I had to admit. The lawyer went on to say that since I was seventeen it was illegal for me not to be home with my biological mother if she wanted me home. He added that she had never abused me and had no police record.

It didn't look good for me. I had run away from home, and my mother, a homeowner, wanted me back.

Then it was Sonny Herbert's turn. He wasn't even a lawyer. "Judge," he said, "when Jeff Ruby was a freshman he had F's and was sitting on the freshman football bench. He needed a change of environment and rented a room and supported himself. He has held a full-time job at Perkins Pancake House for four years, now has straight A's, was co-captain of Neptune's football team, made first-team all-state, is currently unbeaten in wrestling, has never once gotten in trouble, and is a model student. He's better off where he is now than where he was before."

The judge agreed, and Sonny drove me "home" to my rented room in Asbury Park.

My football weight was 190 pounds. When my senior wrestling season started. I needed to lose 15 pounds to make weight, since I was slated to wrestle at 175 pounds. My close friend and teammate, Doug Irvin, was moving up to heavyweight, and I would take his old spot. But Jeep advised me to give up wrestling my senior year because the necessary weight loss would lessen my chances of getting a football scholarship anywhere. I was already relatively small at 5 feet 11½ inches and 190 pounds. I didn't go out for wrestling senior year.

Harry Schaeffer was Neptune's head wrestling coach as well as our running back coach. Jeep had brought him along to Neptune from Pennsylvania. Coach Schaeffer wasn't happy about my decision, so he spread a rumor that I didn't go out for wrestling because I was afraid Joe Bongiovani would beat me out. Joe was a big, tough, Italian kid who played tackle on our football team. The rumor spread throughout the school, and kids confronted me with it all the time. After two months of this, I couldn't take it anymore. Coach Schaeffer's strategy had worked. The season had already started. Joe was in wrestling shape and he was winning. I had a lot of catching up to do and now twenty pounds to lose. Jeep just shook his head. I defied my hero, but I got down to 175 and won back my spot. I went unbeaten and was ready for the state tournament.

My grades got better every year. I had failed my freshman year, but after living on my own I finished my sophomore year with an 84 percent. My junior year I reached 90 percent and then 94 percent my senior year. My first Rubyism was, "Privation is the bread of the strong."

Being a runaway was good for my athletic life, my work life, my social life and my grades. I've never regretted it.

CHAPTER SIX

FATHER FIGURE

George Michael, 1988

George Michael worked as a waiter at his father's Mediterranean restaurant. The father fired his own son for serving too-large portions too often. As a singer George had better "chops" than he served at his father's restaurant. The song "Father Figure" went to number one on Billboard's *pop charts.*

I never heard from my first father figure, "Gui Bordeaux," after his arrest. He was in the North Jersey Mafia, so there is no telling what happened to him. I had idolized him before I knew who he really was. Believing that he had once played hockey for the Montreal Canadiens, I bragged about it to my friends when I was eleven years old. And when someone told me that they had checked and could find no Gui Bordeaux who had ever played for the Montreal Canadians, I just figured he hadn't looked hard enough. Gui's talent as a chef impressed me, but what really made me look up to him was that I literally had to look up to him. He was about 6 foot 3 inches tall. He was the kind of man that a boy wants for a dad, a man's man. Best of all, he took a liking to me.

Only one other man took me places with him when I was growing up: Bob Juska. My mother dated him, and I think he was divorced with a son much older than I. Bob was Catholic and took me to church with him. He was a florist whose Arcadia Flower Shop was next door to the restaurant my mother owned in Asbury Park. The sign in his store window proclaimed, "Say it with Flowers." He was a wonderful man. I remember one day we played putt-putt golf together somewhere far from home.

At Neptune High School, when I was fifteen and living alone

away from home, John "Jeep" Bednarik entered my life. He was the school's head football coach and my homeroom teacher. He was married and had a son a couple of years younger than I was. Jeep had been hired to turn the school's football program around. Neptune High was then a basketball powerhouse, but it had always had losing football teams. Jeep had coached at Easton High School in Pennsylvania. Easton was a nationally known high school football powerhouse. Like my "Mafia dad," Jeep was big in stature. When I saw his tattooed forearms (I called them tree trunks), I wanted forearms as big as his. I also secretly hoped that Jeep and my mother would get married. I wanted Jeep to be my dad, just as I had wanted Gui to be. Jeep was my new father figure.

Jeep was from Easton, and of Slavic descent. He was not an academic, just a straight-talking, no-nonsense guy. He drove an inexpensive car and had a mutt named Too-Too. He reminded me of one of my favorite songs, John Conlee's "Common Man."

Jeep was drafted by the Baltimore Colts, but a knee injury ended his professional football career. His brother Chuck, of the Philadelphia Eagles, was one of the greatest players in NFL history and is in the Pro Football Hall of Fame. Chuck's legendary tackle in a championship game against the New York Giants ended Frank Gifford's career.

"I took Jeff under my care and took care of him all through high school," Jeep told Robert. "Jeff was kind of popular with the other kids. He liked to have fun, and you never knew what you were gonna get with him. It was sometimes tough for people to understand him. He was alone most of the time, and there wasn't anybody to really look after him. He worked hard, starting at 4:30 a.m. at the pancake store.

"I loved the kid, and we were like father and son. He never

went against me, and did all I asked him to do. Except, of course, for taking up wrestling when I advised him against it. I thought he shouldn't get into something he'd never participated in before and get distracted from his studies. On the other hand, he'd never played football before he came to Neptune, either, and he got to be very, very good at it. He's a competitor. I was always very proud of him."

Jeep filled a need at the most crucial time in my life. I was a teenage runaway in the "runaway" 1960s, a period *Life* magazine described as one of "Dissent and Disobedience." It was all about LSD and psychedelic drugs, the Vietnam War, protest music–and assassinations. The '60s was also the worst decade for a teenage kid to be without a parent's supervision.

The teen years, I believe, are the most critical in any kid's life. I compare a kid to a building. A building is a product of blueprints that were drawn long before the building was completed. In my judgment, the blueprint for a man is drawn when he is a teenager. Parents are the architects of the child. They have to make the correct "change orders" before the building is completed.

By wrestling and playing football in high school, I learned a great deal about myself, and it stayed with me for the rest of my life. While others partied and smoked cigarettes, I lifted weights by my-self. Weightlifting for football was not required in those days. In fact, it wasn't universally agreed to be a good thing. I curled every day so I could have forearms like Jeep's. I did sets with 155-pound weights. Wrestling was an even tougher test because it was mano-a-mano. I also learned to sacrifice and to do without. Sometimes I couldn't eat or even drink water, because I always had to make a prescribed weight. I ran in the shower in sweats and took Ex-Lax to lose weight. I'd spit to lose weight. What I learned from these sports prepared me for the competitive business world.

Football and wrestling taught me the value of self-discipline and teamwork. I was part of a team working toward one mutual goal: winning. I also learned how to be a leader. Jeep even asked me to conduct the football team's summer workouts because it was illegal for him to do it when school was not in session. My teammates who smoked in the parking lot before school would drop their cigarettes behind their backs when they saw me coming, because they knew I would chew them out. I became co-captain of the team. Jeep had changed me from a loser into a winner. What was it that turned me around and allowed me to turn losing restaurants into winners twenty years later? I look back now and understand. It was very simple. For the first time in my life, I wanted to make someone proud of me. I finally had someone I wanted to impress.

Jeep knew that I worked in restaurants, and he told me about a place that boiled its steak. I told him he was mistaken. He said he would take me to Midge's and prove that they sliced the beef very thin, boiled it in one big pot and then made steak sandwiches out of the meat. I told him he didn't know what he was talking about. "You don't boil beef if you're using it for steak sandwiches," I insisted. From a young age I was a ballbuster, no matter whom I was talking to–even my football coach, my hero.

More important to me was the fact that I was actually going to get to drive alone with Jeep Bednarik all the way from Neptune, New Jersey, to Easton, Pennsylvania, have dinner together and drive back with him.

When we arrived, Midge himself greeted us. He asked Jeep if I was on the football team. Although Jeep didn't know it, his answer became a defining moment in my life; it changed my life forever. He simply told Midge the truth: "Jeff is a second-team center on our freshman team." After that night, I vowed I was never going to be second-team anything for the rest of my life. My attitude became,

"We never declared a national holiday for our vice president."

When we left, after seeing the thinly sliced beef cooked the way Jeep had described, Midge walked us to the door, said goodbye and wished me good luck. With my coach's words still echoing in my head, I replied, "Don't worry, I'm going to do great." I became Neptune High School's first all-state guard and linebacker.

Every kid wants his parents to come to his games. Jeep was our school's head football coach so, obviously, I got to play in front of him and that motivated me. He also came to some of my wrestling matches, so I made it a point not to lose. I never really learned many wrestling moves. I was just tough and aggressive. I called it "brute force and fuckin' ignorance." I was like Pete Rose: determined to win. I feared losing so much, I wouldn't allow it to happen. I was confident because I knew I was strong from all the weightlifting. My success in football gave me confidence in wrestling and vice versa. Jeep gave me confidence too. I found out early that if you think you will win you probably will.

Confidence gives you a damn good head start. Confidence will get you through damn near anything. Confidence will also make you tough. I was always considered the toughest kid on every team I played on. Ed Marinaro was an all-American running back at Cornell and the runner-up for the Heisman Trophy. He went on to play seven years in the NFL. He told the Cornell football team, in a pregame talk years later, that Jeff Ruby was the toughest guy he ever played against. I had to tackle him in practices for two years, so he knew.

Bob Valenti coached me at Cornell and later coached the Green Bay Packers and the Pittsburgh Steelers. He said that, except for all-pro linebacker Greg Lloyd of the Steelers, I was the toughest player he coached. When you're not very fast, very big or very athletic, you better be damn tough and sure of yourself. I was two out of five, tough and confident. I got my toughness and confidence from Jeep Bednarik.

One of my first wrestling matches was at Christian Brothers Academy. My opponent at CBA, Chris Massa, a senior, was one of the best in the state. He was also the only opponent who ever came into our locker room to say hello to me before the matches began. Jeep made the trip to CBA, a big wrestling school. The place was packed, including priests and brothers in religious robes. Whenever the match was close, the Catholic kids did the sign of the cross. I'm sure I was the only Jew in the entire arena.

I was losing 2-0 when Massa and I both went out of bounds, and he did the sign of the cross. I decided it was time to convert. I did the cross thing, too, but I did it backwards or upside down. Everyone laughed, and a priest sitting next to Jeep turned to him and commented, "I guess this kid is a recent convert." Jeep replied, "No, he's a Jew." I ended up losing to the Christian kid, 3-1.

I was living at the Ocean Grove rooming house when my relationship with Jeep began. Later in my life, fatherless teenage boys would begin similar relationships with me. Boys are instinctively drawn to men who are successful, look tough, and are someone we would love to call "Dad." A child is like freshly poured Jell-O. It needs to be molded by someone to end up in the shape you had hoped for. They may put a hand on our shoulders or even pick us up if we have a broken wing, and stay with us until that broken wing is mended and we are able to fly again. It was my good fortune that Jeep took an interest in me. I found a sense of purpose and I saw a future for myself.

At no time did I need someone more than I did one winter morning in my senior year of high school. My brother, Wayne, had called me the night before and asked me to pay him a visit at Monmouth College. It was a cold night and a twenty-mile motor bike ride

A school portrait from my days at Neptune High School

from Asbury Park. I had a wrestling match the next day, but I went to see Wayne anyway, since I seldom got to see my brother. That night he told me that my father was not Lou Kranz, as I'd always thought. I rode home and cried all night in my eight-by-ten room and never went to sleep. The next morning I told Jeep my devastating news. I had a difficult time explaining myself because I was crying so hard I was hyperventilating. I said I wasn't going to wrestle that afternoon; I was too exhausted since it had been two days since I'd slept.

Jeep's handling of my problem was more effective than it would have been had I been sent to the school psychologist. He just looked at me and asked some questions: "Are you still first-team all-state in football? Are you still unbeaten in wrestling? Were you co-captain of an undefeated football team; the first unbeaten team in Neptune's history? Do you still have all A's this year? Are you still supporting yourself through high school with no help from anyone? Does everyone in this school still admire you for what you have been able to do?" I nodded my head "yes" to all his questions, and then he asked a final one. "What difference does it make who the hell your father was?" I stopped crying, just like that, and decided to wrestle that day.

I was undefeated, but I hadn't yet pinned any of my opponents. This time I knew I was too damned tired to last three rounds. I would have to pin the kid quickly or lose my first match. I pinned him in thirty-seven seconds and went home to bed.

Every boy needs a man.

CHAPTER SEVEN

PRESSURE

George Michael, 1988

Billy Joel ate at both The Precinct and The Waterfront in the late 1980s. About twenty years later he came to Cincinnati for the opening night of his touring Broadway show, Movin' Out. *His father-in-law, Steve Lee, who lives in Cincinnati, told Billy he would take him to a great steakhouse. Billy said, "I know the place. It's owned by Jeff, a Jersey guy."*

In my senior year at Neptune High School, 1965-66, I was still cooking at the Perkins Pancake House on the Asbury Circle at Route 35, and I thought that I might have a future there. But first I needed to go to college and play football. Jeep Bednarik said that the universities of Maryland and Alabama were possibilities. He had a good relationship with "Bear" Bryant, the legendary Alabama coach, and had even talked to him about me. But I had always wanted to go to Cornell for its world-famous hotel and hospitality school.

I had played linebacker and offensive guard for Neptune High and made first-team all-state on a talented, undefeated team that played in New Jersey's largest division—Group IV. Jack Tatum of Passaic, New Jersey, also played linebacker and graduated from high school in 1966. He did not make all-state that year, but he went on to become an All-American at Ohio State, and an all-pro with the Super Bowl champion Oakland Raiders. My pal Phil Villapiano was still a sophomore at a nearby Jersey high school and hadn't achieved his full growth yet. He later went to college at Bowling Green, and he, too, became an all-pro with the Oakland Raiders.

At 5 feet 11½ inches tall and 190 pounds, I wasn't big enough for the National Football League, so that dream would be a stretch. Getting a Cornell education seemed almost equally impossible. I wasn't smart enough or rich enough to go to Cornell. Ivy League schools did not give athletic scholarships, so it didn't matter how good I was at football.

Neptune's head guidance counselor, Gene Minor, told me I had no chance of getting accepted at Cornell. To his credit, my personal guidance counselor, Nick Napolitano, never told me that. But I saw on *ABC News* that Cornell had the lowest ratio of admissions to applications that year. I finally had my first television set; a girl had given me her nice round-screen black-and-white set after her family bought a new one. The first thing I learned from my first TV was that Cornell was the hardest school in America to get into.

My SAT (Scholastic Assessment Test) scores weren't high enough for Cornell. I could get into a college, but not the school I had wanted my entire life to attend. I took the test several times, but I got flustered every time and couldn't get my scores up high enough. I never seemed to have enough time to finish answering the questions. Thirty-five years later I learned that both of my sons were diagnosed with ADD (attention deficit disorder) and ADHD (attention deficit hyperactivity disorder). They got them from me. As my friend John Rijos told Robert, "Jeff has the attention span of a two-year-old."

My last chance to retake the SAT came at the end of our wrestling season, the *same day*, in fact, as the state championship finals. I was undefeated at Neptune and was training for the state tournament. What I had learned most from high school sports was how to be part of a team and how to be a winner under pressure. Coach Schaeffer created pressure by daily posting a news photo of Matt Florio from the *Star-Ledger* on the glass door of the coaches' office, so every boy could see it. Florio, from Middletown High School in our county, was the only high school wrestler whose picture appeared in the paper every day leading up to the state championship. For good measure, and for my benefit, Coach Schaeffer would circle Florio's photo. I don't believe Matt Florio had lost a match in his four years at Middle-town. If I were to reach my goal of winning the state championship and staying undefeated, I would have to beat the best wrestler in the state before I even got out of our regional tournament.

I couldn't be in two places at the same time. If I beat Florio I would have a real dilemma: take the SAT again or go for the state championship. I would cross that bridge when I came to it. Nobody thought I could beat Florio anyway, and I was a kid who could never avoid a crisis. Despite a five-minute delay after I sprained my ankle in the second period, I did beat Florio, 3 to 1, in the regional final. Now I faced the biggest decision of my life. I was mad at myself for even going out for wrestling. Jeep hadn't wanted me to go out for it in the first place, and he especially did not want me to wrestle in my senior year.

If I won the state semifinal match against a kid named Jim Detweiler, what would I do next? Take the SAT again? Just not show up for the state championship title match? Who's ever done that?

Having been the only wrestler to beat the number-one seed, Florio, I was confident I could win the state title. I was already the most-publicized athlete in the county. *The Asbury Park Press* loved me, and it would be a big story for them if I won. But something had to give. I'd achieved one of my three high school goals by becoming all-state in football on an unbeaten team. Two of my goals were left, but I could reach only one of them. I could become New Jersey's high school wrestling champion for 1966, or a Cornell student, class of 1970, but not both.

It was stressful not knowing what to do. I lost weight. I changed my mind by the hour and didn't really make my decision until the day of the semi-final match. I needed to go to Cornell University, and to get there I would have to throw a match. It was tough, with my classmates, teammates, coaches and teachers coming up to me, congratulating me on my big victory over Florio and wishing me good luck in the next round, while I knew I might take a dive. Winning the matches was more in my control. I wasn't as confident about being accepted at Cornell, even if my SAT scores went up.

When I took the mat in the semi-finals I still had mixed emotions. I wasn't sure I could go through with the "fix," or wanted to. I certainly didn't know how to lose on purpose—in football or wrestling. I knew I wasn't going to let Jim Detweiler embarrass me. I wasn't going to let him pin me or even get me on my back. After a zero-zero tie in the first round, I escaped in round two to get a point. I let him escape in round three and get "riding time" to win his three points. Detweiler beat me, 3-1, to wrestle for the state title. He won that championship match 15-3. I would have destroyed that other kid, whoever he was.

Senior year wrestling—with more than my opponent

When the SAT results finally came back, my scores were closer to 1600 than my usual 1400. A suspicious Mr. Minor called me into his office and grilled me about my improvement. He as much as accused me of having someone else take the test for me. He conducted a full investigation by interviewing my closest friends and my girlfriend, Linda Jernstedt. But nothing came of it, and there was nothing Mr. Minor could do except to watch me go on to graduate from Cornell. I'm sure he kept track of my status up in Ithaca. When Toby Keith came out with "How Do You Like Me Now?" I thought of Mr. Minor.

Jeep helped my cause a lot by calling Cornell's head football coach, Jack Musick, and telling him that I would be a sure starter for his team if I got into the university.

My biggest remaining problem was financial. The Parents' Confidential Statement I sent in showed no income at all. Jeep told me it was the first time they had ever seen that. But someone told me that H.J. Heinz awarded $1,000 scholarships to a hotel/restaurant school. I went to the library to look it up and found that most of the winners went to Cornell. There was still time for me to apply. Once again, it came down to beating someone else so I could win. What lies ahead of kids after school is the same thing they faced growing up: making the teams and making the grades.

As I read the Heinz scholarship materials, it became clear that thousands of students from across the country applied for this stipend every year. Only one student was chosen from each of the four regions of the country, and one of those four was named the Grand Winner. I completed all the forms and questionnaires. I wrote the required biography, and the school provided my academic record and a list of my extracurricular activities.

I was working at Perkins one summer day when I got a phone

call from Jeep: "You've been accepted at Cornell." He said coach Jack Musick himself had called with the news. The Heinz scholarship was the last hurdle I had cleared successfully, and this one I had done on my own. I was the Grand Winner.

My challenge had just begun, however. I still wasn't sure I was intelligent enough to be successful at Cornell. Could I make it there academically while playing football and working? Would I graduate? Every Ivy League graduate I've ever met has told me the same thing: it's harder to get into an Ivy League school than it is to stay in.

You're telling me!

CHAPTER EIGHT

THE TIMES THEY ARE A-CHANGIN'
Bob Dylan, 1964

"How does it feel
To be on your own
With no direction home
Like a complete unknown
Like a rolling stone?"
"Like a Rolling Stone," Bob Dylan, 1965

This song played on the radio the year of my seventeenth birthday, right in the middle of the tumultuous decade of the 1960s. Needless to say, I related to the lyrics.

In 1962, a Jewish kid from Minnesota named Robert Zimmerman changed his name to Bob Dylan, and he has remained the most influential American musician in rock 'n' roll history. Dylan's lyrics spoke to millions during an era of social unrest, political upheaval and radical change. He told John Lennon that Lennon's music "said nothing." After that, the Beatles took a radical new direction, from "I Want to Hold Your Hand" to "Revolution."

"My decade" began innocently enough in 1960 with a song written and recorded by Cincinnati native Hank Ballard. But Ernest Evans (aka Chubby Checker) did even better with the song in 1962. Dick Clark asserted, "The most significant rock 'n' roll record of all time was "The Twist", because it was the first time in musical history that all generations could admit they liked rock 'n' roll music."

I don't know how we went from Chubby Checker to hippies,

yippies, flower children, Black Panthers and the SDS [Students for a Democratic Society], but we did. In the words of the Gilbert O'Sullivan song, I was "alone again, naturally" and resisted the temptation to join the fray.

Two days before my twelfth birthday in 1960, rock stars Eddie Cochran and Gene Vincent were driving from Bristol to London after a concert, to catch a 1:00 a.m. plane home to the U.S. Their car skidded into a lamp post and Cochran was killed. They had just finished a sold-out ten-week tour, and Cochran had just completed what would be his final recording, "Three Steps to Heaven." Eddie Cochran was inducted into the Rock & Roll Hall of Fame in 1987. My close friend Ben Scotti produced the motion picture *Eddie and the Cruisers* in 1983, and its 1989 sequel, which was based on Cochran's tragic death.

In a Tom Brokaw HBO documentary about the 1960s, actor Tom Hanks said that rock 'n' roll was the "signature of the decade." Rock and roll also fueled a cultural revolution. Graham Nash said, "When rock 'n' roll came along, it gave kids something that they felt was theirs." Funny, forty years later, Nash and his musical partner David Crosby asked conservative me to join them at their table in my restaurant.

Billy Joel grew up in the 1960s. In his number one single, "We Didn't Start the Fire," the lyrics cover more than one hundred events from 1949 to 1989. Billy recapped the '60s decade in a four-minute, 49-second song, "The fire" is a metaphor for the turmoil and conflict of the period.

The year that I ran away from home, 1963, was the one that historians called the year that changed the world. Martin Luther King delivered his legendary "I Have a Dream" speech during the civil rights March on Washington in August.

In November of that year, President John F. Kennedy was assassinated in Texas by Lee Harvey Oswald. I was a sophomore in high school. I was in gym class when they made the announcement.

I turned twenty in 1968, the year from hell in the United States. A *Time* cover story blurb read, "The Year That Changed the World - War abroad, riots at home, fallen leaders and lunar dreams." Americans were riven by the Vietnam war and by race, age and culture. President Lyndon Johnson wanted no part of reelection. Martin Luther King and Robert F. Kennedy were assassinated within nine weeks of one another.

During my senior year at Cornell, the "Kent State Year" of 1969-70, the FBI reported a total of 1,785 student demonstrations, of which 313 were building occupations. (I had had some experience with one of those at Cornell the year before.)

The late 1960s got pretty "groovy," thanks to the widespread use of marijuana among the youth, and a more limited use of acid, or LSD, which was actually legal.

By the end of 1968, there were more than half a million U.S. troops in South Vietnam. In the summer of 1969, there were that many hippies at a farm near Woodstock, New York, protesting that war with music. Today they are called Baby Boomers.

Five days after what is still America's most historic concert, the nation was riveted by what remains its most infamous murder spree. A Cincinnati-born hippie by the name of Charles Manson became a father figure to five young girls and convinced them to murder people they did not know. The victims were renting a house that was owned by Doris Day, a singer and movie star, who was also born in Cincinnati, and her husband Marty Melcher.

I was only turning twelve when the 1960s began, and was only twenty-two and just out of college when they ended. I didn't go to war, nor did I march in favor of it or protest against it. I drew a high draft number and never got called up, although I was the right age. I was in only one incident that was labeled a race riot, and my involvement was inadvertent. I remember our murdered leaders and the music of the time. But much of what I know about the troubled decade, I've learned about later. In my opinion now, the 1960s were not about peace and love. Although millions of sober and committed Americans protested for civil rights and against the war, many of those marchers were so high on drugs they didn't know what they were protesting or advocating.

By accident of birth, I chose to run away from home and raise myself at the age of fifteen in the most fucked-up decade in the history of our country, and I pulled it off. It made me who I am today. Montgomery Gentry had a song for that, too. It was called "Something to be Proud of."

CHAPTER NINE

ROCK-N-ROLL RUBY

Johnny Cash, 1954

I still recall being interviewed my first day at Cornell by a man named Dave Duncan. As I sat across the desk from him, the first thing out of his mouth was, "What brings you to our doors?" I was nervous because I didn't think I was smart enough to be there. All I could think to say was, "I hitchhiked." When I got my bearings, I told him, "I like people. I grew up in the restaurant business. I've wanted to come here all my life."

My freshman year I lived in a dorm. My roommate, Frank Bennett, was from Philadelphia, and he was the fullback on the freshman team. He was always creating new games to play, so I called him "Games" Bennett. Directly across the hall, our neighbor was a short kid named John Brown. He was always running around the hall in nothing but his tight white "jockeys," like a rabbit in nothing "butt" his briefs, so I named him "Rabbit Ass." A kid down the hall, Rick Jay, would come into our room and show us card tricks. He appeared on *The Johnny Carson Show* and became one of America's most renowned magicians, later making it to Broadway and Las Vegas as Ricky Jay. A movie documentary on his life and work came out in early 2013.

Cornell had fifty-one fraternity houses, more than any college in America. Show me a frat house and I'll show you a party. So, when we began rushing fraternities we went to a lot of parties. My buddies and I often got on stage and sang with the band. At Delta Upsilon, the fraternity I pledged, the upperclassmen told me I was good and should start my own band. They also advised me not to include my friends in the band. (In my sophomore year, I took their advice on both counts.)

My freshman year football jersey was number 66, the same number I had in high school. I was the starting linebacker. More important, I was attending Cornell's world-famous Hotel/Restaurant School. What going to Harvard means to a lawyer, going to Cornell means to a restaurateur. I had accomplished my goals. Everything was great–until the Princeton game.

Princeton played the single wing, and I was moved to middle guard for that game. My mother came to that game, the first time she had ever come to see me play. It was also her last game. She could hear my painful scream echoing off the building. On an isolation power play up the middle, two players blocked me at both sides of my knee. The blocking back came over it, followed by the kid with the ball. My knee snapped, and it was "game over" for me. I rode back on the team bus after stopping for dinner somewhere. The ten-hour bus ride didn't help. The New York Giants surgeon, Dr. Anthony Pisano, did the surgery.

I wasn't agile enough ever to play linebacker again, so I became Division I's smallest defensive tackle for the rest of my Cornell football career. (Whenever we played Harvard, I was across the line from Tommy Lee Jones, who was an offensive lineman for his team.) Dr. Pisano turned out to be involved in an NFL gambling scandal that launched an FBI investigation and prompted the policy whereby teams must announce to gamblers the likelihood of its injured players playing in the upcoming game.

"I met Jeff when he was eighteen," Tom MacLeod told Robert, "and knew him all through our freshman year at Cornell. He was the first guy I'd ever met my age who had to take care of himself. He was a pretty rough character as a freshman; he was undersized, but a real tough guy. He was advanced, not necessarily social- ly, but in terms of taking care of himself and carving out a life for himself. I met a self-made man before I even knew what that was. He wasn't much into girls or drinking; he was really into caring for himself. He was financially independent at a very young age, and that really impressed me. He always had money and bought his own stuff. He never leaned on his friends or asked us for anything. That self-sufficiency must be in his DNA.

"Sophomore year, Jeff and I were roommates with three other DUs in the fraternity house. One day he showed up with a brand new lime green Dodge Charger he had just bought. I couldn't believe it. I would have had no idea how to buy a car back then. I didn't have my first car until I was twenty-six. Other guys had cars, but their dads had bought them. Jeff was in a different league from the rest of us. He couldn't sing a lick, he couldn't play an instrument, but he started a very successful band."

Santo Laquatra, one of our roommates at DU, my freshman counterpart at linebacker and fellow "Hotelie," became my best friend throughout college. He reminisced for Robert. "We freshman foot- ball recruits met before school even started, and I was struck both by his incredible blue eyes and the chip on his shoulder. Pound for pound, he was the toughest guy I've ever seen. We freshmen players washed dishes and served at training tables to earn our keep. Our team members became close, and we produced a hell of a pledge class for Delta Upsilon, the jock house at Cornell. Those of us who are still alive are friends to this day.

"We didn't have football scholarships, but we did have grants based on our parents' incomes and need. They gave us cash each semester, and we paid our tuition and other expenses out of it. In the spring semester, Jeff used his grant money to buy the famous lime green car. To make up for the money he needed for school, he started his band, which became the hot band on campus. They were a truly excellent group of men. Jeff had a voice that went right along with them."

I was the front man and the main lead vocalist, and I handled the bookings. Our musicians included one older Cornell kid, Steve, a music major who played lead guitar. I found a drummer at Trumansburg High School. Jeff Legnini had long hair and sang lead on The Young Rascals songbook and other rock tunes. I sang lead on all the soul music. Steve came up with the band's name: The Lavender Hill Mob, after the 1951 Oscar-winning movie starring Alec Guinness. We were the only band in the region that booked itself. We kept all the money. We made three hundred dollars a night in 1967 dollars and played more gigs than a lot of better bands. My barber, who never let me pay for a haircut, owned an upscale restaurant and lounge off campus called The Red Carpet. He hired me to sing there. I brought my guitar player along and made money on the nights our whole band wasn't booked.

Our band's first gig was at The Heidelberg in Collegetown on a Monday night. The club was owned by a German guy named Joe van Boven, who had a black group that did the music I liked. They weren't drawing many people, so he told me he would give me "the door," meaning that we would keep whatever was collected in admissions. If it was only twenty dollars, we'd split twenty dollars among the six of us. Joe would not pay us anything additional.

Santo Laquatra spread the word all over campus that "Rubes" was going to be at The Heidelberg. I had an accounting exam that night and needed extra time to finish it. I needed so much extra time that it was past the hour my band was supposed to start playing. Jeff Legnini didn't sing lead on enough songs to start without me. By the time I finished, got into my costume and ran to The Heidelberg, the place was so crowded it was almost impossible to get to the stage. They started chanting, "Rubes, Rubes." We rocked the Heidelberg, and I never counted so much money. The owner then decided if I wanted to play at his bar anymore, *he* would get the door and we would get a flat $300. We played there every Monday night. It was extra cash we could count on, and the gig gave us priceless visibility from which we booked many frat parties.

Singing with my band at Cornell, The Lavender Hill Mob

With my blue eyes and Jersey background and singing lead with my own band, I was going to be the next Sinatra.

One of my proudest memories of my four years at Cornell University took place at Hobart College in Geneva, New York. A booking agent called to book our band. The agent said he wanted us to be the opening act for Sly and the Family Stone. I thought he was full of shit and hung up. He called back and apologized for being disconnected on a long distance call. He was serious. From the hundreds of bands in upstate New York, Jeff Ruby's band, The Lavender Hill Mob, was chosen to open for Sly and the Family Stone. They were inducted into the Rock & Roll Hall of Fame in 1993 and were one of the greatest bands of their era. At Woodstock they were the band that brought the crowd to its most thunderous applause. This was the group that invented funk and influenced Prince, Rick James, George Clinton, Bootsy Collins, et al. Our band did many of their tunes.

We made the long drive to Hobart and got set up. By then we had been informed we would also be playing after Sly's show, as well as before it. Then my bass player broke his string and couldn't play. The crowd was jammed into the school gym, and they were getting rowdy and restless and yelling for us to start performing. The later we started, the later the hottest funk group in America would start.

"Screw it," I said, "I'll get Sly's bass strings." I went to his "psychedelic" bus to ask for a couple of bass strings. When I opened the door, I thought I had entered the steam room at Cornell's football building. Sly and the entire Family were "Fuckin' Stoned." I introduced myself and asked him for the bass strings. Sly was cool and accommodated me. Thirty years later he came to one of our restaurants with his friend and my partner and pal, Hall of Fame bassist, Bootsy Collins.

We played everything on our play list that was not a Sly and the Family Stone tune. That meant we didn't play "Life," a song that frat houses always made us play three or four times a night. It was our best tune.

Joining Delta Upsilon was probably the best long-term decision I made at Cornell. Rushing DU began with hazing. We had to eat goldfish right out of the fishbowl. I can't remember how many goldfish I was forced to eat. And that was before I had ever even heard of sushi.

DU had seventy-two brothers, of which thirty-two lived in the fraternity house. It was a close-knit unit that included many football players. The DU stereotype around campus was very misleading. The "dumb jock" image was downright unjust. Although our binding interest was in athletics, the brothers had a multitude of interests and were individuals in their own rights. The athletes, in fact, were some of the best students and deepest thinkers in the house. Delta Upsilon finished eighth out of fifty-one houses in academics. Our single favorable reputation was that we had the closest brotherhood at Cornell. We had few factions in DU, compared to most of the other houses on campus.

Tom MacLeod was the smartest guy in our room. He started as a defensive back in football for three years and was an All-East pitcher on Cornell's baseball team. Tom was from St. Louis, and I was from New Jersey. After graduation, we both ended up in Cincinnati. Back at DU, I used to make cheesecake for my frat brothers. Tom suggested that I package my cheesecake and sell it nationwide. He said it was better than Sara Lee, the company that sold more cheesecake than anyone else in America. He knew mine was better, and he wasn't even in the hotel and restaurant school. He was in the School of Agriculture.

Tom eventually became president of the bakery division of

Sara Lee. He still had no idea how to make cheesecake. He told Robert, "When I was running Sara Lee, we made 250 cheesecakes a minute. Jeff made good cheesecakes, too, but he didn't make them quite as fast."

My counterpart at linebacker was Santo Laquatra, from Pittsburgh. As my closest friend and my roommate, he got me through hotel school. Santo later made my crucial interview with Winegardner & Hammons, Inc. (WHI) happen. My other close pals were Brooks "Wally" Scholl and Ken Snyder. Santo, Brooks and Ken were the three wonderful guys who prevented me from showing up for an important job interview with Sheraton Hotels in Boston. They had planned skydiving for that day. I had an airplane reservation with a representative from Sheraton waiting for me at Logan Airport. They didn't want to hear it.

A twenty-one-year-old male can be called a "chickenshit pussy" only so many times. We drove to Elmira and took a quick lesson. No one would be diving with us. We went solo. We made it safely, but we prayed for "Rat," Dem Van Tyle, whose chute didn't open. Dem remembered what he was taught about using the reserve chute, and he landed more or less safely in a tree. (Sadly, Dem is the only one of us no longer alive.) Had I gone to that Sheraton interview, my life might have taken a very different course. Still, I'm glad I took that all-important second "dive" in my life.

My freshman year at Cornell, I met the man who would have the most influence on my professional life. Erik Kamfjord was a 6 foot 2 inch, 265 pound former lineman at the University of Virginia, and one tough Norwegian. He was at Cornell getting his master's degree in business administration and was responsible for the varsity football team's training table. As part of paying my way through Cornell, I worked at the training table.

I wore Italian knit shirts, like the ones they wore in *The Sopranos* three decades later. I never wore jeans. I was into clothes and into myself. I seemed to be one of the few kids at Cornell who didn't belong there, and who didn't have Daddy sending him money whenever he needed it. I had to work for everything I had, which was mostly clothes at that time.

Back then, in 1967, the term they used a lot was "hot shit." I suppose I thought I was a hot shit. Erik and I had a run-in one day when the team showed up for dinner, and he couldn't find me. My job was to stand behind the counter and dish out food, cafeteria style, as the players slid their trays along. Sometimes, however, I would mosey over to the Statler kitchen and talk to the employees who weren't students. The cooks there would give me a slice of prime rib, and Erik would come in and catch me eating in a private VIP room all by myself. "You're not the only one who was all-state," he yelled. *Everyone* here was all-state. Get your ass to work."

Erik punished me by assigning me to the ice cream station. They were running out of ice cream because players were taking cups full of it back to their frat houses or apartments and leaving them outside on their window sills to stay frozen. My job was to make sure that they took only one ice cream per person. I got into a fight with a player who wouldn't listen to me about the new "one ice cream" policy. When Erik pulled us apart, he scolded me. It seems I had just fought with Freddy Devlin, who happened to be the captain of the varsity football team and an All-Ivy League linebacker. "Use some common sense when you apply a rule," Erik warned. I yelled back that there shouldn't be a double standard.

Erik is now the CEO of Winegardner & Hammons, Inc. (WHI), the large hotel management company, having been with the firm ever since he left Cornell forty-five years ago. He recalled to Robert,

"Since the Ivy League had no such thing as an athletic scholarship, the freshmen football players were required to work at a job that paid them by the hour. Jeff was a hotshot who thought he didn't have to take this job seriously. But I saw right away that he was intelligent, and he could be hardworking when he wanted to be. I thought to myself, *this guy's gonna go places.* So I was very surprised, when I returned to Cornell three years later seeking applicants for WHI, that Jeff did not sign up for an interview."

Although most of my close friends were in my class at Cornell, occasionally I found a good friend in the classes a year or two behind me. Craig Lambert, now with Marriott Hotels, pledged DU when he was a freshman and I was a sophomore. He was my football teammate as well as my fraternity brother.

Ed Marinaro was two years behind me at Cornell, but he was from New Jersey, and he was Italian. Italians and Jews have a connection, and two people from Jersey can certainly relate. Eddie and I were meant to be friends. He became the best running back in America, and a runner-up for the Heisman Trophy. His NFL career, however, was much more successful than that of the Heisman winner that year, quarterback Pat Sullivan from Auburn.

After seven years in pro football, Ed became a successful actor, starring in the TV police drama *Hill Street Blues*. We still stay in touch. When I am "roasted" for televised charity fundraisers, Ed flies in at his own expense to be on the dais. He is the funniest and most ruthless of all the roasters. He also still holds NCAA rushing records. He does not, however, hold the Cornell record for the most classes attended. That record is held by a dog named Spoof, a stray I took in. Spoof followed me to my classes and actually attended more of them than Ed Marinaro. Poor Spoof never even got a diploma. If Ed got one, Spoof should have gotten one.

I took Spoof home with me from college every summer. In Holmdel, New Jersey, where I worked as a broiler man at the best steakhouse in the area, I often took Spoof on errands with me in my convertible. One day I had to run in someplace for a minute, so I leashed him to the console's drive shaft, so he wouldn't jump over the side onto Route 34. When I came back, he was hanging motionless over the side of the car. His feces were splashed on the asphalt. I ran to Spoof and put him in the car. I gave my dog mouth-to-mouth, then I got him to the nearest vet. Spoof made it through okay, but I almost had a heart attack.

The car Spoof almost died in was my first car, a '60-something yellow Ford Galaxy convertible. I knew the car was jinxed the day I met the Nationwide Insurance agent at my mother's apartment to sign the papers. After he left, I got in the car and drove it from the parking lot to my mother's front door, where I stopped and quickly ran in to get my wallet. When I opened the apartment door to leave, I noticed that the car was driving itself down the street. I ran after it. It made a right turn down a grassy hill and headed straight toward a solid brick apartment building, just as I tried to jump in. Before I could catch up to it, the "yellow bird" turned into a parking lot and smashed into a parked car. I called my new insurance agent. Not only was I his quickest claim ever, I was his first and only client ever involved in a two-car accident with nobody in either car at the time of the accident.

John Rijos, who is co-president and COO of Brookdale Senior Living, the largest such operation in the country, was a freshman at Cornell when I was a senior. Although he later became a good friend and was my "enforcer" when I went to the auction to buy the historic building that became Carlo & Johnny, I didn't really know him at school. But he apparently knew about me. As he told Robert, "Jeff was a legend on campus, a great football player and a member of one of the wilder fraternities. He loved to sing in front of a band. He had then, and he still has, a reputation as a tough, swashbuckling guy with no filter whatsoever. But as I later found out, he's just a sweetheart. He doesn't lose friends."

CHAPTER TEN

BURN IT DOWN

Linkin Park, 2012

In my view, the most courageous American civilian of our time was Martin Luther King Jr. He insisted that to achieve their civil rights, blacks must demonstrate peacefully. For his efforts he was called an "Uncle Tom." He was stabbed near his heart by a black woman and physically attacked three other times. His home was bombed three times, and he was thrown in jail fourteen times. His hate mail alone would have been enough to make any other man give up. One letter said, "This isn't a threat but a promise. Your head will be blown off as sure as Christ made green apples." J. Edgar Hoover accused King of being a communist. The FBI bugged his home. He was investigated, interrogated and humiliated.

I was a sophomore at Cornell when King gave his famous "I've Been to the Mountaintop" speech in Memphis on April 3, 1968. King's speeches were all memorable, and he remains one of the most quotable leaders in our country's history. This speech sadly proved he was a prophet: "I've seen the Promised Land. I may not get there with you, but I want you to know tonight, that we as a people will get to the Promised Land."

King was assassinated the following night. By week's end, 168 towns and cities had paid the price for the murder of the most eloquent proponent of racial harmony, civil rights for all, and non-violent protest in America. Within a week, American cities experienced arson, bombings, looting and riots such as America had never seen before.

On April 8 the news spread on campus that buildings were burning in the Collegetown section of Ithaca. We later learned that our venue, The Heidelberg, had burned to the ground in retribution for King's assassination. I thought, *Poor Joe van Boven.* My next thought was, *Come to think of it, poor us.* We kept all of our band equipment at The Heidelberg. We no longer would have the income from playing there every week or benefit from the exposure it gave us. Now, all the rioting and racism had affected me directly.

I turned twenty-one at 7:30 a.m. on April 19, 1969, in my junior year. My birthday fell on the Saturday of Parents' Weekend. My brother, Wayne, and his wife, Diane, made the trip to Ithaca to be there for me. Early that morning, someone shook me and told me to wake up. I opened my early morning eyes.

My roommate, Santo Laquatra, recalled to Robert, "We had been to a party the night before and got home around two in the morning. A few hours later, the phone rang in our room. The SDS [Students for a Democratic Society] and some black radicals had taken over Willard Straight Hall, Cornell's student union building."

The Straight was the nerve center of our campus. Everything happened there. It was where we ate, gathered, and studied. Visiting parents stayed there. Now it looked as if students and parents would not be able to use our social center over the entire Parents' Weekend. The radicals had kicked everyone out, including the parents, locked the building and taken control of it.

"Let's reopen it," I said to Santo.

I began my walk alone up the steep steps to the street and then up the hill to The Straight. I circled the building and eventually found a small, divided-pane window with one panel of glass missing. This allowed me to put my hand in and crank the window open. The college radio station, WVBR, broadcast from there. Inside, however, a black kid stood guard. He told me I couldn't come in. I told him, "I'm a magician." The "guard" took off running.

Climbing out the The Straight window in my Cornell Football jacket

Upon entering The Straight, I pushed away the desks and chairs that were blocking the window. Eight other DUs entered behind me. We proceeded up a winding staircase through a door that led to the kitchen of the Ivy Room. I was looking for doors that might lead to the outside. Had I found one, I would have opened it and let others outside know that they could now get in. I thought that people wanted to get into The Straight and were angered by the action of the AAS (African-American Society). I believed that the University and the majority of its students were behind me. Never during this incident did I think I would be condemned for my actions.

While the nine of us DUs were hopping over steam tables and food counters, two other whites, one of whom was not a member of Delta Upsilon, had also come in through the window and were looking for us, intending to join us. After exiting the WVBR studio, they had taken a wrong turn and gone up a different staircase. The building was a labyrinth of doors and staircases.

Unbeknownst to us, these two were confronted by three or four blacks who told them to leave the building. As the whites stood there, a group of fifteen or twenty more blacks came running down the stairs. At that time, the DU fraternity member, Owen Snyder, was hit across the face with some type of heavy bar and knocked to the floor. The other white kid helped him to his feet, and both fled to the WVBR room and escaped through the window. (Owen was treated by a dentist who had to push his teeth back into place.)

Meanwhile, back in The Straight, we continued to advance from the Ivy Room kitchen through to the Ivy Room itself. We opened the doors that led to the stairs to the main lobby. It was at this point that we first encountered the blacks. I started up the stairs and met them on about the third or fourth step. One of them lifted an iron fireplace poker over my head and told me if I took another step he would crush my skull. I grabbed the club and held onto it. He then ordered me to get out of the building. He said I didn't belong in there.

"You're wrong," I replied, "That's the whole trouble. We both belong in here, together. Neither one of us has a right to say it is ours alone." I asked him if we could talk it over and straighten things out. One of the blacks, a teammate of mine, said, "Jeff, what are you doing here?" I said, "What are you doing here, my friend?"

Blacks lined the stairway, yelling. I stood in front of my brothers. In the meantime, more blacks appeared on the scene, many
of them leaning over the railing above us and spitting down at us.
Others started pushing each other down the stairs carrying clubs and
pool cues. One yelled, "Kill 'em, make examples of them." I said to
myself *Happy fuckin' birthday.* Then I called out, "We don't want to
fight. There are only a few of us here. We want to talk."

The black man who was in front was 6 six feet 8 inches tall
and weighed about 250 pounds. He told us to get out or we would
get killed. I told him we would leave. He then told the other blacks
to let us leave peacefully. Some listened to him; others did not. As
we began to retreat, someone yelled, "Get those white bastards, kill
them motherfuckers."

One DU, Barry Stacer, tried to open the glass door in order
to leave, but a black girl tried to pull him away from the door. He
brushed her aside effortlessly and started to open the door again
when a black male hit him across the head with a hammer. (The
media reported that a white man had attacked a black woman.) The
black cocked his arm, ready to strike Barry again, when another DU
noticed this and started swinging at him. A flurry of fights broke out.
Most of the DUs started running, looking for a way out of the building.
The blacks chased them with clubs that had knives attached to the
ends of them. A few blacks, however, held others back, telling them
to let us go. I was surrounded by blacks, but I was never struck, nor
did I ever hit anyone. My eyes were open, however, and every time
I was confronted by a black I would say, "Don't try anything." Twice I
pulled blacks off my fraternity brothers.

One of my roommates wasn't so lucky. He was attacked by
five blacks and had a liquid thrown in his face. He fell to the floor, his

eyes burning and face red. As he started to crawl away, another DU came and helped him up and led him away. More fights broke out. I tried to stop that by telling the DUs to keep their mouths shut, but violence was inevitable. It was like the Alamo. They had 165. We had nine. They had rifles, shotguns and bandoleers. We had our fists and one small window, five floors below us.

After the building had been occupied for thirty-three hours, and the AAS threatened still more confrontations, a seven-part agreement was reached between the AAS and the University. Steven Muller, vice-president for public affairs, defended the decision to sign the agreement to avoid "a growing and imminent threat to life."

It was never my intention to fight. The frat brothers who came with me were good kids. One was a sophomore who was my fraternity "little brother" and was also from New Jersey. My "little brother" didn't help our cause by getting up on a pool table, swinging a pool cue and yelling, "Come on, nigger" to a guy coming after him. I yelled to him, "Shut up." All eight of my frat brothers were hospitalized. Uncharacteristically, I was probably the only one who kept his composure.

I later learned that the tall man I had confronted on the stairs was Harry Edwards, one of the most notorious and defiant black radicals in America at the time. He had earlier received his M.A. and Ph.D. from Cornell on a fellowship, but I think he had come to us this time all the way from the University of California, Berkeley, the birthplace of campus protest. Edwards was the author of *The Revolt of the Black Athlete.*

One year earlier, he had inspired the legendary raised-fist Black Power salute. At the 1968 Mexico City Olympics, medal winners Tommie Smith and John Carlos, wearing black gloves, raised their fists during the medal ceremony and the playing of our national anthem. Edwards tried unsuccessfully to boycott those Games, but failing that, engineered the salute instead. A photographer captured the incident, and the Olympians were thrown off the U.S. team, but the image became iconic.

Ronald Reagan, who was elected governor of California in 1966, had declared Edwards "unfit to teach" and guilty of the "appeasement of lawbreakers" when Edwards was an instructor and coach at San Jose State College. He had spearheaded a group to "physically interfere" with the opening game of San Jose State's football season if his group's demands weren't met. The game was canceled, and Edwards called Reagan "a petrified pig, unfit to govern." By 1970, Edwards was an assistant professor of sociology at the University of California, Berkeley.

All of my previous interactions with the press had been positive and were mostly about sports. I had never seen the dark side of the media. I didn't know about their biases, use of falsehoods, and arrogance. On April 22, ABC radio incorrectly announced that "Four thousand armed blacks [had] seized Barton Hall" (where the basketball team played). ABC not only got the wrong building, there were only 250 blacks enrolled at Cornell at the time. A Syracuse TV station reported that Cornell's President Perkins had resigned. Unfortunately, that too was incorrect. Early radio reports said that forty blacks had taken over a building and twenty white football players wielding clubs and pipes had forced them out. I admit that sounds a lot "juicier" than reporting that one hundred or so African-Americans occupied a building, and nine whites without weapons went in to talk to them about opening it back up for Parent's Weekend. Logical thinking would suggest that, if we had gone in intending to fight, we would have brought more than nine unarmed kids.

The New York Times reported that Delta Upsilon had no Jews or blacks in the fraternity house and that there were no parents in The Straight when the blacks took it over. The *Times* story was wrong on both counts. Delta Upsilon had pledged black students in the past and had a number of Jewish members besides me. I later spoke with parents who were awakened in The Straight that morning. They told me that their doors were beaten down, and they were forced into one large room "like cattle." They said blacks holding clubs with knives attached to the ends told them that they would be killed. One parent begged an attacker to go easy on an elderly man with a heart condition. The heart patient was then shoved to the ground.

Because our lives were threatened, and because the Black Liberation Front demanded it before they would sign any agreement to give up occupancy, President Perkins agreed to release our names to the Black Panthers. As a result, for the rest of the semester DU had bomb scares, death threats, rocks thrown at us, and "Strangers in the Night" prowlers. We parked our cars facing out, in case we needed a quick escape.

Campus police had actually allowed the blacks to bring arms into The Straight that day, saying that if they attempted to stop it, "we would have found ourselves in a position where we would have been open to the possibility of scuffling or incidents around the periphery [of the building]."

"We were pariahs," Santo told Robert. "Girls spit on us and people called us racists. The DUs paid a price for a long time. Legacy admissions used to be standard at Cornell, but only one of our DUs' children got into the university. One of our daughters, who had straight A's, didn't make it into Cornell."

"The stories about this incident have gotten so screwed up over the years," Tom MacLeod, our roommate who was president of DU at the time, told Robert. "The stories have changed in favor of the dramatic. A handful of our guys were in the building for five or six minutes at the most. A lot less happened there than was later talked about. There were no heroes on any side, including the Cornell administration, which became completely intimidated and cowed. The SDS was the worst, most radical organization on campus. And it was not real bright of our fraternity to get involved. DU became a target for the rest of our college careers."

The seizure of The Straight made the front page of *The New York Times*, and I recognized one of the group's two leaders, Larry Dickson. In photos he was featured with his rifle raised, declaring victory. Larry lived in Asbury Park, and I had driven him home once on Christmas break.

The May 2, 1969, cover of *Life* read "Cornell: Guns on Campus." Eight inside pages of dramatic photos captured the brigade of blacks leaving Willard Straight Hall with rifles and shotguns over their shoulders and bandoleers strapped across their chests. A photo showed me exiting the window, wearing my Cornell football jacket. My head coach, Jack Musick, wasn't happy about that. I told him, "Coach, I just got our football team more publicity than we got all of last year."

We nine, and our whole fraternity, were a law-abiding group of young men who expected law and order to be upheld under any circumstances. Taking over buildings was not our thing. We would not have been justified had we taken that type of action. However, we felt we were justified in entering The Straight with the intention of re-opening the doors for the students and parents and possibly communicating with blacks with whom we were friendly, particularly black football players. Athletes have great respect for one another and have been brought closer together by both the competitiveness and the cooperation required by their work. Blacks and whites have become more united through sports than in any other area. They play, work, eat and sleep together as a result of their work. In The Straight that morning, however, there were only two black football players. Both of them were freshmen with little influence in the AAS. One of them was incapable of communicating with us. The other one did try to hold off some blacks who were attacking us.

My DU brothers and I had felt it was time for the "silent center," the "DU jocks" and what we thought was the "heart" of the Cornell community to act. Although we were only nine in number, we assumed that we represented the majority of the campus and that their lack of participation was due mainly to fear.

We were wrong. When it was all over, the nine of us stood alone. Most of the student body, which we thought we were representing, condemned our actions. They thought we were racists looking to bang heads. The fact that we were all football players from a fraternity with no black members *at the time* reinforced this misperception, which the media—including the campus paper—encouraged.

Certainly the news coverage of the event was increased by the entrance of white students into The Straight. That made it a national story. While we did receive telegrams and mail from all over the world supporting our stand and our courage, the overwhelming opinion seemed to be that Cornell, one of the greatest universities in the world, was a racist institution. The earlier burning of a cross on campus and the whites' attempt to "overtake" the blacks by "force" made bigger stories and sold more papers. Sensationalist reporting took over. When three whites and a black came out of the building with blood on their faces, the cameras started snapping. Distortion of the event and one-sided reporting caused many people to condone the blacks' seizure of Willard Straight Hall and to condemn any opposition to it by students, faculty or administration.

Only blacks and their sympathizers were interviewed about the incident for stories in the *Cornell Sun*. None of the *Sun's* reporters interviewed me or any of the DU members who were with me.

The *Sun's* sympathy with radical ideals had been apparent since the seizure took place. The campus paper's attacks were directed only toward conservative or moderately liberal whites.

Five or six black leaders were interviewed, and they claimed that they brought guns into The Straight only after "scouts" had spotted eight carloads of guns and ammunition being loaded in the DU parking lot. Had the *Sun* investigated, they would have found that at the time the blacks claimed they saw the "guns" being loaded, members of my band–ironically, a soul band–were loading their six cars with musical instruments and equipment for a party where we were to play that night.

The *Sun* failed to report that I was told I would be "shot full of lead" if I didn't get out of the building immediately. At that particular time, the blacks claimed they had no guns inside the building. The *Cornell Sun* also neglected to mention the fact that campus police had counted only four rifles taken into the building by the occupiers, although more than fifteen guns were brought out upon their departure.

The blacks claimed that the cross burning incident, the "attack" by white students, and the "carloads of guns" were all linked and clearly illustrated the presence of tense racism on the Cornell campus.

Both the Ithaca police and the campus police said they believed that the campus cross burning was an act by either the SDS or the by AAS themselves, "in a move to set the stage for the planned seizure." The campus police also stated that they had picked up five blacks for setting off fire alarms the Friday night before the occupation.

The efficiency with which the blacks captured and secured the building and the fact that it was Parents Weekend clearly indicated that the takeover was not impulsive, but was a well-prepared and well-organized plot.

The purpose of the occupation, it turned out, was to gain five African-American students amnesty for their participation in a *previous* demonstration.

By no definition am I a racist. I would have taken the same action no matter what group had seized The Straight. My fraternity brothers who entered the building with me felt the same way. We totally disagreed with the university's surrender of justice under threats and coercion. The university had confused the right to dissent with license to disrupt and destroy. Until the administration learned where to draw the line, we could expect further revolt and repercussions.

The rest of my junior year at Cornell essentially didn't exist. The nine of us were not permitted to attend any more classes that year. Academically I received an "S" in every course for the semester. I imagine the "S" stood for "Surrendered."

I addressed many groups on campus over the following weeks, talking to both black and white students. I was (finally) interviewed by most of the major newspapers. My purpose was to set up lines of communication, to answer questions and to explain Delta Upsilon's position on the worst crisis in the history of our magnificent Ivy League university, founded in 1865. I was just a Jersey boy in the silent center and was never a political guy. I was a "rock jock," a football player by day and a lead singer by night. Now it seemed I was speaking on behalf of the white community at Cornell. I reminded my audiences that the only lyrics that ever came out of my mouth were lyrics to black music.

After the smoke had cleared, I got in my Dodge and "got out of Dodge." I left President Perkins and headed back to Perkins Pancake House in Asbury Park, where I returned to scrambling eggs. Soon, President Perkins was fired for his mishandling of the crisis. It seemed that the Board of Trustees wasn't crazy about students using violence and rifles with telescopic lenses as a way to get your protest record expunged at Cornell.

CHAPTER ELEVEN

KENTUCKY FRIED BLUES

Nirvana, 1977

The summer of 1970, after graduating from Cornell, I was back in Asbury Park working at the Perkins Pancake House. I got an offer from my old Cornell freshman year boss, Erik Kamfjord, who now was with Winegardner & Hammons, Incorporated (WHI), the owners of thirty-seven Holiday Inns around the country. I had refused to interview with Erik when he came recruiting for WHI my senior year, because I felt he would reject me, given our history three years earlier. Santo Laquatra, my DU roommate and best friend, persuaded me to see Erik. Santo assured me, Erik viewed me favorably.

"I was now a vice president at WHI, overseeing fourteen Holiday Inns," Erik told Robert. "We took chances and gave young guys very responsible positions, trying to change the culture of the company. We particularly wanted athletes, because they were used to being part of a team. As with recruiting for any sports team, sometimes you win and sometimes you lose, and sometimes you get a bloody nose. I was pretty sure Jeff had matured in three years, and I was ready to take a chance on him. I laid out the prospects at Holiday Inn for him and told him it would be a very competitive situation, which I knew would appeal to him. If someone did well, he got promoted in two years and sent to another location. Because I knew what Jeff had his heart set on, I reminded him that all of our hotels had restaurants in them."

WHI wanted me to start in Syracuse, a prospect which did not interest me. I wanted to stay with John Angeles, the owner and manager of the Perkins where I had been working since I was fifteen.

We had a good relationship and I thought I could work my way up to assistant manager.

But Erik persisted. He kept calling me at Perkins, urging me to hurry up and make up my mind. My decision would affect his decisions on other candidates and their careers. I finally agreed to go to Syracuse and talk to him. WHI wined and dined me at their Syracuse Holiday Inn. I saw a great show at their rooftop supper club and spent the night in their penthouse suite with a beautiful girl. One night in Syracuse was great. The rest of my life was something else again. I told Erik that if he wanted me he would have to put me in Cincinnati, which happened to be his company's headquarters. When he asked why, I told him that the Cincinnati Reds had been my favorite baseball team since I was eight years old, and I wanted to see some of their games. Little did I know then that Reds legends Johnny Bench and Pete Rose would eventually make my first restaurant possible or that Sparky Anderson would consider me his "son." Erik agreed to my "demands."

So, in August of 1970, I packed my little white suitcase (still bearing the legend "No Riders") into my lime green Dodge Charger RT with racing stripes and the noisy glass-pack exhaust, and I drove south and west. I had twenty dollars and owned one suit. I stopped at a grubby Perkins "cafeteria" for lunch. It was nothing like the Perkins in Jersey. Ours was clean and a restaurant I was proud to be part of. I slid my tray down the counter and asked for the meatloaf. The lady's response was, "Please?" I was taken aback. In Jersey we just said, "Gimme some-a dat." In this town apparently you had to say, "I'd like some meatloaf, please." I apologized and said, "May I have some meatloaf, please?" Days later I learned when someone in this town can't hear you, they say "Please?" rather than "What?"

I stayed at a Holiday Inn in Fort Mitchell, Kentucky, while I looked for an apartment nearby, just across the Ohio River from Cincinnati.

I couldn't believe this place I had just moved to. Even the names of the streets had me questioning the likelihood of my fitting in here: Turkeyfoot Road, Buttermilk Pike, etc. And the towns! There was a sign for Big Bone Lick, and a town somewhere in the state was called Rabbit Hash; another one was dubbed Hazzard. I thought *What the hell am I doing here?* This was a far cry from the Jersey Shore.

On my first visit to Downtown Cincinnati, I heard a commotion across from Shillito's Department Store. I looked over and saw a little old black lady lying in the street, moaning in pain. I ran to her side and knelt down to comfort her. Then some guy came over giving the impression he wanted to help, but he grabbed the woman's purse and started to run. I caught him, threw him to the ground and said, "Shame on you." I returned the purse to the lady, and she was grateful.

Another night I left the Holiday Inn in Fort Mitchell, at 3 a.m., heading north to Cincinnati on I-75's "Death Hill." The car in front of me was swerving all over the place. I passed it carefully, so I wouldn't get hit. The driver was obviously drunk. A couple of minutes later, in my rearview mirror, I saw the car smash into the rock mountain on the passenger side of the highway. The car flipped upside down and began to smoke. I backed up and got out to help. A man, a woman and four children were trapped in the car. I could hear them crying. Knowing that their car could blow up at any second, I climbed in and pulled the kids out. An ambulance arrived and the adults were pulled out. I followed them to the hospital and stayed there all night, because I wanted to know if everyone would survive. They all did. I later learned that the male driver had told the cops I had run him off the road. The cops, of course, knew better, but I thought to myself, *What the hell kind of town is this? I can't even help people around here.*

I decided to go back home to Jersey and re-think just how badly I wanted to see a Reds game. "Pack up all my cares and woe, here I go…Bye, bye blackbird." AGAIN!

90

CHAPTER TWELVE

STARTED AT THE BOTTOM

Drake, 2013

Erik managed to settle down his problematic project–twenty-two-year-old me. At his urging, I returned to Cincinnati. One of the first things Erik made me do was get rid of my green Dodge Charger. He told me it was not a proper car for someone who worked for Holiday Inn. He had me buy a black Pontiac Grand Prix. My first job for Erik was at the Holiday Inn Downtown, on Linn Street, as the junior assistant innkeeper. Dick Whittaker, another Cornell graduate, two years ahead of me, was the assistant innkeeper.

Dick was living at The Forum, where many young professionals, professional athletes, radio jocks and hot girls lived. He let me sleep on his couch, and we split the rent. The Forum had a bar on the grounds, and I visited it one night. As I stepped up to order my Jack Daniel's, I noticed all these young chicks sitting around. One was even sitting on top of a guy. I figured there were too many girls for him alone, so I walked over. I wanted his "spillage." The guy was Johnny Bench.

I had watched Bench play against Cornell when he was with the Reds' minor league team in Buffalo. I introduced myself and invited him to come up to the Holiday Inn rooftop showroom, Top of the Inn, as my guest sometime. When I went back to the apartment, I told Whittaker that I had just met Johnny Bench. Dick had lived there for two years and hadn't yet met him. He busted my balls at Holiday Inn every day about my meeting Johnny Bench, so when I got a phone call one night and was told it was from Johnny Bench, I took the call with suspicion. When the caller said, "This is Johnny Bench,"

I said, "Hi, I'm Richard Nixon." It *was* Johnny, though, and he wanted to take me up on my offer to visit Top of the Inn.

We junior assistants were permitted to "comp" up to $150 per month each to buy hotel guests a drink or dessert, etc. Johnny showed up that evening with ten people. The Top of the Inn was a supper club that offered a lavish prime rib and crab leg buffet and acts that appeared on Johnny Carson's *Tonight Show*.

"I think we used up his allowance for the whole year that first night." Johnny told Robert. "It was only my third year with the Reds, and Jeff was a rookie in the hotel business. He was a go-getter from the first, and one of those guys who wore well. Word got around that there might be free drinks for athletes, and many of the other players and even a couple of coaches started coming in for a cocktail after the game. That Holiday Inn also became a place for players to meet for breakfast. The marketing strategy was that the Reds would bring in the girls, the girls would bring in other guys, who would bring in the money. It was brilliant for Jeff's career.

"Being around Jeff, you were always laughing. He did great impersonations; he really wanted to be Jackie Mason. Jeff had a lot of fun in life, and if there was a party anywhere, you wanted him around. He made life easy. You could trust him, but he had this macho thing and was a brawler, so you didn't want to mess with him."

Every relationship starts by simply saying "hello." Johnny, over time, became one of my best friends, my business partner, and my daughter Britney's godfather. I was in his first wedding. It was my job, along with Bengals first-round draft pick Mike Reid (now a country music song writer and Grammy Award winner), to be sergeants-at-arms at the front door of the church. Our responsibility was to make sure that no one crashed "the wedding of the century" in Cincinnati. No one did.

Rickelle and I were married in Reuven Katz's back yard, next door to Johnny's house. Johnny was the best man in our wedding. Reuven became my friend and attorney because Johnny introduced me to him.

Johnny Bench was best man when Rickelle and I married

The only autograph I ever asked Johnny for was on the mortgage for my first restaurant. More than anyone else, he made The Precinct possible. He also introduced me to country music. Both of these things have made my life better. And Johnny's and my relationship has motivated me to be successful.

* * * * *

In front of my Holiday Inn, 1971

The next summer, 1971, I became the assistant innkeeper at the Holiday Inn Riverfront in Covington, Kentucky, where I received a call from Erik. He told me that the Cincinnati Reds manager Sparky Anderson was staying at my motel and asked me if I had met him. When I told him that I hadn't, he responded in his typically stern Norwegian voice, "Then *meet* him!" I walked right into the dining room and there was Sparky, sitting with someone, having breakfast. I introduced myself, and Sparky said, "Sit down, son," He then introduced me to his breakfast companion, the outstanding and controversial college basketball coach Bobby Knight.

Thirty-five years later, Knight came into Jeff Ruby's in Cincinnati for dinner with St. Louis Cardinals manager Tony La Russa. Tony had been to our restaurants often, but when I introduced myself to Bobby Knight and said, "It's a pleasure to meet you," he said, "I met you at Holiday Inn in 1971 when I was with Sparky Anderson." Bobby Knight remembered meeting me, but I didn't remember meeting him. Say what you want about Knight, he earned my respect that night. He once gave my son Brandon a nice "directional" talk to help steer him right.

Sparky Anderson became like a dad to me. I ran all my problems with my girlfriends past him. Sparky won back-to-back World Series with the Reds in 1975 and 1976, and he won the 1984 World Series as manager of the Detroit Tigers. He knew how to manage, motivate and lead men, some of whom had huge egos. I learned from him.

When I got promoted to managing a larger Holiday Inn, in Sharonville, Ohio, Sparky moved there with me and brought his coaches with him, even though it wasn't convenient to the stadium. In his book about the 1975 Cincinnati Reds, *The Machine*, Joe Posnanski described how Sparky's coaches hated the "hotel in some bedroom community that was a pain-in-the-ass thirty-minute drive from Riverfront Stadium in Downtown Cincinnati....'It just didn't make sense,' they said. 'Jeff's there,' Sparky said, 'and we go where Jeff goes.' 'But,' they said to him, 'we're talking an hour of driving back and forth on Interstate 75.' 'Jeff's there,' Sparky said, 'and we go where Jeff goes.'

"Sparky loved that kid," Posnanski wrote. "Sparky would never forget having lunch at the old Holiday Inn, the one that was near the ballpark, and he saw one of the hotel employees leaning on his mop, not doing a thing, the sort of laziness that always set off Sparky. He thought America was sinking because of shiftlessness…and was just about to say something to this sluggard when he heard that voice dripping with New Jersey: 'Hey Pally! If you can lean, you can clean! Get moving!'

"That was Jeff Ruby, a mouthy Jewish kid who had gone to Cornell. Sparky called him 'bubula' – Yiddish for 'babe.'

"'Bubula,' Sparky whispered to Jeff over dinner that night. (That was another thing: Sparky often whispered when he talked to Jeff, like they were sharing a secret). 'People don't know, Bubula. They think they know this team, they think they know the Big Red Machine, but they don't know anything. Bubula, we're going to be good. We're going to be really good. You have to follow your stars. I'm telling you, the stars will win it for us this time.'"

On the night of July 13, 1975, the Reds' ace pitcher Don Gullet broke his thumb pitching against the Chicago Cubs. The next morning at breakfast, Sparky told me Gullett would be out for two months. I said, "This is horrible. We're in real trouble now." Sparky just kept on smiling, as he had been throughout our breakfast, which puzzled me. I asked him, "What are you going to do now?" He put down his fork and said, "Bubula, I'll tell you exactly what's going to happen. Now they're going to find out what a real genius I am."

When Gullett went down, the Reds were in first place by 3½ games. The team went on to win the league, with 108 wins and 54 losses, and they beat the second-place Dodgers by 20 games. That year, the Reds beat the Red Sox in arguably the greatest World Series in history. It was the Reds' first World Championship in 35 years. Sparky led the Reds to a four-game sweep of the Yankees the following year, becoming the first National League team to sweep a World Series since the 1921 New York Giants. In two years, Sparky had managed the Reds to as many World Championships as they had had since they were founded in 1890.

But then, after consecutive second-place finishes to the Dodgers, Sparky was fired by Reds general manager Dick Wagner. I asked Sparky what reason they gave. He said, "They didn't give me one and I didn't ask for one." That was Sparky Anderson. I, on the other hand, reacted by destroying all of our Cincinnati Reds promotional literature, posters, brochures and schedules. Winegardner & Hammons had a long relationship with the Reds. The team gave us tickets to games, and all of the motels along I-75 in Ohio and Kentucky advertised the Cincinnati Reds. Our motels were full when the Reds were in town. When Roy Winegardner heard about my rampage, he called Erik Kamfjord and ordered my "execution." I got a "stay" when Erik explained the relationship Sparky and I had. Sparky and Erik had become friends, too.

The 1975 World Series is still considered by many baseball fans to be the best in history. The Reds were playing the Red Sox at Fenway Park, and I flew to Boston to see games six and seven. There was a long rain delay during game six, and the Reds waited, along with me, in the dugout. The game was eventually rained out.

During the wait, Pete Rose instigated a playful one-on-one between Johnny Bench and me. I was wearing my Cornell football jersey.

As Johnny told Robert, "It wasn't a wrestling match; he'd been a wrestler, and I can fight but I can't wrestle. It was more like a grizzly bear and a polar bear going at it. It certainly wasn't a good idea. Sparky and I could have been banned from baseball for life."

"Some of us got really angry with Jeff," Joe Morgan, the Reds second baseman and the National League's MVP for both 1975 and 1976, told Robert, "going at it with Johnny like they were two linemen testing each other's strength. If Bench got hurt we'd be in trouble. Some guys were laughing at this fight, but it was not funny to me. I yelled at Jeff, who I'd really just become aware of in the clubhouse that day. Back then, a lot of guys, friends of players, were allowed in the clubhouse—that wouldn't happen today.

"Back home in Cincinnati, Jeff and I became friends. He knew the city better than I did then. There are very few people in Cincinnati who don't know who Jeff is. He knows a lot of important people; he's gotten around. But he's not a politician, shaking hands with everybody. He's a business person. Most of the time what he does is real.

"The secret to his success is no different from anyone else's: attention to detail and working hard to get the job done. He understands the restaurant business, which is very difficult to understand. He has the perfect recipe for success: he knows people and is able to hire the best people to work for him.

"I've heard about the difficult side of him, but I've never seen him confront anybody. My relationship with him is as a friend. Often it's just the two of us, watching a game or a match or having a glass of wine."

Several other players got knocked over in what had turned into a real battle, before Sparky finally heard the commotion and came running from his office to pull Johnny and me apart. Some cameramen heard it, too, and filmed every minute of it. Sparky said, "Jeffrey, this is my catcher. This is the sixth game of the World Series. I need this man. Thank God I got to those photographers. They promised me they wouldn't let the pictures get out. I could get fired."

Sparky Anderson tries to stop my "fight" with Bench during the 1975 World Series. My roommate, Doug Flynn, is in the middle of the picture looking on

Not only did the pictures get out, they made the front page and two inside pages of the New York *Daily News*. The photos also appeared in other papers around the country. "Boys Will Be Boys" was one headline. "Boys Will Play on a Rainy Day" was another. I never got to see Game Six. I was afraid if I stayed another day in Boston, I would get fired by Holiday Inn for missing too much work. So I missed the famous Carlton Fisk home run in the bottom of the twelfth. I spent three days in Boston, and I never saw one game of the greatest World Series ever.

The Reds' former manager, Dusty Baker, and I met when he was with the Los Angeles Dodgers and came to play Cincinnati in the 1977 season. Dusty told Robert, "Jeff can rub people the wrong way, but I've always gotten along with him. He is a pretty complex guy. He walks a thin line between strong and stubborn. He's very public and very private. He has a warm heart and can be open-minded and all for the equality of the common man. But he can also be an autocrat, and you never want to have political discussions with him. He's both King John and Robin Hood at the same time."

* * * * *

While I was working at Holiday Inn South in Fort Mitchell, Kentucky, as an assistant, a sixteen-year-old Beechwood High School kid named Gary Ginn was one of our busboys after school and on weekends.

Gary recalled to Robert: "Jeff had been there only a few days, but he was a take-charge person from the moment I met him. It seemed like he knew more than the innkeepers. He didn't have any patience, and he had a quick temper. He got in a lot of fist fights. When he and I would butt heads, he told me, 'I can hit you, but you can't hit me.' He'd fire me and then ask me when I was coming back to work.

"Jeff taught me to cook, starting with his cheese cake. The chef, who had been there for twenty-five years, didn't want me—or Jeff—in his kitchen. He yelled at me, 'get back, get out,' and came at me with a chef's knife. Jeff got him in a hammerlock, took the knife away, and fired the chef, which he really didn't have the right to do. But the innkeeper and the regional manager both backed him up, and the chef stayed fired.

"Ten years later, at The Precinct, where I was his assistant

100

manager for the first two years, one night he fired all the chefs and sent them home. 'We don't need them,' he said. And we didn't. He and I did all the cooking that night. It was a wild time at his first place. Someone shot a bullet shot through the window at The Precinct when we first opened.

"After we had a robbery at gunpoint at the Fort Mitchell Holiday Inn, Jeff asked me to get him a small gun, just in case we were robbed again. I showed him how to use it, and he put it in the bottom drawer of the innkeeper's desk. What Jeff didn't know was that the innkeeper was so afraid of guns that he took the clip out of it, so when Jeff later used it to chase after a second robber, the gun wasn't loaded."

It was Labor Day, and everyone had checked out. Other than Janice, a gorgeous blonde at the switchboard, I was the only employee on the property. I was sitting at the manager's desk in the office just off the lobby when a guy walked in the open door and pulled out a Colt 45 with a barrel as long as a chopstick. He came up to me, pushed the barrel of the gun against my head and shouted, "Where's the safe? I want the weekend money." I told him that I was just an assistant and didn't have the combination to the safe. He called me a liar, and we started arguing. He kept threatening and I kept bluffing. I had no intention of letting that SOB steal our money. Besides, I don't take orders from people. If I wanted to take orders, I'd wait tables at our restaurants.

"Open the safe or I'll blow your fuckin' head off," he yelled. I said, "Now you're really fucked." He still had the gun in my face but he wanted to know how he was fucked, so I explained, "You kill me, you still don't have your money, but you'll be in a helluva lot more trouble than you are now." He then ordered me to get up and walk to the front desk. As I walked, I turned my head to the left and mouthed, "Call the police," to Janice so she could read my lips. I'm not sure

Janice knew how to read *The Kentucky Post*. I hired her to look good and she did a very good job of that. Now, however, she was getting blonder by the second, and I needed someone with some common sense. The bandit took what little cash was in the drawer and began to walk away.

When he got to the lobby, I slipped into the office and got my gun. The bandit was just going out the front door, and I was face-to-face with him through the plate glass window. We took aim at each other. Just as he was ready to shoot, I ducked my head back into the office and came back out and took aim at him again. We kept this up, like they do in the movies, until he took off. I ran out the door and chased him.

Just then, my friend Joe McNay drove into the parking lot, with his twelve-year-old son, Don, and eleven-year-old daughter, Theresa. He especially wanted Don to meet me, and we had planned to have dinner that night. Joe rolled down the window and asked me what was going on. I told him, but I kept running after the guy. I don't think Janice ever did call the police.

Don McNay, who is now fifty-four and a journalist for the *Huffington Post* and an author based in Richmond, Kentucky, vividly recalled that incident of forty-two years ago and told Robert, "The robber was running as fast as he could across the parking lot, and Jeff was chasing right behind him. When Jeff came into the dining room for dinner he was huffing and puffing, although he was only twenty-three and in good shape. His shirttail was hanging out. The robber had gotten away. Dad asked Jeff if the robber had a gun, and when Jeff said 'yes,' Dad asked, 'What were you going to do if you caught him?' For once, Jeff didn't have a quick response. If it had been anyone else, they wouldn't have run after an armed man.

"He didn't own the hotel. He was only in charge of it for that day. It wasn't his money that was stolen. But by putting his life on the line chasing the robber, he showed the same guts, inner drive and determination that led him later to create some of the most successful restaurants in the Cincinnati area.

"Jeff pushed Cornell really hard at me that night at dinner, even though I was only twelve and not thinking about college yet. (When the time came, I did get accepted at Cornell, but they had no money for scholarships, so I went to Vanderbilt.) But what I really remember most about that night was the furious chase across the parking lot. My sister and I laughed about it for years afterward. To this day, every time I go by the original location of that Holiday Inn, I think about it and smile."

The police caught the bandit, took him to the police station, and the SOB still escaped.

"After eleven years working with Jeff at three different Holiday Inns and The Precinct, I was ready to move on," Gary Ginn recalled. "I had always wanted to open my own restaurant, and eventually I did, several of them. After two years at The Precinct, seven days a week, twelve hours a day, I really wanted my own place. In 1983, I started as the manager of a 400-seat night club, The BBC, and took a couple of Jeff's bartenders with me. Jeff said it would really be disloyal if I put steak on the menu."

Gary took my creation "Halibut Forte" to a Cajun place called Dee Felice, and now that dish is on menus all over the Midwest.

My first full innkeeper's position was at the 104-room Holiday Inn in Mason, Ohio, about twenty minutes north of Cincinnati. It was a "sleepy hollow" motel with a Sunoco station nearby, off of I-71. My motel guests were the guys building the Eiffel Tower for the Kings Island amusement park being developed nearby. My predecessor,

John Minello, had left to join his family at their well-established Italian restaurants in Cleveland.

I continued John's hugely successful Italian Night on Tuesdays, and added a French Night. I was the chef for both nights. We were the smallest Holiday Inn in the company, and we served close to three hundred people on Tuesday nights in "Mayberry," offering authentic Italian food, which John had taught me how to cook. There were no *réchaud* burners at any Holiday Inn, so I cut a number 10 can in half and put Sterno inside of it. I wrapped the can in aluminum foil and did my tableside cooking with a frying pan on top of it. I used Sexton brand flambé instead of brandy. In Mason, Ohio, back then, that was French enough.

For months, everything went smoothly with my improvisations. Then one night something went wrong. I held the red plastic pourer from the flambé bottle too close to the flame and the pourer popped out of the bottle, creating a huge flame of its own. It took off across the dining room like a flamethrower. The restaurant was quite busy, and naturally everyone's heads turned in surprise and bewilderment. The "jet" pourer finally landed on some guy's plate. The missile had hit its target. The flame had gone out, and the diner wasn't upset at all. He looked over at me, and I just said, "I'm sorry, that was supposed to land on someone else's plate." We were lucky that nobody got hurt.

Today, there are more students at Mason High School than the population of the entire town back then. I worked my way up to regional director of the seven Holiday Inns the company owned in Greater Cincinnati. My territory stretched from Middletown, Ohio, to Florence, Kentucky.

With Erik's help and encouragement, I pioneered the night-club industry in Greater Cincinnati. There hadn't been any places for the twenty-five and up crowd to go for nightlife in this city, until he gave me rooms to work with. Other than in Los Angeles, Miami or New York, no one had seen anything like Lucy's in the Sky, on the rooftop of the Holiday Inn Downtown. It was the city's Studio 54. In Covington, we opened Dr. Potts in an old banquet room in the motel's basement and featured Las Vegas show bands.

"Jeff took off and ran with it," Erik told Robert. "The company provided the stage and he filled the stage. Pretty soon the tail (the clubs) was wagging the dog (the hotels), thanks to his aggressive, creative management and his friendships with the sports teams. In the late 1970s, when the old business model for clubs began to shift from live entertainment to discotheques, Jeff, who was always a fast learner, presided over the transition—even though he preferred live music and didn't like using the word 'disco.'

"He and I had a father-son relationship, and before his marriage he spent Thanksgiving and other holidays with me and my family. But Jeff didn't get any of his promotions at Holiday Inn because of me. He got them by delivering an outstanding performance."

In 1993 I was one of just two members inducted into the Nightclub and Bar Hall of Fame in Las Vegas. The other was Hugh Hefner.

When I joined the team at Winegardner & Hammons, their Holiday Inns were largely unionized. In every subsequent union de-certification, I was either the innkeeper at the motel or the regional director responsible for it: Holiday Inns North, Downtown, Riverfront and South. To assist in the decertification elections, Erik brought in the renowned Memphis labor law firm of McKnight Hudson. Cincinnati was the headquarters for the hotel/restaurant union, and the maids, laundry workers, dishwashers and cooks had been members for their entire careers. The majority of the employees were African-American, low-paid, hourly workers. The elections boiled down to voting either for their union or for me. These were no different from any other elections; the outcomes depended on likeability and whom the voters trusted most.

The campaigns were intense. The union told our employees lies about the company in order to get their votes. At Holiday Inn North, only the laundry workers were unionized. The laundry room was about one hundred yards from my office. I had a very good relationship with those workers. They were mostly black, and all of them were women. I felt confident that they would decertify the union they had belonged to for more than ten years. The unprecedented vote totals at the four Inns were 73-0, 54-1, 37-0 and 63-1 in my favor. I was not satisfied, however. I kept trying to figure out, *"Who was the one?"*

The upside of my eleven years at WHI was learning a lot about the business from Erik; making many friends like Sparky Anderson, Pete Rose, and Johnny Bench; and meeting many beautiful girls. I met both the girl I lived with for five years and the one I married at Spanky's in Sharonville, Ohio. I was in the business of finding good-looking girls and getting them to come to my bars to attract men and their money. It was accidental that I fell in love with two of them.

The downside of those eleven years was that I spent them at Holiday Inn, not the Ritz-Carlton. Let's face it, Holiday Inn does not provide the epicurean background investors are looking for when they put their money behind someone like me, who wants to open his first restaurant. Since my prior experience had been mostly at Perkins Pancake House in Asbury Park, I hadn't followed the best-designed career path after Cornell. Cincinnati was a city with as many Mobil 5-Star restaurants as New York. Was I really ready to open my own place in this market?

Ready or not, I was itching to do it. Erik told Robert that I was "winging it for the last couple of years at Holiday Inn." What I was really doing was scouting locations and learning as much as I could about the stand-alone restaurant business.

Buddy LaRosa, Cincinnati's oldest living restaurateur, has owned family-style Italian restaurants since 1954. He now has seventy-two operations, grossing $160 million a year. Buddy told Robert about meeting me on an airplane going to London on a restaurant junket in the late 1970s:

"On the plane going over, this chubby, curly-haired kid was sitting next to me. I didn't know who the hell he was. He knew me, but I didn't know him. He started asking me questions about running a restaurant. He was polite and respectful, and he had a degree from Cornell, which impressed me. I'd been a boxing coach, used to working with kids, and I'd had many great mentors myself, so I was happy to tell him what I knew.

"Once we got to London, we were pretty much on our own. But everywhere my wife and I went, on a tour bus or to a restaurant, there was Jeff, with more questions. He picked my brain every day, absorbing it all like a sponge. When he asked me what the most important thing about owning a restaurant was, I told him it was the orchestration of it, like putting a symphony together. Everything the customer's going to see or experience has to sparkle. Once the customers come in, it's got to be like show business, like opening night. I told him you have to get great people to work for you, train them well, pay them extra well, and give them benefits. Pay attention to all the little things. Anybody can be successful, but you've got to start early and work late and make a lot of sacrifices. Even then, you're not going to hit a home run every time.

"A couple of years after we met, Jeff brought the New York steakhouse experience to Cincinnati with The Precinct. Sure, you're gonna pay eight dollars for a baked potato, but in New York you might have to pay twelve. The quality impresses, long after the price is forgotten.

"Recently, I read a story about Jeff's philosophy of running a restaurant, and some of it sounded awfully familiar. I love him like a son, but I'm not taking any credit for his success.

"He's like Toots Shor. He's got the magic."

CHAPTER THIRTEEN

MRS. BROWN, YOU'VE GOT A LOVELY DAUGHTER

Herman's Hermits, 1965

I was managing the Holiday Inn North in Sharonville when the most beautiful girl I had ever seen walked into Spanky's, the Inn's bar and club. "It was nineteen-seventy somethin,'" as the song goes, and I thought to myself, *This is the girl I want to marry.* Her name was Susan Brown, and it was love at first sight for me. She was with a huge, chiseled, good-looking dude much younger than I. He was the Cincinnati Bengals' number one draft pick that year, a defensive tackle named Bill Kollar. The twosome looked like they were made for each other. He was probably twenty-two and she had just turned twenty. I figured I only had one chance to meet her, so I made my move, Bill Kollar notwithstanding. You don't get a girl like this without a fight.

It took me some time to land Susan. Aside from Kollar, she also had a boyfriend. Ross Bunch was a tall, good-looking trumpet player in a show band called Cops 'N' Robbers. I booked Cops 'N' Robbers just so I could see Susan. One night Ross and I were standing next to each other in the men's room and didn't say a word to each other. He knew what was going on with Susan and me.

She eventually moved in with me, and we lived together in my house in Loveland, Ohio, for about five years. We made great love in Loveland. My Cincinnati Red housemate Doug Flynn said his girlfriend remarked, "I hope you're as good as they *sound*." Susan still reminds me about those days. I still remind her that she was "Downtown Susan Brown."

I tried to slip an engagement ring on her finger in Aruba, but she wasn't ready. I tried again at the Magic Wok in Kenwood, and again she said, "No." I tried to propose to her in three different countries. We were seven years apart in age. I was thirty and ready to settle down, but my girlfriend was twenty-three and was not yet ready, as she made very clear. Mrs. Brown, you've got a stubborn daughter.

"Jeff was laser-focused and very persistent," Susan told Robert Windeler. "When he puts his mind to something, that's the way it's going to work out. He had turned thirty and had his house. He wanted to get married and have kids. Jeff was used to getting what he wanted, and he did get what he wanted—just not with me. I was still in my early twenties, and I wasn't ready to do any of that yet. Back then I was going to live life to the fullest and be dead by forty. I was kind of bratty about it. I told him, 'Don't give me a ring, or it will be over.' He tried again in Hawaii and I still said no. I didn't even want to see the ring. I never did see it. I understand it was really nice."

I finally gave up and told Susan to move out, and she did. Be careful what you ask for. With her gone, I was so depressed I couldn't stay focused on work. My boss, Erik Kamfjord, knew what was wrong with me and called me into his office. Seven Holiday Inn general managers were not getting direction from their boss because I, now the regional manager over them, was a freakin' mess over the break-up with Susan. I had lost the love of my life, and now I would lose my job if I didn't snap out of it. "If the drinking don't kill me her memory will," as George Jones sang. I hoped Susan would call me. She was still working at our corporate headquarters Downtown, at the job I got her as WHI's receptionist.

I was awakened at about 3 a.m. one night by a pounding on my front door. I hoped it was Susan wanting me to take her back. I walked to the door, thinking about my plan of action along the way. I took a deep breath and then opened the door to see a beautiful young girl standing there. It wasn't Susan. It was another good-looking girl I knew who had had a fight with her boyfriend. She wanted to be with me that night, so I accommodated her.

When Susan and I broke up, Sparky Anderson reminded me of the Michael Masser-Ron Miller lyrics sung by Diana Ross in 1973: "We don't have tomorrow, but we had yesterday." I responded with, "That's all well and good if she would 'touch me in the morning.'"

Susan is married to Drew Gitlin, a former pro tennis player she met at Spanky's. They have two terrific kids and live in Los Angeles. Susan and I remain very good friends.

CHAPTER FOURTEEN

THE FIGHTIN' SIDE OF ME

Merle Haggard, 1970

The song hit the country charts the year I graduated from Cornell and hit the road for Cincinnati. The fightin' side of me, however, began much earlier than 1970.

My propensity for fighting started with the Spinach Fights. Every kid I knew watched *Popeye the Sailorman* cartoons on TV. Every time Popeye got into trouble he would open a can of spinach, gulp it down and kick ass. Bluto was his antagonist and was three times Popeye's size. It was a David and Goliath concept, good vs. evil, and Popeye would be getting the shit kicked out of him until he could find his can of spinach. Then it was "game over" for the evil Bluto. When I was about eight, I would get a can of spinach, get on my bike and go looking for fights. I got in a fight every time someone looked at me funny. One guy who looked at me funny and started giving me a hard time was a real "Bluto." He was huge, about one hundred pounds heavier, a foot taller, and much older than I was. I got off my bike, ate my spinach and got the shit kicked out of me. He kicked me in the head with his work boots while I was on the ground. It didn't faze me. The next day I was back on my bike with my can of spinach. I liked being David. Goliath was big, but David had balls.

In the summertime, the kids from Neptune High went to the beach at Avon-by-the-Sea in the afternoon. Out-of-towners went everywhere else. A fight broke out on Ocean Avenue in Bradley Beach one night. A group of Syrian older kids from New York were fighting some underclassmen from Neptune High when I drove by on my motorbike. I stopped, of course, and started whaling away, protecting my boys. The cops came and I was the one they arrested. At the trial, the two cops told the judge I resisted arrest and tried to flee. The public defender then asked me to stand up. "Your Honor, take a look at this kid and take a look at these two policemen. Do you think if this kid tried to get away he would even be here today?" I was found not guilty.

At our forty-fifth high school reunion, Len Renery told a story about me that I didn't recall. Apparently he's been reciting it at every reunion, none of which I attended until the forty-fifth. Len played baseball and was a soccer star at Neptune. He went on to play professional major league soccer for seven years. Since he remembers the story and I don't, let him tell it as he told it to Robert. I don't even remember going to this game, let alone the incident that followed. But Lenny has no reason to lie about it, and it sounds a lot like me.

"Jeff was what you'd call a big man on campus. He hung with a prestigious crowd," Len recalled, "although he wasn't arrogant or unkind in any way. Everyone knew Jeff Ruby. We were in the same class and had a cordial relationship, even though we didn't hang out together. One summer afternoon in 1965, between our junior and senior years, I was sitting on a bus at Asbury Park station with a baseball buddy of mine, waiting for the rest of the passengers to get on. We were headed to New York and a Mets night game at Shea Stadium. I saw Jeff Ruby walk by, his Neptune varsity jacket hanging over his shoulder, and I yelled out the window to him. He asked where we were going. When I told him, he wanted to know who the Mets were playing. When I told him it was the Cincinnati Reds, he asked if there was any room on the bus. Next thing I knew, he was boarding.

"As the bus rumbled up the Garden State Parkway, then along the New Jersey Turnpike and through the Lincoln Tunnel, I got to know more about Jeff Ruby's upbringing and self-sufficiency. At Port Authority Bus Terminal, we hopped on a subway out to Queens and our seats in the third deck at Shea.

"I was pleased when the Mets won, but Jeff wasn't. He was, indeed, a Reds fan even then. The game was long, and we didn't get back to Port Authority until 11:45 p.m. The last bus for Asbury Park had left at 11:30; the next one was not until 6 a.m. My buddy George and I made collect calls to our displeased and concerned mothers. Jeff didn't need to make such a call.

"We walked around the still-dangerous Times Square for an hour, damned glad Jeff Ruby was with us. Then we bought tokens and rode the subway rails to kill time until dawn. By 3:30 a.m. the platforms were deserted, and our subway car was empty, except for the three of us. Jeff and George were both asleep, but I couldn't keep my eyes closed. Every time the train pulled into a station and the doors opened, I held my breath. I breathed a sigh of relief when no one got on.

"Then, somewhere in the Bronx, it happened. The biggest, ugliest, scariest dude I'd ever seen got on, sat down directly opposite me, and kept staring. Then he got up and said he wanted to sit where I was. I told him that there were plenty of other seats, but he said 'I want that seat, mother-fucker.' I got up and slid down to the seat next to Jeff. The big man got up again and walked down the aisle toward me. I woke Jeff up, and now the big guy was standing in front of us, as the train clattered into another station.

"Jeff didn't speak a word. He rose from his seat in a movement so rapid that it shocked me. His Neptune High jacket slipped from his shoulders and fell to the ground. Like a hawk on a rabbit, Jeff's hands fastened on the lapels of the big dude's jacket just as the train pulled to a stop. If I was surprised at the speed and purposefulness of Ruby's action, the giant was shocked to the core. Jeff marched the seven or eight yards to the door of the car, the giant securely in his grasp, too surprised to struggle. As the train doors opened, Jeff Ruby tossed the big man through the air and out the door. He landed on

114

his back on the platform, the look of shock still on his face. The doors closed and the train continued on.

"My life was saved. I turned to Jeff to say a simple 'thank you,' but he was asleep again, his Neptune letter jacket draped over his head and shoulders like a blanket."

* * * * *

At Neptune High School we were equally split racially at a time when segregation was still in force. The word "black" wasn't being used widely yet. I got along with all of the Negro kids. I was called "the Duke" of the school, which meant I was the toughest kid at Neptune High in a fight. Wesley Walker was the toughest Negro kid. The kids, both black and white, wanted the two of us to fight, like Ali vs. Quarry, just to see who would win. Wesley didn't show. Thank God for that. What a stupid idea.

There were three types of white kids at Neptune High: greasers, bookworms, and jocks. Most of the whites were greasers. The same thing was true at Asbury Park High. At this time, at the Jersey Shore, we grew up playing hopscotch with real scotch. Sometimes I'm surprised that I lived to reminisce about it.

What I find interesting is that I recall very few of these incidents. My friends' memories are always of a fight I was in that I can't remember. In the following story, which took place in my sophomore year, I don't even remember the bar, let alone the fight. Craig Lambert, my fraternity brother and football teammate at Cornell, recalled it, however.

"When I was a freshman and rushing Delta Upsilon, I went to this bar in Ithaca. I got into a fight with an employee there. He happened to have a harelip. He beat the hell out of me. When I told Jeff about it, back at the fraternity house, he insisted that we return to the bar. The place was crowded, so it took a while to find the man with the harelip. When a guy finally approached Jeff and asked him, 'Are you lookin' for me?' Jeff asked him, 'Do you have a harelip?' The guy said, 'Yeah, why?' Jeff knocked him out with a right hook, turned to me and said, 'Let's go home.'"

When Erik Kamfjord hired me, he said what he liked about me was that I was a "street fighter." But I don't believe he knew just how that was going to manifest itself for the next eleven years in the bars at his Holiday Inns in and around Cincinnati.

Three years later, when Erik came back to Cornell to recruit, I didn't sign up for an interview with him because I remembered the times he had caught me eating prime rib and goofing off. There was no way I was going to give him the pleasure of denying me a job offer. My roommate and closest friend, Santo Laquatra, did interview with Erik, and he finally persuaded me to sign up for an interview. Santo claimed that Erik had told him he really wanted to see me, and Santo insisted that Erik liked me.

Erik had followed my career at Cornell. He knew about the injuries that I suffered in football and how I fought through them. He had watched me grow and mature. I asked him, "What about what happened my freshman year?" "You were an eighteen-year-old kid," he said. When I went to work for Erik, his slogan was still "One Ice Cream," just as it had been my freshman year at Cornell. It meant simply "keep costs down, Jeff." For the eleven years that I worked for him at the Holiday Inns in Cincinnati, I needed a man like Erik. He became my mentor and made a big difference in my life.

The problem with bars is that you have to deal with drunks. The problem with me was that I wasn't very good at it. People behave differently when they drink. I become friendlier and more

116

conversational. Some are just the opposite. Sometimes it takes only a couple of drinks to turn them nasty. I never handled those situations well, but, in my defense, every fight of mine was the result of one of my employees being hit or verbally abused. I always had my employee's back, even if it meant I had to put someone else on his back.

I was managing the Holiday Inn in Sharonville, just north of Cincinnati, the company's largest motel. It consisted of many buildings sprawled over many acres. I named the new bar Spanky's, and it became the hottest singles "boy-meets-girl" joint in Greater Cincinnati. At happy hour, General Electric and Ford workers filled the place. At night my formula was: good-looking babes, ballplayers, businessmen, and barflies. Hotel guests, of course, chose to stay at my hotel because of Spanky's. That was Erik's best reason for not transferring Jeff Ruby out of Cincinnati. I'm sure of it. His company had hundreds of managers, and when they got promoted they usually had to move to a motel out of state. Maybe he knew he had better keep me close, because I would get into too much trouble out of state. I was getting into a lot of fistfights in Cincinnati.

Erik was a friend of Sharonville's Police Chief Nuss, so when the chief gave Erik a call my boss wasn't alarmed. Nuss told Erik that business was great since that new kid had taken over, but they'd never had so many police calls to break up fights in the hotel's history. The chief said, "Erik, every time we show up, your manager is at the bottom of the pile." Erik decided to have the regional manager, my direct boss, Joe Cooper, meet with me. The meeting was scheduled for 6 p.m. Mr. Cooper didn't tell me what the meeting was about.

Happy hour was packed that night. Sharon, the sweetest little gal, was a bartender for us. She came over to me to tell me a guy wouldn't pay his bill. He had accused her of padding it. I had decided that I had to stop getting into so many fights. I'd try a new approach. I wouldn't confront these drunks in front of people. Maybe that's what

I was doing wrong. I'd politely talk to them away from their friends so they wouldn't be embarrassed and couldn't show off. Maybe that would work.

I politely asked the gentleman if I could talk to him, and we walked to the hotel's front desk. I was cordial and attested to Sharon's integrity. It worked. He gave me his credit card, and I ran it through at the front desk. As I walked back to Spanky's, I felt a shove from behind. I immediately reacted with a right hook, and that guy hit the ground head first.

Birdie Griffey was our hostess and saw the entire incident. "Jeff, I think he's dead!" she screamed. Birdie is Ken Griffey Jr.'s mom. Her husband was Ken Griffey, a Cincinnati Red and my friend. Birdie needed a job, so I gave her one. Kenny Jr. and his brother Craig were my water boys when I played very semi-pro football in Cincinnati. Ken Sr. was then going back and forth between the minors and the Reds.

The guy I had just hit was lying on the ground unconscious and turning purple. A thin straight line of blood streamed down his face. Entering the lobby for our six o'clock meeting was Joe Cooper. It was a very narrow corridor, so Joe had to step over this guy to get to me. "I guess I'm a little late for this meeting," he said.

I had thought about giving the patron mouth-to-mouth but changed my mind. I yelled to our security guard, "Smokey, do something!" He just stood there in shock. The paramedics came and took the guy away.

Across the driveway from the Holiday Inn in Sharonville was a workout gym and golf driving range called Golden-Tee. I became friends with the kid working in the weight room and let him have a room at my house in Loveland. He was much younger than I and not

118

making much money, so I didn't charge him. The kid looked up to me, and I thought he was a good kid.

That all changed when I was told he was in one of my hotel rooms with my girlfriend. I couldn't drive fast enough to my house to confront him that afternoon. When someone I've been good to does something like that to me, I take it personally. I'm no different from a prostitute. If you fuck me, I'm gonna make you pay. This kid was built. He lifted weights and was in his mid-twenties. When I got home he was asleep. I woke him up, said good morning, and hit him square in the face. Blood spattered the walls and ceiling and all over me. His pretty face was unrecognizable. He certainly wasn't handsome enough for my lady anymore. He grabbed some towels, wrapped what was left of his face and drove himself to Bethesda North hospital. The truth was that both he and my girlfriend were mistakenly told there was a party going on in our party suite. The kid suggested since they were there they should have sex. My girlfriend said no and told him, "Jeff will find out (which I did) and will kill you (which I almost did)." "He's crazy," she said (which I was). The kid agreed, and they didn't have sex after all.

I later rented rooms to Doug Flynn and Rawley Eastwick of the Cincinnati Reds' famous Big Red Machine, for seventy-five dollars per month each. The only thing we fought about was the music each of us played in our rooms. I had my R&B, Rawley had his hard rock, and Doug had his country (before I liked it). It was a small, $43,000 house with tiny bedrooms.

The late Sparky Anderson, a Reds manager, liked to tell of the time he was staying at the Holiday Inn Downtown, and I got into a fight with someone outside the front door. Sparky came out to stop it. "Jeffrey, the snow is red. It's over, Jeffrey," he said. That dude had punched out my thin, under-matched assistant, the late Mark Patrick. May Mark and Sparky both rest in peace.

One night at Lucy's in the Sky, I got word that one of the Cincinnati Reds, Champ Summers, was staying at my Holiday Inn and had my girlfriend in his room. I was furious. I got a master key, charged in and threw this well-built player to the ground. My girlfriend jumped out of the window and onto the thirteenth floor ledge overlooking I-75. I pulled her in and threw her out of the room. Over breakfast the next morning, I told Sparky what had happened. Nothing more was said, but a week later Champ Summers was traded.

Trouble has a way of finding all of us occasionally. I just happen to have a more difficult time hiding from it than most people do. On Sundays it knows how to find me at Paul Brown Stadium. Taylor Swift wrote a hit song, "Should've Said No." I should think of that before I lose my temper. I need to say, "No, Jeff," to myself more often.

One Sunday, two guys crashed our company's Owner's Suite at the stadium during a Bengals-Steelers game, right next to my twenty guests. I was sitting, watching TV and talking on the phone when I noticed these two guys helping themselves to our food. The Bengals offer a "Best of Jeff Ruby's" package to their suite owners as one of the dining options for the games. These two crashers were "dining fine." I went up to the guy in his twenties and asked who he was and who said he could be there. My concern was that damn near everyone says they know me or know someone who knows me. I didn't want to overreact. I then asked, "What are you doing?" He replied, "Eating." That did it. When I tried to wrestle him to the ground and he didn't go down, I felt like I didn't "have it anymore," so I just gave the jerk a good right to the face.

The punch knocked him back so far his head hit the wall just below the TV. His friend took off and ran out of the stadium. I told someone to get security. In minutes, stadium security, the Cincinnati Police, Hamilton County Deputy Sheriffs, and Bengals representatives were in my suite and outside my door. I don't recall how many cops asked me if I wanted this asshole arrested. I said, "Not at all." My Kentucky attorney, Phil Talliaferro, was in our suite that day, and he dealt with the kid over the next few days. Most of the food had ended up on the ceiling, and the kid had done nothing about hitting me back. I still "had it."

There's something about Pittsburgh Steelers games that particularly incites Bengals fans. At one Bengals-Steelers game at Paul Brown Stadium, I had another "should've-said-no" moment. I was wearing my custom-made Steelers jersey with Ben Roethlisberger's number 7 on the front. On the back, however, I had had Koch Sporting Goods stitch "Worthlessburger." While I was walking up the ramp with my two surrogate sons, Nick and Jake, a guy yelled something unprintable at me. I charged through the crowded ramp. I suppose he yelled at me because I had a Roethlisberger jersey on. He saw only the front. I asked if he was the guy who had yelled at me. Surrounded by his six friends, one of them a "gorilla," he confirmed that he was, so I put out my cigar on his forehead. I then stared at him. He stared back and then punched me in the jaw with all he had. "That all you got?" I said. One of his friends said, "That's Jeff Ruby."

Like the Toby Keith song lyrics go, "I ain't as good as I once was, but I'm good once as I ever was."

CHAPTER FIFTEEN

TRAGEDY

Bee Gees, 1979

May 28, 1977, began like any other Saturday for me. I was living in Loveland, Ohio, with my girlfriend, Susan Brown, the most beautiful girl in Cincinnati. I was in love in Loveland. I had just turned twenty-nine, purchased my first house, and been promoted to Regional Manager of Greater Cincinnati's seven Holiday Inns. Life was good.

I had planned to be at one of my hotel's busy nightclubs that evening, the one I had named Lucy's in the Sky. It had a panoramic view of the city from the top floor of our high-rise location. Lucy's was the hottest singles bar in the city. My evening's plans quickly changed, but I couldn't foresee that so much more was going to change that night.

Rick Hauck was one of my hotel managers, and a friend. I had met Rick while we were playing semi-pro football together in Cincinnati, and I hired him as a doorman at one of our bars. He worked his way up to Innkeeper at the Holiday Inn Riverfront in Covington, Kentucky. Rick's girlfriend, Rickelle, turned twenty-one that day, and he wanted to take her to Beverly Hills, a spectacular supper club in Northern Kentucky. The late Jack Lobert, our wine rep, and his lovely wife, Joanie, would also be going. They, too, were friends of mine. Rick called to ask if I would join them.

Now, I went to Beverly Hills only when an entertainer or group I liked was performing there. That night it was singer John Davidson, whom I had no interest in seeing. Rick pleaded with me to go because it was Rickelle's birthday, so I gave in. Rickelle, a dead ringer for actress Heather Locklear, was a cocktail waitress at Spanky's, our club at Holiday Inn in Sharonville. I could get us good seats. Susan agreed to go with us. I told Rick we would pick up him and Rickelle, and meet Jack and Joanie at the club.

Beverly Hills was the most notorious nightclub in Kentucky's history. It had opened in 1935. Pete Schmidt, an ex-con who had served time for shooting a cop during a raid on Pete's huge whiskey still during Prohibition, created a luxurious restaurant and an illegal casino in Southgate, just outside of Newport, Kentucky. He called it The Beverly Hills Club, and he operated a still out in back there, too. Prohibition was over by then, but most people couldn't afford brand-label liquor and continued to buy the homemade stuff. The club's success drew the attention of one of the most powerful crime syndicates in the country, the Cleveland syndicate. Among the syndicate's leaders was Moe Dalitz, a boyhood friend of Jimmy Hoffa, a member of the notorious "Purple Gang," a partner of Meyer Lansky and Bugsy Siegel in their New York operations, and a power in Northern Kentucky bootlegging. Dalitz owned many Las Vegas casinos and was a force in gambling in Cuba until Castro overthrew Batista in 1959.

The Cleveland syndicate offered to buy the club and make Schmidt a partner. When he refused to sell, Mafia hit man Red Masterson burned the place down in 1936, killing a young girl.

Schmidt rebuilt the club in 1937, reopening it as the Beverly Hills Country Club, although it had no golf course. The syndicate, however, was not to be denied. Their soldiers held an armed robbery in front of customers, they publicly urinated in Schmidt's other establishment (which I took over sixty years later), and they kept up the pressure, causing Beverly Hills' business to suffer. Business got so bad that Schmidt sold the place to the Mafia in 1940, for next to nothing. The new Mafia owners brought in name entertainers such as

Frank Sinatra, Dean Martin, Marilyn Monroe, and Ozzie and Harriet Nelson. Newport, Kentucky, was the first "Sin City," and was essentially the precursor to Las Vegas, where all the Newport gangsters ended up.

A. B. "Happy" Chandler, Kentucky's governor, declared in 1958 that, "The people of Newport have a right to have it dirty." Chandler was re-elected. You could do anything you wanted, but if you talked to the law you went into the Ohio River in a concrete body cast called a "Newport night gown." The Northern Kentucky Mafia was known back east as the "Cornbread Cosa Nostra." But everyone who got in their way went fishing with Fredo, because the local Mafia paid off cops and bribed judges.

When Dick Schilling bought the property in 1969, he changed the name back to Beverly Hills. In 1971, the union set a second fire while the place was being remodeled. Kentucky's "good ole boys" network of corrupt governors, judges and cops prosecuted no one, just as they hadn't in 1937.

Frank Sinatra Jr. was the opening night act for Schilling's new Beverly Hills. I went with my girlfriend Susan Reddick, a student at the University of Cincinnati. On that opening night, I could not foresee that six years later I would also be there for their *closing* night, with another girlfriend named Susan. I'm still desperately seeking Susan, any Susan.

It was a sultry night in Greater Cincinnati on that Saturday of Memorial Day weekend in 1977. I was still wondering why I was going to Beverly Hills see John Davidson. He certainly was a star, especially among middle-aged women, but he'd never had a hit. There wouldn't be many other twenty-nine-year-old men in the audience. My previous forays to this club had been to see two of my favorite groups, The Righteous Brothers and The Four Tops, and I'd also gone to see the comedians Redd Foxx, Phyllis Diller, and Woody Woodbury, whose album was titled, "Booze is the Only Answer."

If that night hadn't been Rickelle's twenty-first birthday, I wouldn't have gone. Twenty-one is a special birthday, and I wanted to be there for Rickelle. Another thing I didn't foresee was that, in five years, almost to the day, I would end up marrying Rickelle instead of Susan.

We didn't have dinner before arriving at Beverly Hills, and we didn't eat in their restaurant. We went straight to the Cabaret Room where Ron Schilling had our table reserved in the front row facing center stage. If Sammy Davis Jr. had been performing, it would have been a religious experience for me.

The comedy team of Teter and McDonald had begun their opening act some time before we arrived. I ordered my usual Jack Daniel's Black Label (never green) with a splash of soda and a twist. All of a sudden, a young employee appeared on the stage and grabbed the microphone from Jim McDonald. At first it appeared he was part of the act. He said, calmly, "I want you to look to my right. There's an exit in the corner of the room. I want you to look behind you. There's an exit on the back wall. And I want you to look to my left, because there's an exit in that corner. There's a fire at the front of the building, and I'd like everyone to leave the room." The kid handed the microphone back to McDonald and walked off the stage.

I told everyone at our table to follow me, and I jumped onto the stage to exit the way the comedians did. A busboy told me that I couldn't exit that way, so I jumped back down. I then led our group to our right. I brought my companion, Jack Daniel's, along with me. I wanted to keep my drink while we waited outside before returning to our table. We were stopped by another busboy telling us we couldn't go that way either. Once again we changed directions.

When I saw 6 foot 4 inch, 350 pound Scott Schilling running like hell toward the Cabaret Room, I decided it was time to distance myself from my friend Jack Daniel's. At that moment, I realized the severity of the fire and figured that we probably would not make it out. We now were behind hundreds of people who were all trying to exit through one door. Rick looked at me and said, "Jeff, we can't go this way." I told him that we had to, because we weren't allowed to go the only other way. He had persuaded me to go to Beverly Hills in the first place, and now he convinced me not to listen to a busboy and to go the way that I had previously chosen. The best seat in the house for a show is the worst seat in the house for a fire. We changed our course for the fourth time, and once again a busboy confronted us. "You can't go this way," he said.

Susan Brown recalled to Robert Windeler, "Jeff being Jeff, told the guy, 'Fuck you. We're going this way.' Jeff doesn't stop for anyone, he just doesn't. That's who he is. He led us into the hallway where there was a wall of white smoke. It was very dark in there, and packed with people. It was very hot, like standing too close to a barbecue. I kept rubbing the back of my hair because it was so hot my hair was going to singe up. I thought, *I have to call Mom before she hears about it on television*. My father had been killed in a plane crash a few years before at the age of thirty-nine, and I didn't want her to go through something like that again.

"Because I was standing behind Jeff and he had his arms back around behind me, I couldn't see him. I could hardly breathe, because he told me to keep my face pressed to the back of his jacket, and to hold on to him and not let go.

"We got to the stairs heading down to the ground floor, but the stairs were made of metal, and were steep, slightly tilted, and slippery. Since Davidson was performing that night, there were a lot of older women in long gowns, almost falling down the stairs. So everyone else was delayed in trying to escape. I remember Jeff saying, 'If I'm going to die, does it have to be going to see John Davidson?' But once he knew I was safely down, Jeff began to reach for the women and help them down the steps.

"I looked back up and saw the ventriloquists' dummies' heads above the crowd, coming down the steps toward us. The comedians must have grabbed them before they left. The puppet heads seemed to be just floating up high, through the smoke. It was eerie and surreal.

"Jeff is the one who got us out of that inferno. If he hadn't been with us that night, we'd have died in the fire."

I was wearing my very best suit that evening. The suit was the same color as the smoke in the hallway we escaped through, charcoal gray. Fortunately, it was the only thing I lost that night.

The pushing and shoving from behind me started once we got into that hallway. I turned around and, with a throat full of dark smoke, calmly but loudly enough to be heard, told everyone, "If we stay calm and don't push we will all get out alive. If we panic, we will all die." The pushing stopped, and a few minutes later I saw the greatest sight of my life. It was daylight from an open door and the green hillside bearing the Beverly Hills sign that read "Showplace of the Nation." Only a few people got out that door after we did. The indelible memory I still have, like Susan, is of those dummies coming down the stairs on the shoulders of their ventriloquists. After the dummies got out, I didn't see anyone else come out of that door.

People were trapped inside, trying to get out. Thirty-four bodies were found in front of that door, many stacked on top of each other.

To this day, Susan credits me with getting our party of six out of that "furnace" alive. If I hadn't been me, she says, I would have done what that employee told me to do, and the headlines might have read "Fire Claims 171 Lives."

About 3,000 people were in attendance at the sprawling 54,000 square foot, 19-room, two-story complex that night, and about 1,000 of them were in the Cabaret Room. People were stacked like cordwood (both dead and alive) in front of a set of double doors, and more bodies lay on the hillside by the chapel where weddings were held. People who were screaming, "Get me out, get me out," never got out. Back then, doors swung inward, not outward, and there were very few doors for a place with a capacity in the thousands. A family of seven had made the drive from Louisville that day. Only one young daughter returned to Louisville alive.

The fire had started in the room closest to the main entrance, a party room called the Zebra Room. It was the furthest location from the Cabaret Room. A small wedding party had complained about the room being warm and giving off a "funny odor." After their party ended, an employee smelled smoke and opened the room's large, wooden, double doors. She was met with a cloud of smoke and shut the door instantly. Word got out among the staff that there was a fire in the Zebra Room. A waitress reported it to the same busboy who later made the announcement to us in the Cabaret Room. He decided to check it out for himself. He saw smoke coming through the closed doors and immediately headed to the main bar just across the foyer and told those patrons to leave the building. The busboy saved about one hundred lives.

When the Zebra Room's doors sprang open, a "flashover" was created, and the fire got the oxygen it needed to spread. Everything in that facility was combustible: the chairs, drapes, carpet and furniture. The fire department was called at 9:01 p.m.

Thanks to the busboy, people from the other rooms were

already exiting the building but, as they ran past the Cabaret Room, they couldn't have helped noticing that a comedy team was still performing, backed up by an orchestra, and that everyone was enjoying themselves.

What that kid did next was beyond brave, and probably not in his job description. He walked over to Charlie Coslet, the tuxedoed captain whom I knew and who handled our table at the Cabaret Room. He told his superior about the fire and said, "We have to clear the room." Seventy people were still waiting in line to get in, behind red velvet ropes. Charlie told him he would clear the room and asked the busboy to watch the line. While Charlie was gone, the busboy told the people in line that they must leave immediately. They followed the kid's orders. Because this busboy took control, seventy more lives were saved. The busboy kept waiting for people to leave the Cabaret Room doors, but it never happened. The show was still going on, the jokes were still being told, and everyone was laughing, probably including me, Susan and my friends.

At that point the teenager decided that he would have to be the one to tell one thousand people to get the hell out of the Cabaret Room. His courage was transcended only by his poise. He knew that he must deliver the message in such a way that everyone would follow the orders of a teenage busboy, but in a way that no one would panic. He rehearsed his lines as he walked to the stage. When he was finished speaking, I believed that there was a small fire somewhere in the building, but I took my drink with me. Mission accomplished, kid. You "done good," and you saved my life.

The next morning, Susan and I went to Pete Rose's house in Western Hills and watched news of the fire on television for hours. That was when we learned the magnitude of the tragedy. Thirty-three fire departments and 522 firefighters had fought the fire. Bodies were taken to a gymnasium at the old Fort Thomas Armory, which served as a morgue, so families could identify their loved ones. The final body count was 165. We six had barely escaped the second deadliest nightclub fire in America's history.

Unfortunately, it takes a tragedy for us to get things the way they should have been in the first place. After the Beverly Hills tragedy, fire code laws were rewritten and new laws were put in place. Some of the laws over-reached, but most of them were necessary. Fire investigators concluded that the Cabaret Room had exceeded its safe occupancy level by almost 300 percent. There were no sprinklers and no fire alarms. There had been no employee emergency training, and the exit doors swung the wrong way. At that time, there were no such things as fire-rated fabrics and other materials.

Fire code laws weren't the only things that changed in America as a result of the Beverly Hills fire. The way personal liability and tort cases would be tried in American courts would never be the same.

A relatively unknown attorney from Cincinnati by the name of Stanley Chesley showed up at the scene of the fire, but he had to get a court order not only to survey the ruins, but also to prevent what was left of the building from being bulldozed. The club carried very little insurance, so Chesley took an unusual approach for a personal injury case. He went after every possible connection to the fire: contractors, manufacturers of the chairs, tables, carpet, drapes, and just about everything that burned. He targeted not only those that caused the fire but also those responsible for the toxic smoke that killed victims as they tried to escape. Chesley's groundbreaking strategy worked, and he rewrote the book on personal injury litigation, becoming known as the "Master of Disaster." He essentially invented the class action lawsuit.

He went on to become one of the most respected attorneys in America and the preeminent mass tort lawyer on the planet. In the Beverly Hills action, he represented three hundred clients and settled out of court for $50 million. Stan eventually became a regular guest at my restaurants and a good friend. He was even a partner in one of our restaurants.

Chesley's later clients received $4 billion from Dow Corning as a result of health problems from leaking breast implants, $280 billion from the tobacco industry, $300 million from the 1980 MGM fire in Las Vegas that killed eighty-five people, and $200 million for Vietnam veterans in the Agent Orange lawsuit in 1983. He represented the families of 248 soldiers from Ft. Campbell, Kentucky, who lost their lives in an Arrow Air jet crash in Newfoundland, and the twenty-five thousand people who died in the Bhopal gas tragedy in India, at the Union Carbide plant, in 1984. He was the attorney for families of the victims of the 1988 Lockerbie, Scotland, terrorist bombing of Pan Am flight 103. Stan not only was able to obtain a $2.8 billion settlement, it was the first terrorist case ever won against a government. Prior to the 9/11 bombing, it was the deadliest terrorist attack ever on civilians. Two hundred and seventy people were killed.

The other good that came from this terrible tragedy was that, while I was at Pete's house, I saw that courageous busboy being interviewed on television. His name was Walter Bailey, and he was from the small town of Alexandria, Kentucky. I had to do something for the high school kid who had saved my life and the life of the girl I loved. I knew one thing for sure: he needed a job. As it turned out, he also needed a father figure.

He got that job at one of my Holiday Inns, a mentor in me, and a college trust fund that I set up for him with my friend Hy Ullner. That kid is now fifty-two years old and a successful financial advisor living in a Dallas suburb. He calls me every so often, and he visits me whenever he comes to Cincinnati. I suppose I am a hero to the kids I mentor. Walter was my hero, and still is to this day.

Walter Bailey recalled to Robert, "I wasn't even supposed to be working that night, and being underage, I never worked the Cabaret Room. But while I was driving around that day, I heard some deejays on the car radio talking about the ventriloquists and their dummies that were going to be the opening act for Davidson that evening. The dummies were made up to look like U.S. presidents, and the deejays were saying how funny it was. I decided to go into the club and catch some of it. The Beverly Hills management was loosey-goosey, and the Cabaret Room was overcrowded. Soon I was carrying in extra tables and chairs, six or eight at a time, on my shoulder, acting the macho kid, like I did this all the time. When the fire broke out, one of my bosses didn't want to clear the Cabaret Room because a lot of dinner bills hadn't been paid. I knew I was risking my job by working my way to the stage and telling the patrons where the exits were. When one of the comedians handed me the mike, most people thought I was part of the act. But Jeff was paying attention. He later told me that he believed me when I said the patrons were in danger, and that it was not a joke.

"When Jeff called my home to talk to me the next day, I wasn't looking for a mentor, but my father was an alcoholic, my parents were divorced, and my mother was the single parent of four boys. Jeff took me seriously, and we became friends. He talked to me about various jobs at the Holiday Inn, from lifeguard at the pool to room service bellman, to working the hotel's front desk. Jeff and his boss, Erik, thought that might be my springboard to management. But at the time, all I wanted to do was make money to go to college and become a doctor. I wanted the highest paying job. That turned out to be parking cars. I became the manager of car parking at the Downtown Holiday Inn where Jeff had created Lucy's in the Sky, the Studio 54 of Cincinnati. The tips were great. When Jeff left to open The Precinct, I went with him as head of its parking, with ten or eleven valets under me. We were voted the city's number one parking operation by *Cincinnati* magazine.

"I had never been to a professional sports game when I met Jeff. He made a call and set me up for a Reds game, and I went with my mother and younger brothers. We were sitting in Sparky Anderson's seats. The players' wives and Jeff were sitting behind us. When Nick Clooney interviewed me on TV, he asked me who got us the seats. I said 'Jeff Ruby.' I also went to the movies with Jeff and Susan. Jeff made sure I was happy. I looked up to him. As a boss he was charismatic, a good leader who commanded respect and showed confidence."

* * * * *

It's been thirty-six years since the fire, and no one who lived in Greater Cincinnati back then has forgotten the region's worst tragedy. John Davidson lived to talk about it, but he has refused to do so. He lost his musical director, whom I saw being interviewed on TV outside the building that night. But after the interview, he went back inside to get his sheet music and never came out. Davidson also lost some of his band members. He told a reporter, "It was an incredible turning point in my life. I have never spoken about it. I have memories that I don't want to talk about."

Over time people have raised suspicions about the fire. Recently, former Beverly Hills employees, led by maitre'd Wayne Dammert and busboy David Brock, presented compelling evidence that the fire was a result of arson. They also claimed to know who was responsible. A number of other employees and witnesses support their claims, including owner Rick Schilling.

I have met with Dammert and Brock, and they seem to have a reasonable argument. Both men are good, credible people. They have witnesses who saw "workers" in the Zebra Room the day before the fire and, eerily, shortly *after* prospective buyers had been rebuffed in their attempt to purchase Beverly Hills. That sounded familiar. Kentucky Governor Steve Beshear, a good soul, said there was no evidence of arson in the 1977 fire, and the case is closed. I wondered if authorities remembered that it was rejected prospective buyers who burned down Beverly Hills on that same site in 1936. "Those who forget the past are condemned to repeat it."

I don't believe in coincidences. Individually, you can dismiss any one of these fires at Beverly Hills, but collectively there were too many coincidences for me to believe that this fire was an accident.

By the way, the old syndicate boss Moe Dalitz won the Las Vegas Humanitarian of the Year Award in 1976, and died in 1989, of natural causes.

CHAPTER SIXTEEN

LOVE ON THE ROCKS

Neil Diamond, 1980

Rickelle and I met at the same place I met Susan, Spanky's. I was attracted to her instantly, just as I had been with Susan. Rickelle looked like Heather Locklear. Rick Hauck, my general manager at Spanky's, introduced us, and I kissed her on the mouth before I even said hello. Rickelle was working there as a cocktail waitress. Nothing sums up what happened after that better than Human League's lyrics from "Don't You Want Me":

"You were working as a waitress in a cocktail bar
When I met you. I picked you out
I shook you up
And turned you around
Turned you into someone new."

But I had the same problem with Rickelle that I had had with Susan: she was going with a band member, and not just any band member. Steve Ricks was much tougher competition for me than Susan's ex had been. This guy Ricks was a tall, good-looking Elvis Presley impersonator in a nationally known, thirteen-piece band called The Van-Dells. They had played Las Vegas and were legendary in Cincinnati. Rickelle's boyfriend, Steve, was the star of the band's show, and hundreds of girls lined up to touch his sweaty body whenever he bent over to woo them, like Elvis did. This dude even flew his own airplane.

Yet, I followed the same basic game plan. I teamed up with Ronnie Schilling, a nightclub owner and the son of the former Beverly

Hills nightclub owner Dick Schilling. We booked The Van-Dells a few times at our sideline venture, Moonlight Pavilion at Coney Island. This venue held two thousand people and we always sold out for both shows every night. Ronnie and I made a great deal of money moonlighting at Moonlight Pavilion.

While Steve Ricks was wowing a thousand girls out front, I was in the back eating pizza with his girlfriend and making money doing it. Ronnie and I made so much money we were able to book Jerry Lee Lewis, too. Lewis was so drunk in his bus he was an hour late taking the stage. I had to get on the bus and threaten to kick his ass to get him on the damn stage. He told me he wasn't going to play. I told Jerry Lee Lewis, "Play, or I'll break your fingers." He played.

We booked The Van-Dells a third time at the Holidome at my Holiday Inn in Fort Mitchell, Kentucky. When I got there, a little late, Ronnie Schilling pulled me over and angrily warned me to stay away from Rickelle because she and Steve were now engaged. He was afraid I was going to screw up this great money-making run he and I had going. That night, when the Van-Dells went on stage, I took Rickelle to Dr. Potts, the club at Holiday Inn Riverfront in Covington, and convinced her to break her engagement to Steve and move in with me.

A few weeks after Rickelle moved in, she got a call from the city's most respected photographer, the late Jim Brown. He had been hired by the Marriott in Sharonville to do a photo shoot for their brochure and was asked to find a good-looking model in a bikini to lie out on a chaise lounge by their pool. Rickelle was one of two girls, a blonde and a brunette, who would be photographed. Only one of them would be selected by the ad agency.

Rickelle, the blonde, was excited about the modeling opportunity and agreed to show up for the photo shoot. When she got to the Marriott she met her competition. It was Susan Brown, the brunette.

Jim, the photographer, told me that when the two women went into the locker room to change into their swimsuits it took so long for them to return he went in to see what was keeping them. He found them arguing over me. Susan didn't want me back, but she didn't want anyone else to have me either. Jim put a stop to their arguing and got them out to the pool. Rickelle told me she got the job.

I was at the Holiday Inn in Covington one day when Nick Nolte strolled in. He had already been drinking. I had dinner with him and took him to Spanky's for some nightlife. Rickelle and I entertained him all night. He had no luggage, no clothes, no car, and nowhere to go. By 2:30 in the morning, he was wasted and had to stay at my house in Loveland because my Holiday Inn was sold out. Nick Nolte was "down and out in Loveland" six years before he was *Down and Out in Beverly Hills*. I've entertained movie stars, rock stars and jock stars, but none was quite like "Nick at Nite."

Rickelle loved the life I provided, and before long we had truly fallen in love with each other. Before long, Rickelle became pregnant, and just like a girl and me back in college, we agreed not to have the baby. We loved each other, but our relationship was too stormy. Rickelle had been previously married, and I was becoming skeptical about what had really gone wrong with that marriage. When she told me she was pregnant a second time, she insisted on having the baby. I had to make the most important decision of my adult life—should I marry Rickelle and start a family?

At a trial the participants must say, "I do." At a wedding the participants must also say, "I do." Our marriage was like the O.J.trial. The outcome was decided before anyone said, "I do." A judge married Rickelle and me. We should have asked for a jury.

Had I asked Rickelle to terminate her pregnancy, it would have been the third time I had asked a woman to abort my baby. I didn't ask her to, and on December 7, 1982, we had a beautiful baby girl. Britney was living proof that I had made the right decision, regardless of what lay ahead for the marriage. In December of the next year, Brandon was born. Then came Dillon, in 1987. Now there was no way out of the marriage for me. I couldn't leave my kids, at least not until they were grown.

Rickelle's mother lived with us the entire twenty-two years we were married, and I supported her (although she contributed by helping with the children). Rickelle's sister and older brother practically lived at the house, too, and they didn't work. I supported the homeless long before it became fashionable.

Our marriage was seriously impaired by our divergent positions on how our children should be raised. When Brandon was fifteen, I felt it would be best for him if he attended a good military school rather than continue on the self-destructive path he was taking. When I told Rickelle, she went ballistic. I told her I had done a great deal of research and, "I got the brochures." She said if Brandon went to a military school she would divorce me. She made me sleep in the guest room. Brandon did not go to military school.

We separated a year later. When I moved out of our house to an apartment at the Hannaford Suites, I saw my first episode of *The Sopranos* on television. Tony Soprano was having similar problems with his son A. J., and he told his wife, Carmela, he wanted to send their son to military school. Carmela flipped out and threatened to divorce him and made him sleep in the guest room, to which Tony's response was, "I got the brochures." Friends had been telling me for about a year that the Tony Soprano character reminded them of me. After I saw that episode, I thought I must have been a screenwriter for the producer David Chase—and somehow I'd forgotten it.

Rickelle and I tried living together again, but our marriage went from bad to worse. While the dynamics of every marriage (and divorce) are best known to the husband and wife, who are never going to agree on everything, sometimes an outsider can offer perspective. Boomer Esiason, who has known our family since 1984, told Robert that I had said, "I married Rickelle because she looks good, not because she was a Phi Beta Kappa." Boomer's own opinion was, "I loved her. She was the salt of the earth, good people, a beautiful gal. Jeff probably just drove her crazy. Or she drove him crazy. Or both."

It was a relative stranger who finally put my marriage into perspective for me.

Actor Michael Douglas was in Cincinnati for two weeks filming *Traffic*. He dined at all of our restaurants, and we struck a chord with one another. I took him out on the town to other bars. After a few nightcaps at the bar at The Cincinnatian Hotel, Michael and I talked about our dysfunctional childhoods in New Jersey without our real fathers around. He said that was what had made us both become what we were. He said he had been closer to his stepfather than to his dad, Kirk Douglas (although he and Kirk later became closer and worked together).

I've never met a celebrity quite like Michael. He insisted on paying for everything, he graciously walked through two thousand cheering college kids at Las Brisas, from the boat dock to the restaurant, and he wanted to know everything about me. He said that for me to have two restaurants as good as ours in the same city for all these years was an accomplishment I shouldn't take lightly. Los Angeles didn't have two good restaurants with that longevity, he said. One night I asked Rickelle if she'd like to join Michael and me for dinner at The Precinct, along with his publicist and bodyguard. She was delighted to go, but she spent most of the time berating me for devoting too much time to my restaurants and not spending enough time with her and the children.

Michael's last night in town, he had dinner with Steven Soderbergh, the movie's director, and Amy Irving, a co-star, and some others, at The Waterfront. Michael told me he would join me upstairs in our club for a drink afterwards. It was College Night, a Thursday, and we owned that night in Greater Cincinnati. In addition to the crowd outside, we had a few hundred more kids upstairs. And we stayed open until 5 a.m.

Michael came looking for me a couple of hours after dinner, as he had promised. When our drinks arrived he looked at me, and I have never forgotten the first words out of his mouth: "Jeff, you've got problems." When I asked him what kind of problems, he said, "Your marriage." He said he and his pals were shocked at the way my wife had talked to me, and they were impressed at what a stand-up guy I was to just let it go and not let it ruin the evening. He was about to say more, but Amy Irving grabbed his hand and said, "Let's dance." He stood up and told me I was dancing too. I told Michael that I didn't dance, but he pulled me up and took me to the dance floor where we all danced the rest of the night. At 5 a.m. we walked down the ramp over the river. Under his umbrella, in the pouring rain, he thanked me for making his two weeks so great. He gave me a kiss on the cheek and got into his waiting van.

A year later, I decided it was time for me to hear the rest of what Michael Douglas had to say about my marriage. What was he about to say before we were interrupted by Amy Irving and dancing? I called him. I was not surprised when he called me back—from Tokyo—and remembered our conversation of a year earlier. He picked up on it, telling me that Rickelle had no right to talk to me like that in front of people I hardly knew.

"It's her insecurity," Michael said. "She has disproportionate anger. This is your career and you are great at it. She should understand that."

For the first time, it occurred to me that maybe I was not to blame for everything. Rickelle had always said that I was the cause of every argument we had, that I was the "asshole," so I assumed she was right.

In 2003, I realized I had to tell Rickelle I wanted a divorce. There's something about men that many women won't accept. When we're courting them, we fly them in private jets. When we have them, we take them for granted. I've been a hard-working, career-oriented person from an early age. When your career comes first, it becomes like a mistress competing for time with your wife. Divorce becomes inevitable. "Getting Married Has Made Us Strangers" was a Top 40 hit for Dottie West in 1965, because we could all relate to it.

Our daughter, Britney, told Robert Windeler, "I'm surprised they stayed married as long as they did. They're better off apart."

Average White Band had a song called "I've Got Work to Do." Its lyrics wasted no time in the song's first verse:

"I'm taking care of business; woman, can't you see?
Got to make it for you, make it for me.
Sometimes it might seem that I've neglected you.
But I would love to spend more time
I've got so many things to do."

Rickelle recalled events a bit differently. She told Robert, "When I told Jeff I wanted a divorce and he asked 'why?' I pulled out seventeen photo albums of spring break and Christmas vacations with the kids—to Disney World, Sea World and the like—and I said 'I want you to show me where you are in the pictures in any of these albums. You're not in any of them.' One time he agreed to a romantic vacation for the two of us, so I booked two weeks in Venice, including all the restaurants I knew he would want to go to and all the historic places I wanted to see. Three days before we were to leave, he gave his plane ticket to his bookkeeper (this was before 9/11 when you could still do that), so I went on this 'romantic' vacation with her instead of my husband, simply because he didn't feel he could be away from the restaurants that long. That was the beginning of the end for us."

Three months after our divorce, Rickelle called to tell me she still loved me and missed me. I told her that I was so miserable without her it felt like she hadn't left yet. She's smart though. She got the house and a ton of money in the divorce. With the money, she bought a second house to rent out and provide a source of income. Her tenants were our two sons. They asked me if I would make their rent payments. I didn't realize it at first, but I had bought Rickelle a house and was renting it back from her! Strangely, we're better friends now than we were when we married. I still love Rickelle, and to remind her of that, every month I send her money.

"He sent me two dozen roses on the day we divorced," Rickelle remembered, "and a note of apology that he had not been a better husband. We needed to end our marriage, because I never saw him. He never beat me, cheated on me, or abused drugs or alcohol. But after our kids were grown, I was a restaurant widow. And I was too young not to be taking vacations and spending time with my husband."

The strange part of our story is that when I first met Rickelle she began seeing Rick Hauck, my general manager who had introduced us at Spanky's. When I found out about it, I told her she could no longer work for Rick, so she took a job at one of our competitors.

At the Beverly Hills club on the night of the tragic fire in 1977, Rickelle was with Rick and I was with Susan. Before I would allow myself to pursue Rickelle, I repeatedly asked her if it was really over between her and Rick. She always insisted it was, especially after she and Steve got engaged. I eventually had to fire Rick for poor performance, and he moved to Phoenix. We remained friends, however, and when I went on my own and was ready to open my second restaurant, The Waterfront, in 1984, I brought Rick back to manage The Precinct.

Right after I got out of the hospital after my near-death experience in 1987, Rick informed me that he had been offered his own steakhouse in Cleveland by investors who loved The Precinct. Rick left us, did a knock-off of The Precinct, and gave the impression I was involved. He named a steak after me and took the celebrity photos from The Precinct walls to hang on his walls. I figured "what the hell, he's got my concept and I've got his woman." It was a wash.

However, he still has the concept (and now has more restaurants than I do), and I no longer have Rickelle. Worse than that, he's still making money from my concept and I'm still losing money on Rickelle. It's no longer a wash.

CHAPTER SEVENTEEN

AGAINST ALL ODDS

Phil Collins, 1984

In 1972, Tom MacLeod, my old Cornell fraternity house roommate and football teammate, was working for Proctor & Gamble and living in Cincinnati. He was from St. Louis and I was from Asbury Park, but we both ended up in Cincinnati. While I was busy tossing guys out of bars, he was developing Pringles potato chips. Every day he drove Columbia Parkway to work and usually had to stop at a red light at Delta Avenue. An old Romanesque building, once a police station, stood at that corner. Tom suggested that I turn the building into a restaurant, but I never bothered to look into it.

Eventually, three women socialites bought the place and opened Amanda's, a trendy Mexican restaurant with an elite second-floor disco that competed with our Lucy's in the Sky on the top floor of our high-rise Holiday Inn. When their "honeymoon" was over, they came up with a promotion they called "Celebrity Chef Night," featuring a local celebrity on Monday evenings.

I had made a name for myself working at Holiday Inn bars and was eventually asked to be Amanda's chef for a night. I cooked a five-course Italian dinner for what turned out to be the busiest night in Amanda's history. Tables had to be set up in the parking lot to accommodate the overflow crowd. People had come because I was the celebrity chef. I broke their all-time sales record, on a Monday night of all things–and I was their competitor! How stupid was I? People who had never heard of Amanda's now knew where it was, how to get there and what it was all about. I had already done enough things to get fired by Holiday Inn, but this took the cake. Eventually, it did get me fired.

The good news was that I knew these three owners didn't know what they were doing, and that even in good times in a good location they wouldn't make it. I realized that I had just experienced the pre-opening party for my first restaurant, and I had done it at someone else's place. This would turn out to be my modus operandi. I would keep my eye on places that I felt had potential but were in the wrong hands and wait for them to be near death. Then I could get them cheaply. Eventually, people started calling me a "turnaround artist."

In 1980, word got out that Amanda's was for sale, but at the time I was developing a nightclub in Fairfield, Ohio. That project was brought to my attention by Don Sheets, who booked the entertainment for Winegardner & Hammons. He and I had become friends, since I made it a point to see every band before I would book it. A friend of Don's, Bill Minnilli, had a club that had closed, and he asked Don to see if I would take it over. Bill had a reputation and a record, and I had "reasonable doubt" about getting involved with him. Don assured me there would be no problems, and I trusted my pal. A young kid from Louisville, Kent Taylor, wanted to work for me, so I took him under my wing. I named the place Mabel Murphy's. We remodeled the joint. I trained the staff, Kent handled the remodeling, and we were ready to open when Sheets told me that Minnilli was taking it over himself. So we had done all of that for nothing. We were screwed by Minnilli, just as everyone else had been. I had nothing in writing.

In Jersey you can make a deal with a handshake. I've been operating Jeff Ruby's in Cincinnati without a lease for years. I've got bigger fish to fry. I'll get around to it one day.

Erik Kamfjord, the CEO at Winegardner & Hammons, was

both my boss for eleven years and my mentor. I learned a great deal from him. He strongly advised me to stay away from the Amanda's location. He did not see any way that the place could be successful. For one thing, it had only sixty-eight. seats, and even on Saturday nights I wouldn't be able to "turn it" enough times to make up for the slower week nights. Erik said I couldn't generate enough revenue to "cover the nut."

My friend from Youngstown, George Pintea, now CEO of a five-billion-dollar company, went with me to look at the property. The bartender was the only one there. I asked George what he thought.

As George recalled to Robert: "I thought it was a shit hole— fine only if he wanted to raise small farm animals, like pigs and chickens. It looked like a barn, and it was a smelly dump in a rough part of town. It depressed me. We had talked often about his dream to open his own restaurant and how he thought it might not happen, given his background in hot dogs, pancakes and Holiday Inns. But Jeff's an ordinary guy who does extraordinary things. In his field, he's very, very bright."

George thought I was crazy to want to quit my job and open a restaurant in that location. Of course I'm crazy. But as the Waylon Jennings song goes, "I've always been crazy, but it's kept me from going insane."

The only one who really encouraged me to take over Amanda's to start my own place was Gary Ginn, my employee at three Holiday Inns over the course of eleven years. As he told Robert, "I told him to go for it, because I knew that's what he wanted me to say. I knew Jeff like a book."

"Once I saw he was determined to go ahead with Amanda's," Erik Kamfjord told Robert, "I did everything I could to help him. I had always recognized that Jeff had a long-standing desire to own a restaurant, to be the next Toots Shor, and he had done a great job for us in our Holiday Inn restaurants. I surprised him by mentoring him through the whole process of opening his own restaurant, even helping to arrange financial backers. Jeff was almost apologetic about leaving us, but I told him he should leave us, it was the right thing to do.

"Something else I could teach him was to be a complete businessman, to meet his own payroll on payday, and remember that he was going to have partners with whom he had to be honest and straightforward. I knew he was a talented, hardworking individual, and that his close connections with athletes would stand him in good stead. Best of all, he was achieving a lifetime dream. I was pleased I had the opportunity to help him get started, and I'm certainly proud of what he's achieved."

I soon realized two things about Cincinnati. It was suffering from an inferiority complex, and it still didn't know how to light up its buildings. Cincinnati had always been content to settle for a field goal instead of a touchdown. The city also had a shortage of celebrities.

Cincinnati was a German town, and the city's largest developers told me it had a 60 percent redneck population that included Northern Kentucky. Wonderful! A Jersey Shore Jew schmoozing Germans and rednecks. And that was the least of my problems.

Reagan had just become president after Carter. The country was in its worst recession since the Depression. The prime rate was 21.5 percent, the highest in America's history. Inflation had reached 13.85 percent, the third highest percentage since 1947. The unemployment rate was the highest of any time in the post-war era. Our attorney, Reuven Katz, learned that fifty-two liens had been filed on Amanda's (one for each week of the year, I suppose). All of that could change for the better, but what wouldn't change was this joint's location. It was the worst in the city, on the railroad tracks, next to boarded-up, dilapidated houses infested with rats, in a high-crime area. The only other business nearby was a biker bar across the street. When Amanda's customers finished dancing, they were lucky if their cars were still there and they hadn't been mugged.

Nonetheless, Reuven Katz, as my attorney, guided me through all the details in making my first restaurant come to fruition. He told me to find ten partners and to give them each a 4.9 percent share. I would be left with 51 percent, which would give me control of the restaurant.

At the time, I had only two wealthy close friends. My first call was to Johnny Bench. He was familiar with Amanda's. It was near his house, and Mexican was his favorite food. He immediately said, "Sure." Then I called Pete Rose, who said, "You mean you're quitting Holiday Inn, and you will manage it? Then I'll take two shares."

Pete and Johnny were never the best of friends. They merely coexisted on baseball's greatest teams. For them to come together to support me was damn nice. In 1981, no sports figures had more star quality than Pete and Johnny. Finding investors for my restaurant would be a lot easier with Johnny Bench and Pete Rose involved. Johnny brought in Barry Buse and Art Stagnaro. I called my friend Ken Root at Equitable. He introduced me to his partner, Dave Meyers.

As Dave remembered it and told Robert, "I got a call in 1980 saying that Jeff Ruby wanted to start a restaurant and had me in mind as a possible investor. Since I've yet to meet a successful male who didn't want to get into the restaurant business, and I'm in finance, I asked to see some numbers. 'Projections, schmojections,' Jeff said.

"I soon learned that he was aggressive but just short of being

148

arrogant. He was strong and opinionated, with a knack for getting the best out of people. A jock at heart, he was charismatic and clearly able to attract good-looking women and young people to his discos. He's irresistible to the people he wants to be irresistible to. That's part of his puzzling mystique. What's all the more remarkable is that he's not from Cincinnati. They don't usually take to outsiders here, as I know, being an outsider myself."

I couldn't give Dave numbers yet, but I promised him two things.
"Do you like beautiful women?" I asked.
"Yes," he said.
"Do you like great food?"
"Yes."
"I guarantee you will own a restaurant with the best-looking women and best food in this city."
"I'm in," he said.

Dave in turn brought in Dick Roth, Jack Voelker, and mega auto dealer Mike Dever. (Dave later made a fortune at Equitable by getting into a deal using connections he had made through me. He has thanked me repeatedly.) My friend Bob Elkus, who owned the best men's clothing store in town, got on board, and everybody's friend Jim "Squirrel" Stadtmiller, who sold radio time, joined the posse. Squirrel's being involved meant that every good-looking girl in town would be there. Squirrel did nothing but go to bars and schmooze.

Each of the investors put in $10,000. For my share, I had to sell my car for $5,000 and wait for my Holiday Inn profit sharing of $6,000. That was the only money I had. Once I had my ten grand and my ten partners, I had my first restaurant—I thought. Then Reuven Katz called to tell me the deal was off. The lease terms we had agreed to were no longer available because of those liens against the property. If I wanted that site, I would have to get the investors to agree to purchase it outright. Now I had to negotiate all over again, to buy the place, and then persuade the guys to sign their names to a mortgage at this questionable location, during these turbulent times, with the prime rate at 21.5 percent, and with fifty-two liens on the property!

Understandably, Bench walked into Reuven's office to say he wanted to pass on the deal. "Forget about it," he said. "We'll do the next one." Then I told Johnny something I hadn't told anyone: I had been fired from Winegardner & Hammons, Inc. I simply said, "We've gotta buy it. I'm no longer with Holiday Inn." He said, "Okay."

The economy had taken its toll on WHI, and Erik had shifted into austerity mode. One of his cutbacks was to have three regional managers cover the five regions across the country. Two guys would have to be eliminated. Twice I had given Erik my notice so I could leave WHI to open a restaurant. Twice the deals had fallen through. Both times I had gone back to Erik and said, "I want my notice back." Now, I was the logical guy to let go. If Erik hadn't fired me when he did, there would never have been The Precinct.

We purchased Amanda's outright for $300,000. To this day, Lib Stone, one of the former owners, thanks me for rescuing her from all that debt and all those lawsuits. Falmouth Bank in Falmouth, Kentucky, was owned by Barry Briggs, a friend of Reuven's. The bank loaned us the $300,000 at one point under prime. I still don't know where Falmouth, Kentucky is. The ten other investors signed the note jointly and severally, which meant I was the only one not on the hook. We had $110,000 in cash for me to turn a Mexican restaurant into a steakhouse.

Money wasn't going to fix all our problems, however, at least not right away. The kitchen was smaller than the ones our guests had in their homes. Our restrooms were smaller than the kind you see at a gas station. The parking lot was small and unsafe. I had to play with the cards I was dealt, but I didn't have to keep the dealers. I hired and trained a new, young staff that brought enthusiasm and attention to detail unlike anything Cincinnati had ever seen. Upscale places in the city had older hostesses or men as maître d's at the reception desk. I put a gorgeous young girl there instead. Thirty years ago, I thought that's what they meant when they said I should have "a business model." She was a part-time model.

I gave Cincinnati a steak like they had never eaten before, served at a place staffed and patronized by beautiful young women. The Precinct became the city's first national-celebrity-spotting restaurant. It was Cincinnati's Spago, which Wolfgang Puck opened in Hollywood at about the same time.

"He created a menu that was desirable for everyone," Johnny Bench told Robert. "He had a nice, small bar upstairs from the restaurant. It was an easy place for me to come to, being a mile from my house, but right away all the Reds came, too, followed by the Bengals. Soon the visiting ballplayers discovered The Precinct. The girls naturally followed. We had really good partners, who were mostly friends, or became friends. Jeff made it an easy place to come to, with a relaxed atmosphere, great decor and the highest quality food. He was a perfectionist and always had imagination. Very soon we were the hot spot in town."

I had projected full first-year sales of $900,000, which would have reflected lunch and dinner revenue. Then I decided not to be open for lunch. We grossed over $2,000,000 our first full year. I paid the guys back entirely, plus interest on their loans, that first year. I paid the bank back a year later. The investors each now had a permanent investment of $1,500.

We opened The Precinct on September 11, 1981. Our country suffered its worst tragedy on my first restaurant's twentieth anniversary. On 9/11/01, I contributed half of our week-long revenue to the families of the first responders who had perished in the collapse of the Twin Towers in New York, after the towers were struck by two domestic airliners under the control of foreign terrorists.

Looking back, if that landlord hadn't screwed me and Kent Taylor by taking away Mabel Murphy's, I know The Precinct would never have happened, because I would have found another place of employment after I was fired from Holiday Inn.

Kent Taylor started his own steakhouse company, and he achieved greater success than I did. He founded Texas Roadhouse. That's another kid I'm proud of.

This is one of the few surviving pictures from my childhood–a junior high school photo, about 1959

153

Another picture with Cindy Herbst at the Senior Ball in 1966

Me and my lime green Dodge Charger

The five DU roommates at Cornell - "The Chujko Brothers"

Sports have always been an important part of my life. Number 66 since high school, The Yale Bowl, senior year at Cornell, with Tom MacLeod and Ken Snyder.

Coming out of the tunnel - The Yale Bowl, 1968

Rawley Eastwick (#49, left) rented a room in my home
during the days of the Big Red Machine in the mid 1970s

At my wedding - The Precinct, with Cris Collinsworth

Before the Pete Rose Farewell to Riverfront Stadium/Cinergy Field Celebrity Softball Game, September 2002 . I coached 3rd base.

Former Cincinnati Reds Hall of Fame Manager, Sparky Anderson, was the father I wish I had had. He is missed by everyone here in the Queen City.

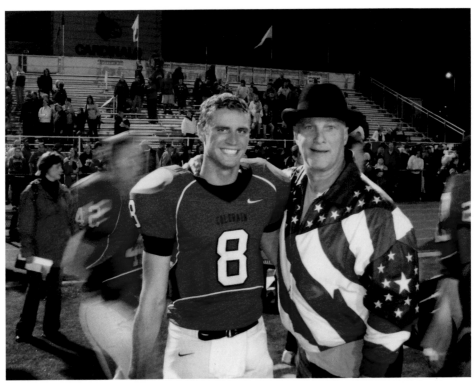

Colerain High School Quarterback Greg Tabar

Holly Collinsworth took this picture of me and Griff Urlage. It was the first time a "dad" had ever attended one of his football games.

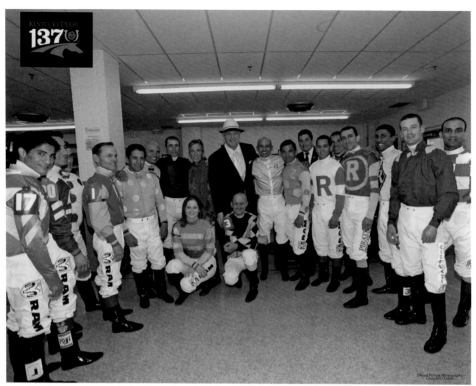

My love of sports has expanded into the fascinating world of horse racing.
I am one of the only people to have the privilege of a portrait taken with
all the jockeys prior to the running of the Kentucky Derby.

Jockey Joe Talamo sports Jeff Ruby pants. Photo © Benoit Photo.

Enjoying a cigar with my longtime friend Marvin Butts, the "Secretary of Defense"

A passion for sports is rivaled only by a passion for music

The two amazing women in my life - Susan Brown (top) and Rickelle

*With my mother and brother Wayne, stepfather Lt. Leon Wurzel,
niece Robin and nephew Scott*

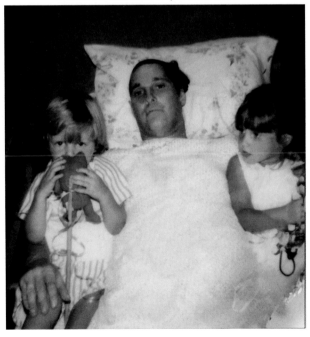

After my auto accident in 1987. This picture survived a house fire.

Never knowing my own father, I tried to be the best father I could be to my three children. This is an early Christmas card.

Enjoying a Reds game with my children in the late 80's

Family portrait from 1991. Gotta love the mullet!
Courtesy of Robert A. Flischel Photography

Fast forward the family portrait to ca. 1998

I'm proud to say all three of my children are now in the family business
Photo by Bruce Crippen

A portrait from Britney's Wedding
Steve Lyons Wedding Photography

Giving away my daughter, Britney, at her wedding in 2007
Steve Lyons Wedding Photography

A telling photo of Rickelle and me at our son Brandon's wedding in 2012
Nate Leopold Photography

From a happier time with Rickelle - perpetual gangster mode!

169

The only thing better than being a father is being a grandfather.
These are Britney's children, Gracie and Hannah

Britney and I welcome Brandon and his wife Christy's beautiful new daughter, Lilly

I've been fortunate to meet, dine with and befriend many famous people over the years. Here I am being interviewed by a young George Clooney, ca. 1982.

Wastin' away again with Jimmy Buffett - the night that almost ended my life

George Burns autographed a cigar that immediately sold at a charity auction...$500

By far my most controversial celebrity photo. Taken at The Precinct, it's highly appropriate to have the jail bars in the background. My only regret is that it does not show his feet as I believe O.J. Simpson to be wearing a pair of the "ugly-ass Bruno Magli shoes" that might have convicted him.

Cincinnati Reds baseball legend, "Charlie Hustle," Pete Rose

My basketball idol as a kid and friend, NBA Hall of Famer, Oscar Robertson

Rickelle and me with "The Iron Lady," Margaret Thatcher

Rocky Balboa himself, Sylvester Stallone, as I present the platinum record "Eye of the Tiger", a song I helped get airplay in Cincinnati

Backstage with "The Gambler," Kenny Rogers, at a performance for my birthday and grand opening of Jeff Ruby's Belterra in 2004

Former prosecuter, Nancy Grace, brings on the fight for justice every night as a legal commentator and talk show host on CNN

Rickelle and me with President George H. W. Bush

Me with President George W. Bush

Academy Award winning actor Michael Douglas at the conclusion of location filming for the 2000 Best Motion Picture nominee, Traffic

Rockin' it with the boys from AC/DC

A recent Kentucky Derby with actor Jonathan Goldsmith.
All we need are dos Dos Equis. "Stay thirsty, my friends!"

Jeff Ruby Cullinary Entertainment has hosted some unique events. Here we are grillling outside The Waterfront. You can see how the skyline has changed since the early 1990s.

The world's largest buffet line stretched across the Purple People Bridge from Cincinnati across to Newport, Kentucky for the opening of Tropicana

182

But my favorite event has to be my 65th Brithday Bash.
Singing "Celebration" with Kool & the Gang.
Photo by Ross Van Pelt

Enjoying the party with my three kids. Surrogate sons Jake Urlage (left) and
Nick Urlage (far back) had a blast - Nate Leopold Photography

There's nothin'like being cool with Kool. Let them eat cake!
Nate Leopold Photography

Inside one of our more recent endeavors, Jeff Ruby's Steakhouse, Louisville
Photo CORE Resources

CHAPTER EIGHTEEN

I'M SO PROUD

The Impressions, 1964

This tune hit the Top 40 on my sixteenth birthday, and twenty-nine years later was featured in the movie *A Bronx Tale*. No song title better describes how I feel about my three kids. They are without question what I am most proud of, much more so than the restaurants. I believe there is nothing more important a man can do than be a good father. In today's competitive life, it's a tough balance, being both a good father and a good provider. My children would not have experienced the life they've had unless they had a hard-working dad.

I'm proud of my accomplishments with our restaurants, but I don't analyze my success in that arena. The restaurant is a team effort. I have partners, lenders, employees and vendors. And where would I be without all of our guests? I've had a lot of help "raising" these restaurants. With my kids, I only had Rickelle (and her mother), and my wife's and my theories of child-rearing were often at odds. Rickelle admitted that I was the better parent, bless her heart. It's easier running a restaurant than it is raising a kid. As Bette Davis said, "If you've never been hated by your child, you've never been a parent."

Britney was born in 1983, on December 7, Pearl Harbor Day. It was also the birthday of her godfather, Johnny Bench. One year and three weeks later, Rickelle gave birth to our son Brandon. So we have two birthdays and Christmas within twenty-one days. My other "baby," The Precinct, was just two years old. This place had better work out!

I had just accomplished my three goals in life: I owned my own restaurant, I was married to the most beautiful girl in Cincinnati, and I was a dad to two gorgeous kids. My restaurant/nightclub was the hottest place in town. Johnny Bench and Pete Rose were among my partners in it. I owned a six-thousand-square-foot house on 2.6 acres overlooking the Ohio River.

Five years later, on the heels of my near-death experience and Rickelle's eight-pound-weight-loss pregnancy, Dillon was born. He's the miracle kid to me. We had a priest and a rabbi in the delivery room. I asked the doctor if my baby would even live, or be normal. He "reassured" me by telling me that Holocaust mothers had delivered normal babies. Dillon was born covered with a white powder that my other babies didn't have on them at birth. I freaked out. Dillon turned out to be a perfectly normal child. As Dillon said to Robert, "My dad and I are both miracles: I was born, and he lived."

I was given the responsibility for choosing the names for our children, and I wanted our kids to have uncommon names. Britney was pre-Britney Spears. The boys, Brandon and Dillon were born before *Beverly Hills, 90210* aired. Brandon was meant to keep my brand going on after I'm gone. Dillon came from the *Gunsmoke* character Matt Dillon, played by James Arness.

After I opened The Waterfront in Kentucky, in 1986, we had the hottest restaurants on both sides of the Ohio River. I turned down countless offers to open restaurants all over America. Hockey great Wayne Gretzky, after just one visit to The Waterfront, told Rickelle he would open a restaurant with me in Los Angeles. But it was more important for me to watch my children grow than to see my company grow. I waited until Dillon was in high school before I made further moves with the restaurants. I knew what it was like not having a dad. I didn't want that for my kids.

Dillon told Robert: "When I was a kid he was home all day—he only went to the restaurants at night—so I could go upstairs and sit in his home office any time I wanted to, even when I was three or four. He never missed one of my football or basketball games from the time I was seven, through high school. He even came to my football practices. He always stressed the importance of exercise, and I know from experience he's as strong as a bull.

"My parents separated when I was in eighth grade. When there was trouble at school, my father was always the one who showed up."

Britney told Robert, "When I was five, we would wrestle in his bed. We'd play hide and seek at the office he shared with Boomer, or at The Precinct. When I played softball and basketball, he came to our games. When I pitched softball, he'd stand behind home plate and watch every pitch. He did a good job balancing work and father-hood. He was strict about my schoolwork, and I have a vivid memory of him forcing me to go to the Methodist church and Sunday school. I fought him tooth and nail on that.

"He also taught me cooking, starting with pasta, and how to scramble a perfect egg. By the time I was fifteen, I knew I wanted to go into the restaurant business. I realized the magnitude of what he does, and I shared his passion for it. I'm ambitious, just like my father, and I wanted to make him proud."

Brandon started playing football at age seven. As he told Robert, "He coached me right away and started coaching our whole team when I was nine, and he was fully involved. I was so young he probably steered me into football, but I loved it right away. I'd heard all his stories of playing football in high school and college. He really pushed us all, and it became important to him to see us all do well in sports.

"The summer I was thirteen, I started bussing tables at The Waterfront. I didn't have a clue what I was doing. I was in way over my head, but I was having fun doing it. I knew then that the restaurant business would be for me. In school, when they asked us what we wanted to be, everyone else said fireman or policeman, or what you'd expect. I said I wanted to be a restaurateur, but the spelling was little botched."

I met with all three children's principals and counselors, and many of their teachers. In our case, those meetings were held quite often. At three of their high schools, I was asked to give speeches. At a fourth, I was called into the principal's office. Like their father, both boys have ADD and ADHD. Brandon was diagnosed by a foremost authority on ADD, Dr. Cheryl Beach, who has doctorates in both cognitive and clinical psychology and serves as the state of Ohio's expert witness on the subject in court trials.

She spent weeks testing Brandon, and her report was as thick as our restaurant training manual. Although no psychologist at Brandon's school had met with him, the principal and her staff disputed Dr. Beach's diagnosis and would not offer him the help he needed and was entitled to. When I threatened to take legal action, the school decided to agree that Brandon had ADD. I wouldn't send my dogs to that school if they began to offer canine training.

Watching my kids grow up has been the most fascinating and enjoyable part of my life. I became a kid all over again and enjoyed their childhoods more than I did my own. I spoiled them by giving them what I never had. Kids are like food: neither, once spoiled, can be "unspoiled." I also learned that you can't make your kids have passion–not even if you think you have excellent leadership skills.

Brandon and Dillon have similar qualities. They know how to treat people. They are respectful, they care, and they give. They are two handsome, sweet kids with big hearts. What more could a dad ask for?

As Johnny Bench told Robert, "Both boys are like Jeff: hard-headed."

Both my boys are also resilient. Brandon was pistol-whipped by some thugs (who were after his Nikes), at the University of Cincinnati, where he was attending school. Dillon was attacked by thugs at two o'clock in the morning at our Downtown Jeff Ruby's Steakhouse. When he fought back, they pulled out their guns and chased him down Walnut Street. I called my friend Tom Streicher, our police chief, to make him aware of the incident, which I assumed had been captured on a city security camera. I found out Cincinnati didn't have any security cameras. The chief set up a meeting with me and certain city leaders. Now Downtown is safer. There are cameras all over Downtown.

Brandon is now the general manager at The Precinct, my first restaurant. He got to re-open it after its final expansion. Dillon is a food server at Carlo & Johnny. When he earns his college degree this year, 2013, he will be evaluated and eligible for a promotion to assistant manager. No degree, though, no promotion. Both boys took their time getting through school. They thought I was bluffing about that requirement.

Marvin Rosenberg told Robert that, "One of the exceptional things Jeff has done is raising his boys. Those kids were in trouble every day, and they could have gone off the cliff. But Jeff's 'tough love' really works."

I had some help from another Marvin, Marvin Butts, my 6 foot 10 inch friend for more than thirty years, who has known my children since they were born. He's my "Secretary of Defense" and sometimes my driver. He was also the kids' caretaker—and my enforcer.

"Shortly after I met him, I drove Jeff to Rickelle, so he could put the engagement ring on her finger," Marvin Butts told Robert. "I drove all three children home from the hospital after they were born, so I've known them their whole lives. Once when the boys had matching black Dodge Durangos, I had to take both cars away from them at the same time, because they'd each done something bad. "I work for Jeff, so I usually call him 'Boss,' but Rickelle's been my friend for just as long. She always said he was too strict with the kids, and he always said she was too lenient. And they were both right."

In one of her high school basketball team's away games, my daughter, Britney, outscored the entire opposing team. I was there, and I was a proud dad that night. But one other moment in her high school career made me proudest of all. The only male black student in the school had asked her to the prom. She wanted to know if she had my permission to go with him to the dance. I asked, "Do you know him, and is he a good kid?" She answered "yes" to both, and I said, "Then go to the prom with him." So the homecoming queen went to a white high school prom with its only black boy. It reminded me of the Chazz Palminteri story in *A Bronx Tale*, and of my own childhood, when they called me a "nigger lover."

Britney is our company's first Director of Guest Services and Development. Like the boys, she has worked every job at our restaurants, and she has worked at every one of our restaurants. Britney has cooked food on national television, done TV commercials, posed for print ads, and turned down opportunities in sports broadcasting. She interned with Erin Andrews, Kirk Herbstreit and Mike Tirico on ESPN. When you know sports as Britney does, and are young, articulate, talented, and drop-dead gorgeous, people want you on national television. But a career as the next Erin Andrews, whom she adores, was not for Britney.

Britney attended the Midwest Culinary Institute at Cincinnati State, after graduating from the University of Cincinnati with a bachelor's degree in religious studies. She made the Dean's List as many times as I got parking tickets at Cornell. She and her husband, Caleb Miller, who was a linebacker for the Cincinnati Bengals when they met, are very religious. That is what attracted them to one another. Caleb and Britney have given me two beautiful granddaughters, Gracie and Hannah.

An ordained minister who runs a non-profit foundation, Caleb officiated at the 2012 wedding of Brandon and his wife, Christy.

Every day, somebody tells me how proud I must be of my kids, or what a good job I did with them. Nothing makes a parent happier than hearing that.

CHAPTER NINETEEN

THE RIVER

Garth Brooks, 1992

In the mid-1980s we had what I described as Greater Cincinnati's "Renaissance on the River." Floating restaurants opened up on the Kentucky side of the river, along with a magnificent, towering riverfront development called River Center, in Covington, Kentucky. Covington not only had finally decided to capitalize on its spectacular view of Cincinnati's skyline, it began creating its own skyline. My pal Bill Butler of Corporex was the pioneer in all of this.

Our unprecedented success at The Precinct had given me visibility, and almost daily I heard how "hot" I was and that I should open a second restaurant. My response became a broken record, "Let's see how long I stay hot; even a fire will cool off."

I made one failed and expensive attempt at collaboration with a barge owner from the Kentucky side of the river. He turned out to be a crook. His concrete barge sank in the middle of the Ohio River, just after I had paid to get out of the deal. Then, with the help of a guy in the marine building business, Doug McGuinnis, I found two tank barges in Mississippi. We brought them upriver and moored them in Ludlow, Kentucky, where we planned to build a two-story restaurant and nightclub on one of them. Doug cut the second barge in half and kept one half for himself. Together we would put an outdoor bar on the other section. It would be open only in the summer.

I certainly wasn't going to open an establishment on the river without giving my partners at The Precinct the opportunity to invest in the floating restaurant and bar. They had taken a chance on me when nobody knew who I was. These men were successful entrepreneurs, and I felt responsible for maintaining these great relationships.

A few of the partners from The Precinct invested, including Pete Rose. New investors such as Bengals Cris Collinsworth and Boomer Esiason came on board, no pun intended. They were regulars at The Precinct and had become friends of mine. The city of Covington agreed to name the street to the floodwall approach to the restaurant Pete Rose Way, and our address was #14, Pete's number. Our phone number was 581-1414.

We spent many months deciding what to call this creation, which would evolve into a three-barge floating complex. I settled on The Waterfront, after the movie *On the Waterfront*. It turned out to be more like *The Poseidon Adventure*. Every imaginable (and unimaginable) catastrophe that could happen to a floating restaurant did, and it didn't take long for them to start happening. Runaway barges wiped out our steel framework as soon as it went up.

The physical appearance of this boat would make a statement to the City of Cincinnati, and I knew it had better make that statement loud and clear. I've never been a "me-too" guy, and I wasn't going to start by being someone with just another riverboat. I interviewed three architectural firms and required them to submit their vision for this 240 foot by 50 foot barge. Dennis Cronin's ATA was the winner.

When passion meets skill, expect a masterpiece. Dennis gave us that. He even tinted the cantilevered window bays blue, so the muddy Ohio River actually looked like Lake Michigan. Our signature rock formation towered above everything else on the river, and water cascaded twenty feet down into a swimming pool on one side and into a lagoon on the other side. I had seen this in a scene from *Scarface*. I found out who had made that rock formation and had them build ours.

Next, I needed to find a restaurant designer, and I found him in Hollywood, California.

Dave Stevens began his career in the motion picture industry as a set designer for directors, including Otto Preminger and Frank Capra. One of Dave's films was *In Harm's Way,* with John Wayne and Kirk Douglas. Dave was also the designer for a few of the Mafia's top bosses, including Carlos Marcello. Dave has designed more than one thousand casinos, hotels, restaurants and nightclubs the world over, and he now works out of Las Vegas. His design for The Waterfront was what we called, in 1986, "*Miami Vice* Deco."

Dave has designed all of my restaurants in the twenty-nine years since we started together on The Waterfront–those that have come and gone, and those that are still in operation. He and I have had our contentious times, too, to put it mildly. As he told Robert,

"I liked the guy right off the bat, but he was a wild man. We've fought like cats and dogs. I used to come to town, have him start in on me, and turn right around and go back to the airport and leave. He's a hell of a lot easier to work with these days. Jeff's ego is equal to anybody else's, but he and I have an uncanny communication skill. We think alike on almost every level. This is beyond valuable in design interpretation. I'd like to think that this level of mutual trust is unique to us, but Jeff has it with anybody he thinks deserves the time and insight that are useful in accomplishing his goals. He gives me a lot of latitude, and we agree that we should never copy anybody else's designs.

"Yet, with Jeff it's always a challenge, He can be a charming, sweetheart of a guy, and he can be a total jerk. He's sixty-five, going on about twenty-eight, in his mind. And that'll never change. And for all his New Jersey tough guy shit, he's as soft as butter and very needy as far as love and affection are concerned. Working with him is like being at one of those twenty-four-hour circuses in Denmark: you never know what you're going to see at any given time. He should have been in showbiz."

The day we were scheduled to tow The Waterfront to our permanent location, thirteen barges broke loose, and they all washed ashore at our mooring location before our tugboats could get there with our restaurant. The Waterfront was hit once by a barge and almost wiped out by another before we even opened.

I believe in omens, so I knew "I ain't seen nothin' yet." I didn't know whether to open The Waterfront or sell it. During the creation period of our restaurants, I learn a great deal about our team. It's like a coach learning about his players long before the first game. I knew the general manager I had chosen was a mistake. He was already lazy, and we hadn't opened yet. I fired him the day before we opened and served as the GM myself, along with all my other responsibilities.

To complement The Waterfront's *Miami Vice* interior, I put all my waiters in salmon-colored tuxedo jackets with white pants. Every one of the waiters was from out of state, out of country, or out of their minds. Their names and hometowns were printed on the nametags they wore, just like the dealers in Las Vegas. At LaBoom, our second floor club, we had real blackjack dealers, all gorgeous girls. They were trained by Ron Jacimine aka Mr. Jacs, a Newport original straight out of Central Casting, who had witnessed his first mob "whack" (by Screw Andrews) at age twelve.

It was smooth sailing for quite a while, and we made so much money one Saturday that at 3 a.m. I called Mark Jahnke, my attorney, because I didn't know what to do with all the cash we had taken in. Our safe wasn't large enough to hold it all, and I didn't want to give the appearance to my partners that I was taking the money home. Mark told me to take it home, and I did.

The next river-related problem came on a busy night at LaBoom. There was a "runaway" barge headed toward us. Boomer and Cris were at the club that night, and they joined me on the second-floor patio to watch the big thing coming our way. It felt like a shark swimming at us at night, and we didn't know whether to "swim" away or stay still. I decided not to evacuate LaBoom. I guessed that the "shark" would not hit The Waterfront. I didn't know then that I would eventually become an expert at calculating this stuff, but I guessed correctly that time.

The Waterfront became a destination that networks chose as a venue. CBS aired the *Evening News* with Dan Rather there. Deborah Norville did her *Inside Edition* at The Waterfront, which also hosted *PM Magazine, Good Morning America*, ABC's *Monday Night Football*, several ESPN broadcasts, and the Disney Channel's "98° concert. I even had my own TV show on the ABC affiliate WKRC-TV, *Sports on The Waterfront*. The *Miami Herald* did a two-page feature story on the place, and *The New York Times, Chicago Tribune, Detroit Free Press, Dayton Daily News, Sports Illustrated, Glamour,* and *Bon Appétit* all found something good to say about The Waterfront. When Cincinnati hosted baseball's All-Star Game, ABC-TV chose us as their headquarters. Tara Patrick (now Carmen Electra) was a regular at the age of eighteen. Britney Spears and Justin Timberlake were there together. At The Waterfront, we served everyone from Michael Jordan to the King of Jordan, and from Ann-Margret to Margaret Thatcher.

Yet, there's something problematic about anything that starts with "Water." For Napoleon, it was Waterloo. For Nixon, it was Watergate. Maybe the fact that water finds its way to the lowest point has something to do with it. I reached the lowest point of my life as a result of the incidents that occurred at The Waterfront. It's where I met my Waterloo. I don't remember this incident at all, but Dave Stevens told Robert,

"During construction our neon guy, Larry Brown, was scamming us. Instead of providing brand new transformers, which Jeff was paying for, he brought in rebuilt ones but invoiced us for new ones. When Jeff found out, he threw Larry off the boat, right into the river. When our painter was falling behind schedule, Jeff threw him into the river, too. They both deserved it."

After my 1987 head injury, I returned to work too soon (despite the orders of my neurosurgeon). I was a maniac. My brain was still trying to heal. The part of the brain that affects emotion and inhibition was irreparably damaged. I thought I was just fine and that everyone else was crazy. Rickelle had me committed to the mental ward at Holmes Hospital. There I sat in sessions with real nutcases, listening to their stories. God only knows how my employees put up with me, even after I got out of the loony bin. I broke more plates than they did, by throwing them at the walls, with the food still on them, whenever guests sent their orders back.

Our outdoor bar on the barge, named Las Brisas, was arguably the most over-the-top food and beverage endeavor ever to open in Greater Cincinnati. Building a two-level floating resort nightclub on the Ohio River on two barges tied together that would be open just three months a year was risk personified.

By the time construction began on Las Brisas, I was not only recovering from two brain surgeries, I was suffering from depression. Nothing in my life was ever as painful as depression. I was convinced The Waterfront was going out of business and that Las Brisas was the biggest mistake of my life. I thought I couldn't have been in my right mind when I decided to do it, but the truth was that I wasn't in my right mind when I was having all those negative thoughts. It almost all came to an end one afternoon at 2 p.m. I had another brush with death.

The weekly Las Brisas construction meeting was at 2:30 p.m. I was driving on the Brent Spence Bridge, high above the Ohio River, approaching Covington's Fifth Street ramp, when something began happening inside my head. Driving in the lane next to me was a friend, Skip Greenberg, who said "hello." I was too incapacitated to reply. I don't know how I got from I-75 to The Waterfront parking lot, but I'm sure God drove the car there, not me. That's the last thing I remember until I woke up in University Hospital.

Pat Dempsey, our assistant manager, saw my car in the parking lot and noticed that I was on the floor of the car and had swallowed my tongue. He told me later he used a pencil to pull it out. The paramedics were going to take me to the closest hospital, but my secretary, Cindy Brown, (Susan's sister) put up a fight and insisted that they take me across the river to University Hospital, so that my neurosurgeons there could deal with this. She informed them of my previous near-death brain injuries. I was supposed to be on phenobarbital, but I had stopped taking it and, as a result, suffered a brain seizure. Skip told Pat he was pissed off that I didn't say hello to him.

I lay in my hospital bed for a few days and thought back to my first close call in Miami Beach when I was about six or seven years old. My mother had taken us to find Walter Ruby, and we checked into the Jefferson Hotel. Before she unpacked, I ran to the pool. Just as I was about to dive in, I quickly stopped. The swimming pool had no water in it. I was glad I had caught that detail. So, I went to the beach and ran into the ocean instead. Suddenly I noticed the water surrounding me was red, and I felt like my foot was coming off. When I made it to the shore, my foot was hanging by a thread. I was hysterical, and nobody knew who I was or where I came from. A kid in a '52 Plymouth rushed me to Mt. Sinai Hospital, and a surgeon was called in from his vacation to save my little right foot. They told me I had cut my foot on a broken Coke bottle in the sand. They sewed my foot, my nerves and my tendons. It took 250 stitches in all. My mother had no idea where I was all this time. She was probably looking for her husband, not me. That was three decades before my even closer call in Florida with Cris Collinsworth, when we were on our reconnoitering mission in aid of creating The Waterfront.

* * * * *

Music is a crucial element in all of our places, but at The Waterfront's Las Brisas it was so important that I auditioned musicians myself and created our own house band. Jam Factor was a thirteen-piece triumph with a four-piece horn section, an incredible rhythm section, and four lead vocalists. From this ensemble came Blessid Union of Souls with lead singers Eliot Sloan and Eddie Hedges, and lead guitarist/vocalist Jeff Pence. They had four Top 40 hits. Rasheeda Azar, the female vocalist, later became a back-up vocalist for Paula Abdul and went on to join Janet Jackson. The keyboard player, Jeff Kazee, went with Bon Jovi. The rest of the rhythm section was every bit as talented. I'm so proud of them all to this day.

At about four-thirty on Labor Day morning, our security guard, Vic Palumbo, woke me up with a call to tell me he thought Las Brisas might be sinking. I hurriedly checked with my friend and partner Mike Zicka, a prominent homebuilder, and he told me I should take it seriously. Palumbo made Barney Fife look like Rambo, and I would probably have gone back to bed if Zicka hadn't been there with his boat. By the time I arrived, all the TV stations were there, and the barge was under water. The only thing sticking out of the river was the top of the waterfall. When the structure listed, it wiped out all of the cantilevered windows on the restaurant's barge.

The investigation began. The cause of the disaster turned out to be a plumber's failure to caulk the exterior of the barge with PVC (polyvinyl chloride), thus allowing river water into the hull and causing the barge to sink.

Runaway barges were attracted to The Waterfront, especially on holidays. The next time it happened was on New Year's Eve at about ten o'clock at night. After receiving the call about an approaching barge, I ran out to Las Brisas to "see what condition my condition was in." Las Brisas, by then, had been fished out of the river and restored since the previous disaster. It was closed for the winter and tied alongside our restaurant barge. If something was going to hit us, it would hit the empty Las Brisas barge. This time, Alan Bernstein went after the runaway barge in his tugboat, attempting to steer it away from us. The Bernstein family owns B&B Riverboats. They also own the Mike Fink, a floating restaurant, and Covington Landing's restaurants. They were my main competitors. Talk about a possible conflict of interest.

I evacuated about four hundred people from the restaurant, but I stayed behind, briefcase in hand. I made certain I had all of my notebooks with my ideas written in them. The barge did hit us and mangled a bar at Las Brisas. When we reopened, I didn't repair it, I just named it the Shipwrecked Bar.

On a Friday night in March 2011, my attorney, Tedd Friedman, called me right after my assistant, Amy Lewis, called. They both wanted to know if I had heard that The Waterfront had broken loose from its moorings and was floating down the river–with all eighty-four of its diners and employees on board. Somehow, I wasn't surprised. Still in my Georgio Armani suit, I got into my car, but I didn't know how I was going to find my restaurant. The riverbank doesn't have a street that runs parallel to it, so there was no way I could follow my boat by car. I crossed the Brent Spence Bridge and looked out at the dark river to see if I could see my restaurant floating toward Louisville. That caused me to miss the first Covington exit. When finally I got to our mooring location, lo and behold, The Waterfront was still clinging to land. The Covington Fire Department, Boone County Water Rescue, the Coast Guard, Covington Police Department, Carlisle's tugboats,

Aquarius Marine's boats, and all the TV trucks were there.

The four local TV stations covered this story live for ninety minutes. The Waterfront consumed the entire eleven o'clock news cycle, with no break for the tsunami in Japan, no Leno, Letterman or Nightline. The news went global. ESPN even covered the event, because Collinsworth was on board. The media sensationalized the story and got the facts wrong, making this incident international news. The initial wrong reports were that we had broken free, hit the bridge and were one hundred yards downstream. They reported that Cris Collinsworth was a former quarterback instead of a wide receiver, and misspelled his last name. But, it all worked out great for us publicity-wise.

Cris had wanted to test the stability of the makeshift evacuation ladder, so he was the first to escape. Cris got off safely, before the women and children. Boomer used that fact to bust Cris's balls on his radio and MSG TV show. Boomer is the ultimate ball buster, a New Yorker.

I convinced the fire chief to let me get on the boat before the evacuation. I wanted to be with my guests and employees to give my support, to apologize, and to confront them face-to-face if they wanted to chew me out. Just the opposite happened. They all just wanted another drink and for the band to keep playing. They couldn't have been nicer and more complimentary about all the great experiences they'd had at The Waterfront and how well our staff handled this particularly exciting dining experience…their final one at The Waterfront.

* * * * *

Or so we thought. On April 19, 2013, my sixty-fifth birthday, we signed a lease with the city of Covington, Kentucky, to re-open The Waterfront at a new location, about half a mile upriver from our old spot. We held a press conference that day to announce the restaurant's comeback. I never realized how much The Waterfront had meant to this Northern Kentucky community, until we began to look into bringing it back. It's a joint effort among the city of Covington, Bill Butler's Comprex Corp. and Jeff Ruby Culinary Entertainment. We won't have LaBoom this time, or Las Brisas. But we will have a second barge with an atrium and a magnificent grand entry. In memory of the late Carl Lindner, my mentor and The Waterfront's lender, we will have a three hundred-seat event center named the Carl Lindner Grand Ballroom. We hope to open in early 2014.

CHAPTER TWENTY

I AIN'T LIVING LONG LIKE THIS

Waylon Jennings, 1980

The Precinct passed the torch across the Ohio River to The Waterfront's LaBoom as the area's most popular singles bar. That meant we had dominated greater Cincinnati's nightclub scene for the entire decade of the 1980s—at two different restaurants, in two different states.

Jimmy Buffett was a regular at The Waterfront and went so far as to revise his lyrics to include our place for the live "Feeding Frenzy" version of his 1979 song "Fins." Buffett was at LaBoom on a night we were doing our weekly lingerie auction. Girls modeled lingerie, and men bought it right off their beautiful bodies. Rickelle, who was in charge of that promotion, made some money off the show, we sold drinks, the models got paid, and a lot of people got laid (later) —while people were eating surf 'n' turf downstairs. It was a terrific concept.

At closing time one night, Jimmy told me he would play and sing for a few of us on the river, if I could get a boat, a guitar and some girls. I told him the only thing that might take a few minutes would be the guitar. By that time we had been drinking and watching half-naked girls all night.

(In July of 2013, twenty-six years and three days later, Jimmy gave a concert at Cincinnati's Riverbend and mentioned our long-ago night on the River. I was in New York City for the All-Star Game when my Twitter followers who were at the concert began tweeting me about it.)

Buffett had a line that inspired me to make things even worse.

He said when he does something wrong and gets caught he says, "That wasn't me, that was my alter ego." I loved that explanation, and so did my pal Jack Daniel's. I was ready to party. I felt that "Come Monday, I'll be all right," in the words of Jimmy's first Top 40 hit. I was really buying Jimmy's "alter ego" line.

Two weeks later, July 13, 1987, I was at The Precinct for a very "soft opening" of our second-floor dessert bar called Café Marvelous. The place ended up being a deserted bar, when few guests showed up. I sat with my friend Tony Kiernan, drinking ice water and wearing my black tuxedo and black Reebok sneakers. Tony was the general manager of WLW-TV, the NBC affiliate in Cincinnati.

One of our employees came upstairs to tell me Rickelle wanted to see me in the parking lot. I told Tony I would be right back, and I went down the back stairs and through the kitchen to the parking lot. Rickelle ordered me to get into the car, because we needed to talk. We never talked, we argued. I knew she was very upset about something. I explained that I couldn't leave The Precinct because it was the opening night of our new dessert bar. That didn't interest Rickelle. She was upset and said we needed to talk now. I "should've said no," as the Taylor Swift song says. Bad decisions make good stories. They can also make headlines.

From the moment I got into the car, she started her accusations about the Jimmy Buffett boat ride. Word had gotten back to her about the girl I was with on that boat. I went as far as I wanted to with that girl that night, and she was hotter than the wasabi at P. F. Chang's. There were two reasons I did not take her to the cabin below to have sex with her. One of them had now become reality: I knew Rickelle would find out. There were too many girls on that boat for her not to find out. She found out I had sex even when I didn't have sex. She said she caught her first husband cheating and that's why she divorced him. Hell, maybe he was innocent, too. More importantly, Rickelle was six months pregnant. I had never cheated on her before and I wasn't going to start then.

I told my wife the truth. The other girl and I "made out" like high school freshmen that night. We didn't even have "Bill Clinton sex." When the boat returned to the dock at The Waterfront, it was "Five O' Clock Somewhere," and that somewhere was Cincinnati. There was no time to take that girl to a hotel. I had to get my tail back to Anderson Township before Rickelle woke up. It was damn near daylight.

Rickelle and I had driven two blocks from The Precinct and stopped for a red light. I told her I had to get back to work and asked her to take me back to my opening night. Rickelle said she wasn't yet finished with me. Again, I told her to make a right turn and take me back to The Precinct. When the light finally turned green, Rickelle turned left. I jumped out of the car as she drove off. I don't know what happened after that, except that I never did get back to Tony Kiernan.

"I wasn't driving very fast, hardly moving, because we hadn't come far from the restaurant, and I had just made the turn at the stoplight," Rickelle told Robert. "We were in a Volvo sports car with bucket seats and the gearshift between us. I told him we were going home to our two little children, that I was pregnant and tired. He told me he was going back to work. There were two cars behind us. The witnesses reported seeing a man get out of our car and stumble and fall on the concrete. I angled the car to protect him from being hit by another car; it was all I could think of to do."

Mike Cowans was the man who found me lying on the pavement. He described the scene to Robert: "I worked the 3 to 11 p.m. shift for the Cincinnati Metropolitan Sewer District nearby. I had just pulled my car out of the plant when I saw headlights coming toward me, erratically moving left to right, about a quarter of a mile down the road. When I got to the car, I saw a man lying in the street, bleeding

205

profusely. There was no traffic. I went to the phone booth that was then across the street from The Precinct and called 911. The fire department, also very nearby, responded that they were on the way. I ran over to the man lying in the street—I had no idea who he was then—and tried to hold him down until the fire department got there. He kept trying to get up, all the while still bleeding. At one point, lying flat on his back, he vomited straight up into the air.

"His wife was screaming and crying, 'I love you so much, please don't leave me.' I couldn't calm her down. Two minutes later, another man stopped, and the two of us held the victim still. Five minutes after I'd called them, the fire department arrived and told us to back off. We did, and they took over. When I got home, I was still covered in the man's blood. I took a shower, and the blood ran down the drain like the scene in *Psycho*."

"He was able to move his head a little, so I knew he was alive," Rickelle remembered, "but he was unconscious. At the hospital, a CT scan showed major swelling in his brain and a crack in his skull. He was in a coma for almost a month. I stayed at the hospital the entire time. I never left his side."

By the time Tony returned to Channel 5 that night, I later learned, the news broadcasts were saying that I was either near death or dead, had been doing cocaine–and even that my pregnant wife, Rickelle, might have pushed me out of a moving car. Tony told his news director that the cocaine part, he knew for a fact, wasn't true and ordered him not to touch that part of the story for the *Eleven O'clock News*.

Meanwhile, as I lay in a coma, my lawyer Reuven Katz summoned private investigator Jim Simon, aka "Rambo," to conduct a thorough investigation. It was so thorough he began in Neptune, New Jersey, to talk to my friends about me. First he wanted to see if my intention was to commit suicide. Simon's investigation was as long and detailed as my stay in the hospital, and it cost six figures. The report was thicker than the Cincinnati Yellow Pages. I never read it; it was too damn long.

When I eventually came out of the coma one morning at about 2 a.m., they moved me out of ICU. Rickelle was by my bedside. My prognosis was still not good, and she had a gut feeling something wasn't right with me. Dr. Harry van Loveren of the Mayfield Institute had performed my brain surgery. I had the best neurosurgeon I could have asked for. He told Rickelle there was nothing more that could be done. "He's in God's hands," the doctor told my pregnant wife with two children, five and four years old.

It turned out Rickelle was right. She saw a tear come out of one of my eyes, and she went to find a nurse. My brain pressure was over 22, when about 10 is normal. I was near death. Rickelle called my second neurosurgeon, Dr. Brad Mullen, at home, and he rushed to University Hospital to perform a second brain surgery. He explained to Rickelle this would be experimental surgery to lower the pressure on my brain, but it was my only chance of living. He was going to insert a metal bolt in my brain. I had fallen into a second coma that was deeper than the first. Rickelle was told she had "to be prepared for death." The hospital sent in a rabbi to pray for me. His name was Louis Weiss, the same name as the man who never admitted to being my biological father.

After that second surgery, I was back in ICU for quite some time. I was given a 10 percent chance of surviving and about a 95 percent chance of being a permanent "vegetable" if I did survive. Had Rickelle not been in my room at 2 a.m. and made the decision to call Brad, and had Brad not gotten out of bed and instead had waited until the next morning, I would have died.

One day Rickelle was in my room with Pete Rose's wife, Carol. Carol was standing over my bed looking at me. Suddenly my eyes began to open, and Carol told Rickelle to come over by the bed. Then my mouth opened, and out came the words, "You have nice tits." They both went crazy.

"Jeff's back, oh my God! He's going to live and he's Jeff again, he's normal," Rickelle screamed. They were my first words since I had jumped out of that car: "You have nice tits." Actually Carol had a much nicer butt. I wasn't all the way back yet.

"I think I played a very important part in his recovery from his accident," Tommy Lasorda told Robert. "Every day I was in town I went to that hospital and made him get up out of bed and walk the halls with me. Otherwise he was just gonna lie there. Nobody could get him out of his bed until I told him he had to get up. I've got a hard head, too."

Tommy, the former Los Angeles Dodgers manager, an American treasure, a wonderful guy, and a dear friend for more than thirty years, was also a great motivator. No one has more stories or is a better joke teller. Like Sparky, Tommy has had a positive influence on my life. I've been through periods of depression, and Tommy has helped me through those times.

While I was still in intensive care after my accident, Tommy walked out onto the field to talk to the second base umpire in the middle of a game in Los Angeles. The Dodgers' announcer, Vin Scully, and the rest of the press box wondered what the hell the home team's manager wanted to talk to the second base umpire about. What they didn't realize was that the umpire, Randy Marsh, was from Covington, Kentucky. Tommy wanted to ask Randy if I was doing any better in intensive care. Tommy didn't tell me that story. Randy, who is now a supervising umpire, did.

No one has promoted Jeff Ruby or our restaurants more than Tommy Lasorda. People often tell me that they have heard him mention me on television or the radio. He has plugged us in *USA Today*. And I've fed him well.

"I knew Jeff before he had all those restaurants," Tommy told Robert. "He was a man of desire, who had goals to reach, and he put forth all the effort it took to be successful in that business. He thought big and accomplished what he set out to do, with courage and determination. He's cocky and self-confident, which is the first step to success. If you don't believe in yourself, you're not going to get there. But he also has a big heart and likes people. Walking into The Precinct or The Waterfront, you always felt those restaurants should be in New York or L.A."

Tommy invited me to stay with him at his penthouse suite for a big pennant series in Atlanta one September. The Dodgers were in a tight race, fighting it out with the Braves for first place in the National League. Tommy told me he was going to put me in a uniform, so I could be a Dodger for a day. That sounded cool, so I went to Atlanta. When I got to Atlanta, he said he couldn't let me wear the uniform in the dugout, after all. The players jumped all over Tommy for breaking his promise to me, so Tommy put me in a uniform and sent me to sit in the bullpen with the relief pitchers.

Late in the game, John Candelaria was warming up. Mark Kreise, the bullpen coach, was catching for "The Candy Man" when the phone rang. Mark was responsible for answering the bullpen phone. It kept ringing, so I finally answered it. It was Ron Perranoski, the former pitching coach. I thought I would add some levity to the game, so I answered, "Tony's Pizza, pick-up or delivery?"

"What?" said Perranoski, "Who is this?"
I repeated the Tony's Pizza thing. Ron hung up and tried

again. This time I said, "Dodger bullpen, how may I direct your call?" This was during a freakin' pennant race in September.

* * * * *

I wanted to leave the hospital, but my doctors said I couldn't. I had to get Reuven Katz to meet with a committee of eight people, including the hospital hierarchy. Papers had to be signed, because I refused to stay in the hospital any longer. "I'm leaving in the middle of the night if you don't agree," I told them.

The doctors ordered me not return to work for about two years, but I returned by Labor Day weekend, less than eight weeks after the accident. For months I went back to the hospital as an outpatient, learning how to speak all over again, how to walk and perform all of the functions our brains are responsible for. I had permanently lost 20 percent of my brain and done severe damage to the brain's frontal and temporal lobes—the areas that affect one's emotions and short-term memory. You no longer think before you speak, and your inhibitions are gone forever.

I refused to take medication to keep me calm, because of its unpleasant side effects. I was supposed to be on phenobarbital to prevent seizures, but I wasn't taking that, either. One of the problems I am left with is a twenty-four-hour piercing noise in my left ear that sounds like a whistling teapot and sometimes a train's steam engine. There is no cure for tinnitus, and many people can't live with it. It's so frustrating and annoying that many who suffer from it commit suicide. I'm so grateful to be alive that I just block it out of my consciousness.

I am grateful to all my speech pathologists, physical therapists, neurosurgeons and neurologists, and the countless technicians, nurses, attendants and employees who put up with a brain-damaged lunatic.

Dr. van Loveren told me I would never be the same, as a result of the brain damage. But I believe that it is not what happens to you in life that matters. It is what you decide you're going to do about it. I see people crossing the street with no legs, and our heroes coming back from the wars with no limbs at all and smiles on their faces. The doctor was right, I am not the same. I'm a better man than I used to be.

Five thousand prayer lines were set up, asking God to save my life, when at one point I was brain dead. I know why I'm alive, and I promised God I would be a better person and do good things for people who needed help. I believe God knew I had done many good things for people, and He knew I could do even more if I had more time.

CHAPTER TWENTY-ONE

I'M DIFFERENT

2CHAINZ, 2012

As Ralph Waldo Emerson said, "He who would be a man must be a non-conformist."

An NBC reporter once called me "a Cincinnati icon who's never at a loss for words." I didn't become an icon by following the rules. I always did things my way. I was able to do it my way because I insisted on it. I created a steakhouse in a way no one had ever done it before. I re-invented the steakhouse, and now steakhouses are done my way. I may not be the best, but I'm better than I thought I would be. You're not defined by how you react when things are good, but by how you react when they are not. I can't remember when things were good before I made them good.

Celebrities had always been paid handsomely to put their names on other investors' restaurants. I did it the other way around, and some of sports' biggest names put their money on me and let me do our restaurants my way. One of the reasons our first place, The Precinct, had previously failed as Amanda's was that their patrons' cars were broken into on a regular basis. The parking lot lies between the railroad tracks and a dangerous street. There were too many punks and too many drunks around. I befriended a big black man named Curtis, who was unemployed. He lived in the neighborhood and knew all the punks doing the break-ins. Curtis was a nice guy, and I liked him, so I hired him to be my night security guard. I bought him a baseball bat and paid him to stand in the parking lot six nights a week. It was a win-win. He had under-the-table income, and we never had a car broken into.

There were four or five young boys living on that rough street, and they always hung around while we were under construction. They looked like the "Bowery Boys" from the 1950s TV show. Naturally, they took a liking to me, and I took time for them. I took them to King's Island and to Reds games. I even took them to my house for dinner with me and Rickelle. About a year later, I got a call the night before our grand opening. The Precinct had been broken into, and our dance club's entire sound system was stolen.

The police searched the neighborhood. They went door-to-door with their investigation, but they were clueless as to who had stolen a $20,000 sound system. Someone had robbed a former police station, for God's sake. I was livid. My opening day "punch list" was twenty pages on a long yellow legal pad. I got none of it checked off. I spent the day looking for my sound system, traveling miles up and down Eastern Avenue. Then it occurred to me to ask those kids what they knew. They said it was James Parks, a seventeen-year-old kid, much older than they. They told me I would find all of the equipment in a basement I could enter from the backyard wooden doors. I carried the scuffed equipment back by myself. I never told the cops, but I told the kid, "I cut you a break, Jimmy. Now cut me one. You follow me?" I never had trouble with the neighborhood's biggest burglar again.

Those young boys are grown men now, and a few still keep in touch. About ten years later at LaBoom, our club at The Waterfront, a strange-looking chick came up and looked at me. "It's Bobby," she said. It was Bobby, one of those little boys who told me where my sound system was and whom I took to baseball games. He was now a girl. "Hi, Bobby, long time no see," I said.

My plan at The Precinct was fine dining with continental cuisine on the first floor and a dance club (don't use the word "disco") on the second. The first name that crossed my mind for the place was

The Precinct, because the building originally was built as a police patrol station in 1901. That decision took all of five minutes. Gerry Foote and Mike Calvin (a female) were my designers. We didn't do too much, but we did use purple, and we used mirrors to make the tiny place look bigger and appear to be busier. When you mirror the wall across from an expensive painting, you now have two expensive paintings that twice as many people can look at. When the mirror was 45 degrees from the mural, the mural became infinite. We managed.

Dave Meyer, a partner with a one-half share, kept bugging me to go to Dayton, Ohio, to see a steakhouse called The Pine Club. I kept telling Dave that I had no desire to own a steakhouse. My passion was gourmet food and fine dining. Steak was steak, not challenging enough. But Dave persisted. He eventually persuaded me to take Rickelle and go to Dayton with him and his wife, Beverly, to have dinner at this Pine Club.

I would describe The Pine Club as a honky-tonk steakhouse. Linoleum floors, plastic menus, vinyl booths, no credit cards, and no desserts. I loved it! Dave was correct. Steak wasn't just steak. Nobody in Cincinnati did steak this good. The Pine Club also did other things well, but not for the kind of clientele I was going after. The manager, Dave Hulme, was gracious enough to show me the tiny kitchen. Dave is now the restaurant's owner. He told me where he bought his meat, and I noticed the seasoning that the broiler man was shaking on the steaks. I knew instantly that it was the "magic dust." That was the secret. I had to get my hands on that seasoning, no matter what it took or how long it took. I called Vic Foreman at Michael's Meats in Columbus, where Dave said they bought their meat. Vic told me nobody knew where Dave got that seasoning. He said it was a closely guarded secret.

I came back the very next Sunday when The Pine Club would be closed, and its dumpster would be full. After a busy weekend without a Saturday pick-up, there would be plenty of empty bottles of that stuff in that dumpster. It was a hot July day in a dumpster in Dayton, and I was swimming around inside as if it were a backyard above-ground pool, with just the rats to keep me company. I wasn't worried about rats. I was looking out for the cops. A hobo came along and started going through the trash. I said, "Hey, this is my dumpster. I was here first." I was arguing with a guy who lived off this stuff. Then it occurred to me to pay *him* to find this fucking bottle. He loved the idea. I drove off and came back every fifteen minutes. This went on for hours. I thought he must have given up, got caught, or he had found it and was opening up his own steakhouse. I just kept driving around. There was no place to go and nothing to do. Nothing in downtown Dayton was open. There is still nothing open in Dayton on Sunday. Dayton is Mayberry with room service.

It was dark when I returned and found my guy, bottle in hand. "You got it! Son of a bitch, you got it," I yelled. I hugged him and looked at the bottle. My next yell was to myself. "Fuck me!" They had taken a fork and scraped the label, so it was impossible to determine what it was and where it came from. I gave my "friend" his fifty bucks and took the damn bottle with me. Maybe a genie would come out of the thing and give me the next clue.

Nobody gets anywhere without being relentless. I was on a mission to get that stuff, and I eventually I did. Having that bottle was a good start. I wish I could buy that hobo a dinner at The Precinct. I've been an advocate for The Pine Club ever since, and give them props every chance I get.

At The Precinct I broke every rule I could. I created our own rule book and put together a manual that eventually made its way around the country. Its cover reads, "The Power of WE." Hundreds of restaurants have been opened around America by countless restaurateurs who have worked for me. About thirty of them started their careers with me. I feel good about that. Unshared success is incomplete success. I taught them everything they know, but I didn't teach them everything I know.

Upscale steakhouses did not cater to women and refused to hire women. They didn't have dance clubs, or kids in their twenties coexisting with millionaires in their sixties. There wasn't a steakhouse on the planet that blended bluebloods with blue-hairs, businessmen, ballplayers, barflies, and babes in miniskirts. And they didn't have barroom brawls, blood on the carpet, and Rolls-Royces in the parking lot. My place was like Friday night at "Dino's Bar and Grill, where the blood will spill" in Thin Lizzy's classic, "The Boys are Back in Town."

Our guests had fights with the clientele of the Delta Café clientele across the street. One guy pissed in our ice machine. I fought with him in the middle of the street. He actually filed charges, and I had to go to trial. He claimed his broken jaw ruined his major league pitching career. They found me not guilty. The next time I saw him, he was in the lobby of an Oakland hotel. I was the guest of Reds manager Lou Piniella when they were playing in the World Series. The ice cube pisser was throwing batting practice for the Reds.

I had a bartender who decided to fill out our comment cards and deal drugs. When I found out, I was so mad that I punched him so hard he went through a swinging door and landed in the walk-in cooler. That punch cost me twenty-five thousand dollars in court. Mike Tyson wasn't paid that much to take one punch.

The Precinct was the first upscale restaurant to put "classless" comment cards on its tables. I was criticized for that. Only the likes of Frisch's Big Boy did that type of thing in 1981. If you listen to critics, you'll never be successful. I wanted to know immediately what we were doing wrong, and many people are uncomfortable telling you to your face. I also learned that our number one competitor in

Cincinnati was the longest-running Mobil 5-star restaurant in America, The Maisonette.

With just sixty-eight seats we needed to turn seats, so I didn't offer dessert. We gave everyone a chocolate-covered strawberry. I needed people to "eat and run," so I had three codes for our food servers, and I would let them know which one we were operating under every hour of the night.

Plan A – They can sell an after dinner drink.
Plan B – They cannot offer an after dinner drink.
Plan C – Put their check on the table and tell them, "Mr. Ruby would like to buy you a drink upstairs in our club." Our guests knew the deal and got a kick out of it when we said that. They always cooperated. Under no circumstance was coffee to be suggested on plan A or B.

I had a rule at The Precinct that no employee was to refer to a patron as a "customer." You will treat these visitors as if they were at your house for dinner. You don't have customers at your house, you have guests. You greet them at the door, take their coats, walk them in, and make them feel special. If someone ordered lobster and we were out of three-pound live lobsters at The Waterfront, I called Morton's and bought one of theirs to cook in our kitchen.

In our industry, owners, managers, and employees usually refer to the patrons as "customers," or they say, "We did X number of 'covers.'" Lumber Liquidators has customers. Bands do covers. We have guests. The Precinct was the first free-standing restaurant, to my knowledge, to stop using the term customer and replace it with guest. The idea came to me because those three women who opened Amanda's thought that because they often had guests over to their houses for dinner, they should open a restaurant.

I also did away with the title "busboy" and replaced it with "server assistant," in 1981. The term busboy was one hundred years old, and it meant boys who bussed, or cleared, a table of its garbage. I wanted these kids to assist the food servers and learn everything the servers did. I wanted them to learn to *become* food servers. Every general manager in our company began with us as a server assistant, including my son Brandon. The term server assistant has now pretty much replaced busboy all across America.

Local entrepreneur Fred Mayerson once asked us to make him a salad with bacon, lettuce, and tomato. The employees referred to it as a "Freddie Salad." We made it our house salad, and it still is. The first BLT salad in America was created at The Precinct.

As far as I know, we were the first restaurant to voluntarily prohibit smoking. My partners were furious with me. We had the busiest, most popular place in town in 1984, and I did something as controversial and unnecessary as that. The problem with having silent partners is they keep forgetting they have the right to remain silent. We were also the first to contact the president of Mothers Against Drunk Driving (MADD) and suggest having an alcohol awareness training class for our staff in 1982. With the bar business we were doing, I felt it would be a good idea.

We were the first restaurants to have defibrillators on the premises. We hold training classes for the defibrillators, CPR, oxygen masks, and the Heimlich maneuver. Dr. Heimlich himself did our training. He's a Cincinnatian, and his son Phil is a friend of mine.

Because I wanted this steakhouse to appeal to women, I hired good-looking young male food servers, server assistants, and what I decided would be called "club hosts," not "bouncers" or "doormen." Those words both have negative connotations. All of our guys looked good. One of the things I had them do was offer their arms and escort ladies to the restroom–another first. Some scoffed at this. We're still doing it, thirty-two years later. I put a bar in the ladies' room with a topless "Chippendale's"-style bartender. If they're constantly going to the ladies' restroom, we might as well sell drinks there too. I cater to women. "No women, no men. No men, no money." That's my mantra. If I was going to have men in the ladies' room, why not women in the men's room? I hired gorgeous young girls to be men's room attendants at all the restaurants. One of the first of them at The Tropicana was a Jersey girl, Kate Wenderfer. That was nine years ago. She is still with the company and now works as a bartender at Carlo & Johnny.

Kate told Robert, "I was eighteen and had come to Cincinnati to study at the School of Design Art, Architecture and Planning at the University of Cincinnati. I needed money for school. Beginning when I was sixteen, I'd worked at Sammy's Steakhouse, a real gangster hangout with no sign out front, in my home town of Mendham, New Jersey. I Googled the best restaurants in Cincinnati and picked The Tropicana as a place to apply. They needed me to start the next day. I was too young to serve alcohol, so I was put in the washroom part of the men's room, handing out towels. We could wear anything we wanted to–so long as it was black and included little shorts, since we had to show a lot of leg and a lot of stomach. After all, there were men in the women's room, naked from the waist up. I quickly went from thinking *what the hell am I doing here. Can't these guys get their own towels?* to thinking it was the best job ever.

"I was there every night from when we opened at five p.m. until about one-thirty in the morning. I averaged two hundred dollars a night in tips. Some guys would give me a twenty-dollar bill, just for handing them a towel! Working for Jeff Ruby, I completely put myself through college in six years. I'm still here, and he's still a per-fectionist. Nothing he does is logical. We've just put in a Jeff Ruby Room at Carlo & Johnny. It's the nicest private dining room, seating ten people. He changed his mind about the table he wanted in there about thirty times."

At Jeff Ruby's restaurants, people must silence their cell phones. Their ringing ruins the ambiance for everyone else. The sign at our front desk reads "Cell Phones are a 'Turn Off.'"

At The Waterfront, I decided to have a sushi bar–in 1987, in Northern Kentucky, of all places. They all thought I had really lost my mind. I became the first owner to have a sushi bar in a steakhouse. It never went out of style, in a city I consider a culinary wasteland.

At The Precinct, I engineered the kitchen hood system to send the exhaust in a direction that provided "aromatherapy" up Delta Avenue, outside our door. People can smell our food at the gas station down the street. When our guests arrive in our parking lot, the aroma whets their appetite.

One problem we had was the noise from our club upstairs. The "disco" music and dancing were pounding down on the restaurant below. (We never used the word disco, but that's what it was.) The subwoofers from the floor above had the shrimp nearly jumping out of the cocktail glasses below. The answer was egg cartons. We bought eggs in gray 12-inch by 12-inch paper crates. We laid the empties throughout the entire ceiling. It was free baffling, and it worked.

I was The Precinct's only manager, and I didn't know what I was in for. I grossly underestimated our business. It was more than twice my projections. I was also oblivious to what was happening in the 1980s drug scene and how it would manifest itself when my place became the hottest discotheque in the city. Every beautiful girl, visiting pro athlete, rock star, movie star, tennis player, and wealthy out-of-state high-roller visited our place to dine, drink and party. Some flew in on private jets to Lunken Airport, just three minutes from our place.

The Cincinnati Bengals made The Precinct their home. The year we opened, the team went to the Super Bowl for the first time in their history. Some of the players bought and used cocaine, and I had no clue. I was running around shaking hands, fixing problems, watching the food come out of the kitchen, seeing that the wrong people didn't get in and the right people did, putting out fires, etc. Nobody wanted me to know anything about the drugs, not even the staff. A lot of them were doing drugs too. And even if they weren't, they weren't going to be snitches.

The FBI even thought the white powder that was my secret steak seasoning was cocaine. My chef calling it "magic dust" didn't help. I went to a clandestine place out of town to pick up the seasoning and put it in my car. It was in a big brown box lined with clear plastic. The plastic added to the suspicion, I suppose. The Feds had a camera on the roof of the YMCA across the street from our kitchen door and watched me bring it inside.

The FBI, I learned many years later, told the Bengals that Jeff Ruby was connected to the Mafia. Not until Joe Valachi *told* Congress there was a Mafia did the FBI even *believe* there was a Mafia. Now they believed I was in it. I learned about the FBI accusation when my future son-in-law, Caleb, was with the team and began getting serious with Britney. He was informed of my "connections" by the team's pastor. Caleb was afraid that he could be marrying into the Mafia.

Major league baseball checked me out before Pete Rose and Johnny Bench were allowed to get into the Precinct deal, friends or no friends. When Cris Collinsworth and Boomer Esiason became my partners at The Waterfront, the NFL did a thorough background check. When I partnered with the Belterra casino in Indiana, the background check started all over again. Every time I go to a high school to give a speech, one of the questions is always, "Are you in the Mafia?" When you're from Jersey, have an accent, wear pin-striped suits, smoke cigars, and wear a hat, everyone jumps to conclusions. A pinstriped suit with a fedora is a classy look, and I'm addicted to cigars and heavy gold jewelry. End of story.

I hired young college kids, and I hired good-looking young girls to serve food. You never found a waitress at a steakhouse in Chicago or New York back in those days. Just a few years ago, Joe's Stone Crab in Miami was sued–and lost–because of that one hundred-year-old, all-male waiter policy. The waiters have been working at those established union steakhouses for twenty years. At our places, we dry-age our steaks on the premises. In New York and Chicago, it looks like they dry-age their waiters on the premises.

Our clientele was so diverse it became part of the attraction. Multimillionaires who had to wear a suit and tie at The Maisonette would pull up in their Rollses or Ferraris wearing jeans and no socks. Singer Frankie Valli was sitting by himself in the back one night, so I joined him. He couldn't understand why I was the only one who rec-ognized him. I told him, "I'm a Jersey boy, too, and I grew up listening to you."

In the restaurant business, the bigger you get, the more qual-ity is compromised. You can hire all the managers you want, but no eyes can see like the eyes of the owner. Being hands-on, I got to know a great deal about our guests: what time they liked to be seated, where they liked to be seated, who not to seat near them, how long they'd wait for a table, what to have on hand at the bar, which server matched up well with them, etc.

The big chains can't do that. From a culinary standpoint, for-get about it. They don't hire chefs, and they buy portion-cut steaks.

I sat next to a guy on a plane who told me he won't go back to Morton's because he doesn't like to see his steak being unwrapped from Saran Wrap before it's cooked. My philosophy is "Guest First." The corporations go by "rules first." And French chefs? I wanna see a French chef in my kitchen like I wanna see a French soldier in my foxhole…with all due respect.

Randy Michaels, the former CEO of the *Chicago Tribune* and WGN, told Robert, "I travel a lot, and there are a lot of great steakhouses in America, but Jeff's focus on the customer spoils you for anywhere else."

A restaurant takes on the personality of its owner. My employees are my cast. They reflect my style. The design, chemistry, and charisma of our restaurants are a reflection of my persona. Our guests share in that personality while they are being entertained in our restaurant. Our company is called Jeff Ruby Culinary Entertainment. You won't find this dynamic at a chain restaurant, and you won't find quite the same quality management and staff that you find at a one-of-a-kind place.

In 2009 *Cincinnati Magazine* ran an issue listing the fifty things that make Cincinnati unique. They listed Jeff Ruby as number twenty-nine, only seven places behind Proctor & Gamble. My friends Marty and Thom Brennaman, the Reds radio broadcast team, were number forty-eight. They should've made the Top Ten. No other individual people made the city unique, according to the magazine.

Cincinnati Magazine thinks I'm the only single individual who makes Cincinnati unique, but they don't think any of my restaurants are "serious." The publication's annual "Best 25 Restaurants" issue (now it's "The Ten Best") occasionally listed one of ours in the teens somewhere. Eventually, I wrote the publisher a letter, politely asking him to leave Jeff Ruby's off of their list, as they did our other places. He complied. The magazine has done stories about me and our restaurants, but neither I nor anyone from our company has agreed to interviews or photo requests.

Cincinnati's best restaurant operators are all friends of mine. Familiarity breeds respect. Dean Gregory, who owns the Montgomery Inn, is a good friend. When they opened on the river, it wasn't good for The Waterfront. One night at his place, Jean-Robert a la Cavel asked me, "You know why you don't make *Cincinnati Magazine's* best restaurant list?" I told him that I didn't know. "Yes, you do," he snapped back. The "Yeah, you do," "No, I don't" back-and-forth went on for a while. "Because I don't advertise in the magazine?" I finally asked. "No, because you're a steakhouse. They don't consider that a *serious* restaurant," he explained. The critic was an artsy foodie liberal who listed her own personal favorites, I later learned. I'm the most outspoken conservative in the city, and I own steakhouses. What was her beef? (The restaurant critic recently departed, and the magazine says it is going in a different direction.)

The Precinct and Jeff Ruby's have a higher Zagat rating than every steakhouse in New York, Chicago, Los Angeles, Las Vegas, Miami, New Orleans, San Francisco, etc.

"OpenTable", our industry's leading online reservation program, collects guest feedback daily. Their 2012 "America's 100 Best Restaurants" accumulated ten million guest surveys. The Precinct made the list. It also made Gayot's 2012 "Top 10 Steakhouses" in *USA Today*. And either Jeff Ruby's or The Precinct was chosen by Cincinnatians, in almost every publication, as their favorite fine dining restaurant. The *Cincinnati Enquirer* restaurant critic, Polly Campbell, has awarded five stars to just six restaurants in Cincinnati. Three of them are ours. I take these things seriously.

The Precinct is Cincinnati's longest-running white tablecloth restaurant. The Waterfront was the second longest-running in the area, and the longest running in Northern Kentucky. Jeff Ruby's Steakhouse has outlasted every upscale Downtown freestanding restaurant. We've reached restaurant supremacy in our market through teamwork and incredibly committed employees who care.

I did something else. I kept it simple. I followed the simple philosophy of a 1975 song by the O'Jays. It was a number one R&B hit and was used in the new millennium at Barack Obama's 2008 campaign events. It is called, "Give the People What They Want."

I understood that the engine that drove people to my restaurants was not fueled by truffle oil. So I kept it simple.

* * * * *

My enforcement methods can be unorthodox. Al Green, one of my favorite R&B singers, was staying with us once when I managed the Holiday Inn Riverfront in Newport, Kentucky. Al fell off the stage while he was singing in Cincinnati. He said he got a message from God, and he began singing gospel music.

Al also got a message from me when he skipped out on his hotel bill. Apparently, Al had no green. He and the band got in his bus and tried to cross the state line into Ohio. I chased them down and made them pay their hotel bill. I remember telling him that I loved his song "Let's Stay Together," but not "Let's Stay for Free."

I'll admit that I can go to some lengths to get what I want. After a few successful years with The Precinct, I was looking to expand the restaurant. The elderly man right next door was interested in selling his dilapidated house. At first, he agreed to sell it to me. Then he suddenly changed his mind. I needed to make him come back to me with renewed interest in selling. So I cranked up the sound system in The Precinct's second-floor disco until two in the morning. We got the house for $35,000 and tore it down. It took me a while to figure out what to do with the property. Years later, I turned it into a turn-of-the-century saloon that was one of the best business decisions I ever made.

When *The Sopranos* aired, another few years later, Tony Soprano's soldiers did almost exactly the same thing: blasting the sound system from a boat, to force owners to sell Tony their house on the shore in Sea Bright, New Jersey.

I talk to billionaires and celebrities the same way I talk to teenagers; I'll put them in their places if I don't like their attitudes. I'd rather listen to Shannon Sharpe interview Lou Holtz than listen to someone tell me what I can and cannot say. None of us is better than any of us. Some of us are just more fortunate. The good thing about starting at the bottom is that you respect those who are still there.

Once in a while my humanitarian instincts and my business attention to detail work at cross purposes. On July 4, 2013, my daughter, Britney, organized a Jeff Ruby Culinary Entertainment outreach event for the disadvantaged, in conjunction with the Cincinnati Dream Center, a non-profit that works with ten thousand homeless, drug abusers and otherwise underprivileged people. Our employees volunteered to serve the food. Some five hundred people showed up on a rainy day in Cincinnati.

"When my father showed up, he cut the line to do quality control," Britney told Robert. "He tasted the coleslaw and pronounced it totally inedible. He wanted to know, 'Who created this garbage? It's no good; 86 it. Throw it all away!' I pointed out that these were starving people who would just pull it out of the garbage and eat it anyway. So he grabbed some mustard and other stuff to mix in and make it edible."

Walter Bailey, the heroic busboy from the Beverly Hills fire, who has known me since 1977, told Robert, "Basically, he's the man; he acts upon what he believes in."

Marvin Butts said much the same thing after my sixty-fifth birthday party. When he was driving me home late that night, I asked him, "Why did 3,200 people come to a party to help me celebrate?" Marvin replied simply, "Because you're *the guy*."

CHAPTER TWENTY-TWO

FLIRTIN' WITH DISASTER

Molly Hatchet, 1979

The business I grew up in is "America's business." More Americans have worked at a restaurant or bar at some point in their lives than in any other type of business. More people own, partly own, or invest in restaurants than they do any other business. Movie stars such as Robert De Niro often own more than one. And yet, excellence in this all-pervasive industry is measured by stars awarded by a gas station company. Restaurateurs become obsessed with trying to capture those precious little stars.

Those coveted Mobil Five Stars are determined in our region by a friendly lady from Ohio who was an elementary school teacher. Fortunately, I was at my restaurant when she arrived for her inspection. From her I learned that Mobil inspectors do not even dine at the restaurants they rate. They just look around. They don't know what the food looks like, tastes like, or if the food servers have all of their teeth. They do look at your wine list, however. Most Mobil five-star restaurants have closed, because they weren't too popular. I never cared about Mobil's stars, because the banks don't accept stars. They take cash.

Restaurants are now a chef-driven business. That, in itself, can be problematic. My own experience with chefs is that 50 percent of them use too much marijuana, 20 percent use too much cocaine, and the rest use too much cilantro. I have spent six figures and three decades working with chefs on their drug and alcohol problems. I've been able to get them to cut back only on the cilantro. Alcoholism and drug addiction are common in the restaurant business. Show me a restaurant with a drug problem, and I will show you an auction. I purchased a few of our restaurants as a result of their employees' or owners' drug addictions. They were doing more drugs than business at those restaurants. The restaurant that later became Carlo & Johnny, I bought on the Hamilton County courthouse steps. It was formerly a drug emporium with a raw bar. The chef was using more cocaine than flour in that kitchen.

Do you remember these words of wisdom from Rocco DiSpirito, in a 2003 American Express television commercial? "Do you know me? I am a chef who already runs two restaurants in New York. Now I'm opening a third on national television in a time when nine out of ten restaurants fail in the first year."

That assertion, now part of restaurant folklore, ran during DiSpirito's NBC reality show, *The Restaurant*. Banks had always considered restaurants a risky proposition for loans, despite the fact that they had no figures to support their apprehension. Now, all of a sudden, Rocco DiSpirito provided the missing "numbers." It had always been difficult for anyone looking to open a restaurant to find financing; now it became even more difficult. What made Rocco's absurd statement hard to swallow was that it came from a chef. If the National Restaurant Association had indeed decided it was time to inform America of the financial precariousness of its industry, its spokesperson should not have come from the kitchen. He or she should have been an owner, or at least a manager. Chef Rocco owned only one restaurant in New York at the time. His was called Union Pacific and, when his second property, the reality show restaurant Rocco 22, opened, Rocco was forced out of both of them.

The reason so many restaurants are so risky has much to do with their chefs. Restaurants have become so dependent upon their chefs that many fall victim to the chef. Chef turnover is a way of life in restaurants. It's also a way of death. "If you live by the French knife, you die by the French knife." When the kitchen door becomes a revolving door, the front door eventually closes. Inevitably, when the chef moves on, the food quality suffers. Restaurants may have their recipes on file, but food is more finesse than formula. The restaurant becomes inconsistent, employee turnover follows, and key employees often depart with the chef. The restaurant's reputation suffers, the media become adversarial, and eventually the restaurant ceases to be competitive in the overcrowded market. The chef is the quarterback, and when the quarterback leaves, it isn't easy to find another who can run the offense. It takes time for the team to recuperate. Meanwhile, the team doesn't play well. I always make sure that my backup chef can do the job when the executive chef leaves.

Now it's all about "celebrity chefs," and every city has one or more. Some may have their own television or radio show or newspaper column. Chefs have always been artists, and now they are rock stars. Culinary artists and recording artists have many of the same characteristics. Most artists are hard-headed and stubborn, but that's what makes them what they are. I let it go and let them be. I can relate. My goal is to take each of our chefs and make him a better, more complete chef after working for me than he was before. I'm like BASF. I don't make the food. I make the food better.

Chefs and rock stars often have even more in common. They're prima donnas, problematic, and peripatetic. When one becomes the star of the show, it's a double-edged sword for the restaurant and its owner. Owners used to worry about other restaurants stealing their chefs. Now chefs open their *own* restaurants. The rock star leaves the band to go solo and become a bigger star. Sometimes, however, the move backfires.

Mick Jagger is the voice, the face, and the star of the Rolling Stones, yet his decision to go it alone was ill-fated. Queen without Freddie Mercury would have been worse than England without a queen, but when Mr. Mercury got pissed off at the band, he went solo. He found out that even having the best voice in the business doesn't guarantee success and decided to make up with the guys.

I give our chefs the freedom to demonstrate their talents, but I have final say on the menu. Giving a chef control of your menu is like giving Hannibal Lecter ketchup. It only encourages his evil doings. I consider it my job to give our chefs exposure and to generate publicity for them. I have made stars out of quite a few of them. Seeing one of my chefs evolve into a local celebrity is very rewarding.

Celebrity chef Rocco DeSpirito's commercial caused a firestorm in the industry. After his TV pronouncement, no one wanted to own a restaurant, lend to a restaurant, develop a restaurant, or invest in a restaurant. After Rocco's spots aired, H. G. Parsa, associate professor of hospitality management at Ohio State University, contacted American Express. Parsa wanted to know what documentation they had to support the percentage of failures claimed in the TV commercial. They didn't have any.

Hotel schools such as Cornell and Michigan State University scrambled to get real numbers and find out for themselves if Rocco was right. In 2003, Parsa conducted a longitudinal study of 2,439 restaurants in Columbus, Ohio, using figures from 1996 through 1999. He found that the failure rate for first-year restaurants was about 26 percent. Another 19 percent closed in the second year, and by the end of the third year, 59 percent had closed. Parsa said he found no study that cited a failure rate anywhere near 90 percent. He said the rates of restaurant closures have remained steady over the years and that not all closings were the result of financial or popularity problems. Everybody who responded to the survey mentioned the immense time requirements of restaurant management.

Most of those closed restaurants didn't die. They committed

suicide. That's how restaurants usually die. And guess who is suspected of pulling the trigger? Nobody knows for sure, but he was last seen wearing a white double-breasted jacket and goofy looking pants.

Two inherent difficulties are unique to the restaurant business. The first is that every customer is an expert. They have been eating all of their lives. Second, if you don't sell it, you still got it and if you still got it, you have to throw it in the garbage because it's perishable. You can't have a "sale" for leftover food.

The restaurant business has the reputation of being the toughest business anyone can choose to make his or her career. I've been in it since I was thirteen years old. No other business comes close to being as competitive. You'd be hard pressed to name a city with as many supermarkets, shoe stores, men's clothing places or appliance stores as there are places to eat. We have over a million restaurants in the United States, and it is still legal to eat at home. In Cincinnati, about three dozen places offer a wide selection of sushi. When I want to find a wide selection of shoes, I have to go to Chicago.

In the USA, the proliferation of fast food chains, casual dining restaurants, upscale steakhouse chains and restaurant clusters has resulted in a nationwide epidemic of mediocrity. Burley Crowe, my former linebacker coach at Cornell, told me something that I've never forgotten: "When you're mediocre, you're as close to the bottom as you are to the top." The restaurant "pool" is so huge in America, owners are forced to hire lifeguards who can't swim.

For many people in America, working in a restaurant is merely a temporary job until their true career is determined. In Europe, workers live for the opportunity to work in a restaurant. In many cases, the job is passed down from generation to generation.

There are three primary reasons why restaurants fail:

1) Absentee ownership
2) High occupancy costs
3) Under-capitalization

Very often, business owners do not work at the businesses they own. Restaurants, however, are not just any business. A restaurant is no big thing. It's thousands of little things. Those little things can make or break a restaurant, and managers usually don't pay enough attention to many of them. Nobody has eyes like the eyes of the owner. If a manager hasn't sat in every chair in his restaurant, he doesn't know what he's missing. That is why the industry went in the direction that it did: "Forgettable food at affordable prices."

Nonetheless, for some reason, almost everyone's fantasy is to own their own restaurant. Rock stars, jock stars, and movie stars have become a significant segment of the industry's high-end ownership demographic.

Robert De Niro, as he does for his films, found two excellent "directors" for his restaurants: Drew Nieporent and Nobu Matsuhisa. The last syllable in Nieporent is "rent," so I assume he negotiated a good lease in New York City for Tribeca Grill and Nobu. Drew, another Cornell grad, also opened Proof, a terrific restaurant just a few blocks down the street from our steakhouse in Louisville.

I wonder if De Niro's *Midnight Run* script in 1988 influenced his decision to invest in his first restaurant, Tribeca Grill, in 1990. De Niro's character, Jack Walsh, is a bounty hunter who hunts down Jonathan Mardukas, played by Charles Grodin. Mardukas is a Mafia accountant who is wanted by the FBI. On the title train ride, De Niro tells Grodin that with the $100,000 bounty he will receive for capturing him he is going to open a restaurant. Grodin tells him that if he were De Niro's accountant he would "strongly advise" him not to get into the restaurant business. He tells De Niro, "a restaurant is a very tricky investment" and that "more than half of all restaurants go out of business in less than six months." Maybe Rocco DiSpirito was the movie's consultant.

De Niro's director in the epic *Godfather* films, Francis Ford Coppola, opened his own restaurants, and they were not the Godfather pizza joints. In fact, Coppola has directed more sequels to his restaurants than he has to *The Godfather*, and he is actually *involved* in his restaurants. He also owns an excellent vineyard in Napa Valley.

Maybe one reason so many Americans have the urge to own their own restaurant is that 50 percent of them have worked in a restaurant. It brings back memories of when we were in our teens or working our way through college. For many of us, it was our first job. Jon Bon Jovi worked at Burger King, Madonna worked at Dunkin' Donuts, and Mick Jagger scooped at an ice cream stand. Stevie Nicks was a hostess at a Bob's Big Boy, Kevin Bacon was a waiter in New York City, and Jon Knight of New Kids on the Block once made Burger King Whoppers.

The nearly one million restaurants in the United States generate more than $516 billion and employ more than 13 million people, or 9 percent of the country's work force, according to the National Restaurant Association. Obviously there is money to be made, and much money has been made by savvy entrepreneurs and by public companies. What is different about our business is that, quite often, the return on investment is not what motivates successful people to invest in restaurants. It may have little to do with money and a lot to do with ego, and these people are equipped with both.

Movie stars certainly are not usually seeking another source of income. De Niro said that he opened Ago in Las Vegas' Hard Rock as a result of his disappointment with that city's restaurants while he was filming *Casino*. Remember when he yelled at the chef in that movie because there weren't enough blueberries in the muffins? Millionaires who become partners in upscale, tony restaurants don't expect to make money. They are delighted if they break even. Why do shrewd, successful, wealthy men put their cash and signature on notes for such a risky investment? Because a restaurant has sex appeal. It can do for a man what shares in Home Depot cannot.

Restaurants can provide investors with perks. Dave Meyers often reminded me that he wanted more perks. If you are a part owner of the hottest restaurant in town, you get to revel in its popularity and instantly you become pretty cool. You may even have a menu item named for you. When Dave noticed that a steak was named after him, he was so happy he called me the next day. (Years earlier, his lovely wife, Beverly, had been honored with a dish in her name.) But course, Dave had a problem with his Steak Meyer. It was the cheapest steak on the menu at The Precinct. Even though I hadn't known that before he called, I told him, "That's because you're the cheapest person I know."

If you own a piece of the "in" restaurant in your city, from the moment the parking valet opens your car door, your guests will know that you are "the man." Your Mercedes stays up front, the maitre d' hugs you, every employee calls you by name, the chef comes to your table, and the staff does everything for you but your nails. Your guests are impressed, your client signs the deal, your girlfriend wants to propose to you, your recruit joins your company, and you are feeling very good about yourself. You don't get all that by telling the valet you own shares in California Closets.

CHAPTER TWENTY-THREE

THE GAMBLER

Kenny Rogers, 1978

I met Pete Rose while I was managing a Holiday Inn in the 1970s. Pete wasn't a drinker, but he came in regularly for breakfast. He was always upbeat, jovial and friendly. He also was the best in history at what he did in baseball: hitting. Significantly, he did it without a great deal of natural ability. He did it mostly with sheer determination. Even his detractors agree on one thing: no one in the history of the game got more out of less than Pete Rose. He epitomized "being the best that you can be." How could that not rub off on me?

"Jeff was and is a real go-getter and very intelligent," Pete told Robert. "He always creates fun, a positive atmosphere, wherever he goes. And he's a great promoter, an expert in P.R. He knows how to sell. His club Lucy's in the Sky was the place to go back then, and he made the same success with another club, Dr. Potts—in a hotel basement! When he decided to start up The Precinct in 1981 and asked me and Mike Dever and others to invest in the restaurant, we all did because of his track record with the clubs.

"He likes to be teased by athletes, and he gives us a lot of material to work with. He's like a nine-year-old when you're trying to keep up with him—and he might burn you with his cigar. I once went with him to his son Dillon's football practice. I looked around for Jeff, and there he was, down in the huddle, telling the players what to do. I told him, 'leave the coach alone to do his job.' But that's the way Jeff is. And that's his football background coming out.

"He loves to text, and to tell you who's just texted him. (We don't care, Jeff.) He likes to think he's the biggest celebrity in Cincinnati, which is why he hates to be seen hanging around with me too much," Pete cracked.

When I was recovering from my two brain surgeries in 1987, Pete encouraged me to work out with him, so I would get back into shape. When he said, "Five more," and I did the five more, he would say, "One more," and then, "One more," and, "One more," again and again.

It was during our workout months that I received the first of many calls from Paul Janszen. I knew Paul, but I didn't know he was Pete's bookie or runner. Paul's "problem" was that Pete owed him $30,000, and wouldn't pay it. Paul thought I was the only one who had enough influence on Pete to get him to pay up. His leverage was that he claimed that Pete had bet on baseball. I told Paul if this were true I would get him his money.

When I informed Pete of Janszen's call one day as we were working out, he shrugged it off. I didn't ignore Paul's assertion, though, and pressed Pete to explain why Paul would call me if it wasn't true. Pete explained that whenever he called in a bet that won, Janszen would say he didn't get the bet down in time, but when he called in a losing bet Paul had always got that one down in time. Pete said he never bet on baseball. Janszen kept calling me, and Pete kept telling me Janszen was full of shit. I decided to call Reuven Katz, our mutual friend and attorney, to see if he was aware of this pending problem his client was facing.

Reuven was already aware of the situation, and he said Pete denied everything. I said that Janszen sounded very convincing to me, and I would give him the $30,000 out of my pocket rather than risk the end of Pete's career. Pete had taken a chance on me when nobody had ever heard of me. He had "anted up" again for me on

The Waterfront. I'd protect him from himself, even if he wouldn't. I told Reuven that Pete had some "initial" problems. Paul had told me if Pete didn't give him the money Paul was going to the FBI, IRS, MLB, CIA, DOJ, and that's a lot of "initial" problems.

Reuven persuaded me not to give Paul the money. Reuven was my friend, mentor, and my attorney. This time he was giving me legal advice. If Janszen's story were true, and I were to pay off Janszen when Pete had committed a federal crime, I could be charged with obstruction of justice. To this day, it weighs on my mind that if I had done what I wanted to do–done what Jeff Ruby would have done–Pete Rose might still be in baseball, as a coach or manager, and might be in the baseball Hall of Fame.

Janszen then "upped the ante" by telling me he had stolen Pete's gambling sheets from his house; they could prove that Pete had bet on baseball. After one of our workouts, I advised Pete of that new revelation over breakfast. Again, Pete said that Janszen was lying. I got another call from Paul, and I told him to meet me and show me the betting sheets. If I saw them for myself, maybe I'd be able to convince Pete. Paul and I met the next day. He had the sheets, all right, but they did not prove to my satisfaction that Pete's bets were on baseball games. Pittsburgh vs. Cincinnati could be football–college or pro. Cleveland vs. Chicago could be Browns vs. Bears; Philadelphia vs. Pittsburgh could be Eagles vs. Steelers. That was what I told Paul, and that's when I bowed out of any negotiations.

I had warned Pete about the seedy guys he was associating with, back when the Reds' spring training camp was in Plant City, Florida. I stayed at his house for quite some time and was in his office when these disreputable dudes came to see him one morning: Mikey "The Belly" Bertolini; Tommy "Gio" Giosa; Pauly "Walnuts" Janszen. They passed the duck test. They all looked, walked and sounded like ducks to me, but it was like water off a duck's back, trying to tell that to my friend Pete. They were making him money by selling his baseball memorabilia.

Rick Hill asked if he could interview me for a book he was writing about Pete. I agreed to speak to him at Highlands High School, where I would be watching Dillon's football practice. I gave him about two hours, and that was the extent of my involvement. I had no idea what his storyline was. I did many interviews during the "Pete Rose scandal": ESPN, Fox Sports, Lester Holt on NBC, local TV, and newspapers. I even had movie offers, asking me to play myself. In these interviews, I was always Pete's advocate, but the media coverage was all negative. P.R. stood for Pete Rose, not Public Relations. That, he screwed up.

When Pete bet on baseball, he bet on his own team, the Cincinnati Reds, to win. It didn't take us this long to forgive Japan after Pearl Harbor. President Gerald Ford, who nearly died when he was serving on the *USS Monterey* in World War II, later pardoned Tokyo Rose, who had served six years for treason for her part against us in the war. America's president could forgive Tokyo Rose, but baseball's president won't forgive Pete Rose.

Pete was offered a temporary suspension from baseball if he admitted to betting on the game. He adamantly denied betting on the game and turned the offer down. He agreed to be "placed on the permanently ineligible" list. In return, "The Commissioner will not make any formal findings or determinations on any matter, including without limitation the allegation that Peter Edward Rose bet on any Major League Baseball game."

The Rick Hill book, for which I was interviewed, had been out for some time, but I hadn't yet bought a copy. When Dave Stevens was in town one day I stopped at the Kroger supermarket near Carlo & Johnny and bought one for each of us. A few minutes into our drive

Downtown, an old friend, Brandt Rogers, called to tell me I was all over the news once again. ESPN's Jayson Stark had just broken a story that Pete Rose blamed me for the ill-advised timing of his admission to gambling on baseball. Stark's announcement came just before the upcoming All-Star game. Pete allegedly said he had given me an advance copy of the Rick Hill book, and in the book he finally came clean. Stark went on to report that Pete said I went on a radio show and leaked the story prior to the book's release. The freakin' book was still lying in my back seat. I had just bought it. I never received an "advance copy" and did not go on any radio show and leak the story. Not only was Stark an irresponsible journalist for not checking with me to confirm Rose's story before going public with it, he also had a thinking problem. Somehow it never occurred to him that if I had leaked it on the radio, America would have known about it back then, whenever "back then" was. If I had done that, the local media affiliates would have been waiting for me at my car. WLW would have been the radio station. It carries 50,000 watts and reaches 37 states. Stark is one more example of why the media's trust rate among Americans is at its lowest level ever, at 21 percent. Pete just needed an out, and he used me. He needed someone to blame. That's what friends are for. We've never even discussed it.

"Whenever anyone called Jeff for a comment about me," Pete told Robert, "he'd go on and on like he was my spokesman. I'm used to it. We'll always be friends."

In March of 2013, I heard from Donny Knepper, an attorney in the Washington D.C. area. He was heading a campaign to reinstate Pete Rose's eligibility for the Baseball Hall of Fame. Knepper was looking for someone in Cincinnati with the connections and the enthusiasm to help in this effort. My name came up.

As Donny explained to Robert, "When we launched www.lift-theban.net, our fan-based, non-profit effort to put social pressure on

240

Major League Baseball to allow Pete Rose to be voted into the Hall, we opened a Twitter account. About half of our followers are in Cincinnati, where we certainly wanted to increase our footprint. When we asked them who best to enlist, everyone said, 'If you want to get something done in Cincinnati, go to Jeff Ruby.' So he was the first person we pitched there. We met with him in April [2013], when we went to Cincinnati for the Reds' Opening Day. We also met with Pete Rose on that trip, so he is aware of us but not involved in any way.

"We're aiming toward the end of 2014, when [Baseball Commissioner Bud] Selig will step down. Whoever the new commissioner is, he will have no ties to Bart Giamatti, who imposed the ban on Pete. Also, in 2014, The Big Red Machine will mark its fortieth anniversary.

"In the meantime we want to return to Cincinnati, establish a media presence and sell our T-shirts to help fund the campaign. (You can't sign a petition, but you can wear your support.) We plan to have a big Happy Hour rally in Downtown's Fountain Square next summer."

Needless, to say, I'll do whatever I can to help the cause. We are a forgiving country. Pete has gone through a cleansing period that has had no shortage of punishment, humiliation, embarrassment and financial loss. It's time to forgive.

"I appreciate the effort," Pete told Robert, "but I think they're wasting their time. There's no question I'd like to be reinstated. I'm getting older, and I've paid my time—twenty-four years. But it's not going to happen, at least not in Selig's tenure. Bud wouldn't let it affect his legacy. Others, with drug and alcohol problems, have been given a second chance, but baseball's been very strict about gambling since the Black Sox scandal of 1919. I took the wrong advice, and I shouldn't have done what I did.

"I've been a Reds fan since early childhood; I grew up in Cincinnati, three miles from Crosley Field. Although I live in Las Vegas now, I get to Cincinnati for ten to twelve home games a season. At last night's game, I was introduced in the eighth inning, and thirty thousand fans gave me a standing ovation. That kind of support means a lot to me."

CHAPTER TWENTY-FOUR

I GOT A NAME

Jim Croce, 1973

Featured in the motion picture *The Last American Hero*, with Jeff Bridges.

I found out that my name was worth something in an unlikely place. In the late 1990s, Downtown Cincinnati was dead. "They" all predicted that my third restaurant would be my first restaurant failure if it was located in the center of the city. All three Mobil 5-Star restaurants had gone belly up. The Hyatt Regency was foreclosed on. The shopping mall changed hands three times, then sat empty. The country's highest Zagat-rated restaurant went out of business in no time. We changed all that. Jeff Ruby's Steakhouse became the first successful fine dining restaurant Downtown.

Marvin Rosenberg and Neil Bortz are co-owners of Towne Properties, a development company they founded the year I had my bar mitzvah. They are visionaries and Cincinnati's pre-eminent developers. Towne Properties was responsible for creating the upscale Mt. Adams residential district. Marvin told me of their company's plans to create a "Backstage District" on Walnut Street. Most of the existing buildings would be torn down to accommodate a performing arts center. He and Neil, who were friends of mine, wanted me to open a restaurant on the site of the existing Frisch's Big Boy at Seventh Street and Walnut.

My immediate response was, "What's going to bring folks Downtown when there's no show?" Marvin had no answer to that question, and I told him I couldn't spend time on any project for a few weeks because I was preparing for our summer opening at The Waterfront's outdoor bar, Las Brisas. I go to Florida to select my palm

243

trees. I interview every potential cocktail waitress and travel all over the country to see the bands I might want to book. I assured Marvin I was interested, but I needed more time.

About two weeks later, I learned that Marvin had chosen his friend Carl Bruggemeier to open the restaurant. Towne Properties would be his partner. The place was to be called Ciao Baby, and it would be an Italian bistro with a bakery. Marvin explained that Carl had raised the money for the project very quickly. Carl had an impressive resume, working for many fine restaurants around America, including the renowned Brennan's in New Orleans. In fact, he had worked at too many restaurants and been married too many times. That told me he had a short attention span.

The first time I walked into Ciao Baby for lunch, it was packed. "He who hesitates is screwed" came to mind, and I briefly regretted not acting more quickly on Marvin's proposal. They had a talented pastry chef who made all of their breads, the food was decent, and the restaurant was clearly a "hip" place. They were getting the "in crowd" and doing a terrific business. But I wasn't impressed with the interior design. It was cold and antiseptic. All the surfaces were hard, and the room had no rhythm. Ciao Baby had no soul, and a restaurant has no chance if that particular quality is absent. You should never name a restaurant Ciao (Goodbye) Baby.

A few weeks after the closing, Marvin and his wonderful wife, Elaine, were having dinner at The Waterfront. I didn't stop by their table right away, since they were still eating their appetizers. Soon their waiter informed me that Marvin wanted to see me. I went to their riverside window table, kissed Elaine, and said hello to my friend. Our conversation naturally and quickly turned to Ciao Baby. Marvin reminded me of something I didn't recall telling him. Apparently I had said that Ciao Baby wouldn't make it, and I would be at the auction. Marvin asked me if I wanted to take over the space. I asked my friend, "You chose to take someone else to the prom last year, and now you'll settle for your second choice?" Marvin loved that one.

Downtown wasn't dead, I decided, it just went to bed early. I had to figure out how to make it stay up later. What I liked most about the location at Seventh and Walnut wasn't that it was across the street from the new Aronoff Center for the Arts. It was that it was within walking distance of my psychiatrist.

Marvin, Neil, and I signed the lease on April Fools' Day, 1999. Downtown was as ready for a good steakhouse as a thirsty cornfield is ready for rain. The obvious risk of my opening a third steakhouse in such a relatively small city was the possibility of its negative financial impact on The Precinct and The Waterfront. That was one of the reasons that thirteen years had elapsed since we created our second restaurant. The lion's share of our business comes from guests at Cincinnati's Downtown hotels. With our new place within walking distance of these hotels, the two further-out restaurants, The Precinct and The Waterfront, might lose business. The alternative was that Capital Grille or another nationally known competitor would lease the Downtown space and grab some of our business anyway.

If someone were going to take that business away from Jeff Ruby, it made more sense for it to be Jeff Ruby himself. An executive from Capital Grille was already looking at the building. The company wanted a corner property and would guarantee the lease and take the space as it was. But Marvin wanted me, regardless of my terms, because he knew it would be better for Cincinnati. The fact that I was even interested in opening at that location led to immense media coverage.

Marvin Rosenberg told Robert, "Jeff and I have been tied together for a long time. When he was single, he used to come to temple with my wife and me on high holy days, even though he wasn't that into his religion. We attended his and Rickelle's wedding, and our son Barry was a parking valet at The Precinct when it first opened in 1981. He'd just turned sixteen and gotten his driver's license. Barry is now forty-eight.

"Jeff was the hottest guy in town, and my partner Neil and I loved him. And we knew that, as a strong local operator, he could be flexible and respond to local conditions. That was very key in our decision. He has become a spokesman for the Downtown entertainment scene. When the politicians do something wrong, the newspapers run to Jeff for comment. Some of the things he says and does make the newspapers, some don't.

"As part of our lease arrangement and believing in Jeff, Neil and I invested in the restaurant. We signed a normal ten-year lease, but nobody has talked about the lease in fourteen years."

Neil Bortz told Robert, "I met Jeff but didn't really know him when he ran the Holiday Inn Downtown and had Lucy's in the Sky on the top floor. Not surprisingly, he made a splash with the club right away. Then, when he opened The Precinct, he hit the dirt running, and he never did call for the second wave of investment he could have had. He did his Jeff Ruby thing, and the restaurant became the place to be seen.

"Our building at Seventh and Walnut was really a C-minus building. Frisch's was kind enough to let us buy out their lease. Carl Bruggemeier, who opened Ciao Baby, was another interesting character, almost as creative as Jeff, almost as much of a nut about details. But he was worse in terms of business.

"Jeff has been just a wonderful partner and a perfect friend. He can be gruff and demanding, but you can always make a deal with him if you're patient. He's like a Damon Runyon character; he likes to be a bad guy with a heart of gold. Coincidentally, Damon Runyon came from Indiana, and his first characters were lifted from Newport, Kentucky, when it had more gambling than Las Vegas—before the Kefauver Commission closed them down."

I decided to go for it.

Since my original Precinct partners had launched my career as a restaurateur, I asked the same group to become the owners of this new, third Jeff Ruby restaurant.

Now I had to create a restaurant from the theatre of my mind. That is a long process that presents many challenges. From the beginning, I am involved with my designer, Dave Stevens, in every aspect of the design. I oversee construction. I interview every employee we eventually hire, and I do their training. I see to the restaurant's marketing and menu development, and I select the entertainment. There is no shortage of mistakes made during construction, and no shortage of stress, either.

I regard a restaurant as an aquarium. To make it look beautiful and draw attention to it, you must stock an aquarium with colorful, unique, and interesting fish. I stocked the aquarium for the Jeff Ruby Downtown restaurant party with about a thousand "fish"–while the place was still in the midst of construction. I hung blueprints and renderings on the bare walls. I let the guests and the music become the ambience.

I began to plan my strategy for the Grand Opening Party. I was going to schedule the opening of the restaurant just so I would have a place to throw myself a birthday party on or around April 19, 1999. In turn, my birthday party would serve as the restaurant's grand opening. That restaurant opening/birthday party gambit worked so well the first time I decided to employ it for later restaurant openings.

Tommy Lasorda had introduced me to Dodger catcher Mike Piazza in his rookie year, over dinner at The Waterfront. Mike and I became good friends, but I didn't realize just how much I meant to him until I went to his wedding in Miami, and found out that he had invited only twenty friends. The reception for one hundred guests was held at the Vanderbilt Mansion on Fisher Island. Mike provided a huge yacht for us to get there.

Mike is one of the nicest and most loyal friends I've ever had. He flies in at his own expense to appear at my charity roasts. Everyone wants to roast me. I have no idea why. I asked Mike if he would come to my birthday/opening party at Jeff Ruby's in Cincinnati. He was still with the Dodgers, and Billy Russell was the Dodger manager. Billy and I were pals, but he told Mike he wouldn't allow him to leave the team, which had an off day in Chicago, to attend my party in Cincinnati. The team was flying to Montreal, and Billy had a mandatory batting practice scheduled there. The Dodgers traveled as a team, and there were no exceptions. Mike told Billy that he had promised me he would be at my party, and he was going to be. Russell told Mike that he'd better obey his manager.

I remember Mike walking in the door, saying, "Told you I'd be here. Tonight I'm going to party like it's 1999," referring to the 1982 hit by Prince, and revived by him and many others over the next twenty years. Phish sang "1999" live at the 1998 Madison Square Garden New Year's Eve party. And of course now it *was* 1999. Mike mingled, took photos, signed autographs, and spoke to the crowd. He then flew to Montreal to deal with Billy Russell.

The party for the opening of the Tropicana in 2003 drew more than three thousand people. The attendees and the buffet tables stretched across the bridge over the Ohio River, from Kentucky to Ohio. I was told it was the longest buffet in history. I scheduled that party so that my friends on the New York Mets could be there, along with the Reds.

For my sixty-fifth birthday, in 2013, I had no new restaurant to open. So I rented the Duke Energy Convention Center, and booked Kool and the Gang as the entertainment. We broke our own Tropicana record with thirty-two hundred people coming for drinks and dancing. (In lieu of birthday gifts, I asked for voluntary donations to a college education fund for the surviving kids at Sandy Hook Elementary School in Newtown, Connecticut.)

* * * * *

I had named my new Downtown restaurant the 7th Street Grill, and the logo had been designed. Our general contractor, Paul Kitzmiller, had been dead set on my calling this place "Jeff Ruby's." In spite of the fact that it had been thirteen years since I'd opened a restaurant, Paul said my name was bigger in Cincinnati than even I realized. His exact words were, "Trust me, Jeff, your name is huge in this town. If you call this restaurant anything but 'Jeff Ruby's' you are making a big mistake." I disagreed.

But I agreed to hand out ballots at the party so that our future clientele could vote for the name of their restaurant. On the ballot were many names I had considered, including 7th Street Grill, Jeff Ruby's 7th Street Grill, along with just plain Jeff Ruby's. Who better to ask for their opinions than CEOs, presidents, vice presidents and other officers of Proctor & Gamble, Kroger, American Financial, General Electric, PNC Bank, Fifth Third Bank, and, of course, pretty girls?

The staff counted the votes after the party, and eight hundred fifty people had checked Jeff Ruby's. At the time, "branding" was not on my mind. I've since learned from good sources in the gaming industry that no one gets more money for putting his name on a restaurant than I do. Maybe it's because with me they get more than just a name. As cocky and arrogant as people rightfully think I can be, back in 1999 I felt that my name was meaningless, and I told Paul so. But he did more than build a restaurant for me. He inspired the birth of my brand, which has expanded greatly over the last fourteen years.

At all of our restaurants, my initials, J. R., are on the employees' neckties, on the wine glasses, and even on the wax paper that covers the butter portions.

In the summer of 2012 I began putting "Jeff Ruby's Steakhouses" on the pants of three top California-based jockeys who ride in the Breeders' Cup and other major races: Joe Talamo, Garret Gomez and Mike Smith, who is in the National Museum of Racing and Hall of Fame. Joe told Robert, "I really think those pants with Jeff's logo are lucky; I've won a lot of races wearing them." Mike won the Breeders' Cup wearing them.

As it turned out, Jeff Ruby's Steakhouse and The Precinct became the company's two biggest moneymakers. The Precinct not only withstood the impact of my new place, it has expanded twice since Jeff Ruby's opened.

* * * * *

When race riots broke out Downtown on April 9, 2001, Jeff Ruby's Steakhouse, for better or for worse, became the background for the demonstrations and picketing that went on every day for a while. One of the demonstrators who was holding a sign told me he had watched my kids for me once. He liked me, he said, and he knew I wasn't a racist. He added, "Rube, we need publicity and if we're in front of your place, we'll get more of it than if we were anywhere else."

For many years, the Riverfest jazz festival has been an annual event in July at our football stadium. It was a non-issue for The Precinct and The Waterfront in terms of business. But Downtown's upscale restaurants typically closed for that weekend, since July is a slow month for them anyway. Since this was my first Downtown restaurant, I held a meeting with our team to seek their advice. Our staff is an ethnically diverse group and includes a number of African-Americans. My house band members were mostly African-American. They all recommended we close, saying we wouldn't serve enough people to cover the payroll—and none of them wanted to work that weekend. Other restaurant and hotel managers in the area were unanimous in deciding not to stay open that weekend.

The jazz festival is attended mostly by African Americans. I love Patti LaBelle and Earth, Wind & Fire, and I have been backstage with them when I attended the festival. Now, for the first time, Cincinnati's black community protested when the Downtown restaurants were all closed. They made particular note of the fact that Jeff Ruby's was closed during Riverfest. Having visibility comes with a price.

The black community viewed our decision, which was based strictly on business viability, as racism. The racial climate became as hot as the July sun. A white cop had just killed an unarmed black kid, and we were in the worst possible kind of national spotlight. Then the city decided to prohibit all vehicles from coming into Downtown during festival weekend. Our weekend business comes almost entirely from the suburbs—by car. What's more, concert-goers could not eat at a two-hour dining experience place and then make the long walk to the stadium in time for the concert. Add the soul food street vendors to the list of obstacles to staying open.

I didn't appreciate the banner that screamed "Ruby is a Racist," and I took issue with one of the protester's comments. I went after him, and a television camera caught our encounter. But several days later, I was sorry to see the demonstrators leave. While they were out in front, we were on TV every night. When they left, business actually slowed down a bit.

Only one TV station covered the meeting I held at Jeff Ruby's with the Reverend Damon Lynch Jr. and five other black leaders. Lynch was the black activist who had organized the protesters, and he was the face of the black community. We had a very good meeting, and I offered to stay open for the next year's jazz festival, regardless of profit considerations. I showed him our black menu with white paper in it and held my arm next to his, saying, "We're just different shades of tannish brown, not that far apart. We both bleed red."

Listening to the other side is essential for communication. If you can connect with people, you can influence them. Influencing others is the key to resolving issues and to success in any profession.

The next summer, every Downtown restaurant stayed open for the jazz festival, and they have stayed open for it ever since.

"Jeff was the Downtown area's unofficial spokesman in the situation," Marvin Rosenberg told Robert. "Most of those involved had a political agenda, but Jeff came at it from a strong personal agenda. He was a very key figure at the forefront of the tragedy, the person who did the most to get the police and the blacks together. He's colorful enough to attract positive controversy. And he's been a big factor in the transformation of our neighborhood; where a welfare hotel once stood there is now a high-end boutique.

"He's the glue that keeps all of Downtown together, and he's an action-getter. Seventh and Walnut turns out to be the hot corner; it's like New Year's Eve every Saturday night. Jeff has made the area into a place that attracts all levels of society. He treats everybody with respect. Not many have three thousand people show up for their birthday party. That party was a positive reflection on a guy who came from nothing, but refused to stay there. His standards are high, and his hard work has paid off. Nobody else even *thinks* on the scale Jeff Ruby does."

CHAPTER TWENTY-FIVE

YOU BELONG TO THE CITY

Glenn Frey, 1985

I've never considered myself better than other people. But I am more fortunate than most. While some are more fortunate than I, I am lucky to be on the right side of the grass. I believe that if you are successful and have acquired affluence, you should give some of it back to the community that gave it to you.

Much of what I do for my adopted home town goes unnoticed, which is just as I intend it. So I was surprised when *City Beat*, a weekly Cincinnati publication, nominated me for Cincinnati's Best Philanthropist as part of their "Best of Public Eye" survey in April of 2013. A few other individuals were nominated, but most of the nominees were foundations. I was honored to be voted runner-up in our great city. Otto H. Budig, whose foundation has made tremendous contributions to Cincinnati for three decades, deservedly won the top honor.

"You can't help someone else without helping yourself," as the saying goes. I always feel better when I make other people feel better. And I must admit it is nice to be thanked and recognized for the things I do for the city. Hardly a day goes by that someone doesn't tell me how much they appreciate the charitable contributions I make, as well as the big city dining and entertainment I have brought to our city.

I don't go looking for trouble, but for some reason, when someone in Cincinnati is in trouble, they go looking for me. They hope to use my many connections and my sizeable heart to get them out of a jam or to help them get something they want or need. When actor

Ryan Gosling was in town for the filming of George Clooney's *The Ides of March*, he asked if he could do a video of me. He interviewed me at The Precinct and at Jeff Ruby's, and his camera even followed me as I sang with the band. The resulting mini-documentary, *Godfather of Cincinnati*, is on his website. *Cincy Magazine* ran a cover story with a similar title. Neither the documentary nor the article had anything to do with organized crime.

We all need someone to go to from time to time when we need a favor. We might need someone who has a connection at a university or someone who can wangle hard-to-get tickets for a concert. It can be handy to know someone who knows someone at a casino, a sold-out hotel, or a company where we would like to get a job. Sometimes people need a recommendation for a good lawyer or a doctor. I get those calls often. I have indirectly saved lives by getting people out of some inadequate area hospitals. Their doctors were misdiagnosing two of my employees and Wayne Carlisle's sister, Beverly. I had two of the patients airlifted across the river from Northern Kentucky to Cincinnati. All of them were in life-or-death situations, and all were saved by different heart specialists or neurosurgeons.

In 1981, we opened Cincinnati's first upscale steakhouse, The Precinct. In 1999, we offered Downtown Cincinnati a place to go after dark when we opened Jeff Ruby's. And when I teamed up with Bootsy Collins, in 2008, we provided Downtown a place to go after "the midnight hour" for the first time in a very long time.

I never thought that Bootsy's would be a money maker for our company. My only motivation was for that restaurant and nightclub to be a catalyst to create a comprehensive entertainment district Downtown. I believed if I opened a second and very different place Downtown, right across the street from Jeff Ruby's, others–entrepreneurs, national chains and small local business owners–would feel more optimistic about Downtown and follow suit. I was right! Every empty space and previously inappropriate use of that prime real estate was leased out. The first bar to open was two doors down, The Righteous Room, followed by Scene right next door. My vision is still for Walnut Street's asphalt to be cobblestoned and closed to vehicles on weekends so folks can walk from place to place, drinks in hand, to Fountain Square. (I think they named it Fountain Square because we are so "square" in this town. We aren't "cool" or cutting edge. Mark Twain supposedly said, "When the end of the world comes, I want to be in Cincinnati because it's always twenty years behind the times.")

But things are looking up. The latest boon to Downtown Cincinnati has been the opening of the Horseshoe Casino, the seventh owned by the parent company, Caesar's Entertainment. Since the casino houses a high-end steakhouse, Jack Binion's, they are competitors of mine. Jack Binion's steakhouses began in 1951 as a family-owned company, and there is one in every Horseshoe Casino.

Kevin Kline, the senior vice president and general manager of Horseshoe Casino Cincinnati, told Robert, "This is the first time we have opened a Horseshoe Casino in a downtown market. People always want to compare, but we're just getting started, and Jeff Ruby set the gold standard for hospitality here. We are attempting to enhance our brand in an urban market by joining Jeff's narrative for the revitalization of Downtown Cincinnati, rather than just competing with him. If we all do well, Downtown does really well.

"Jeff's vision and commitment level exceeds all others. I love his life stories and the history of his restaurants. I admire his sometimes unorthodox pursuit of perfecting his food and his restaurants' environments. If the right chandeliers are in Miami, that's where he goes to get them. I appreciate how he approaches his opportunities. It's never a dollar issue with him."

Pioneers pay a price and carry a double-edged sword. My

new competition around the corner is getting $8 million in "money for nothing" from the city. "Money for Nothing" was recorded by Dire Straits, whose name describes just where I might have been. Attorneys and others tell me I should be livid about this. After I've paid taxes all these years and gotten nothing for free, other restaurants are getting sweetheart deals (tax breaks) and free money (cash contributions to build out the restaurant) in order to compete with me.

"The Banks" is the huge development on the Ohio River surrounded by the Bengals and Reds stadiums. Eight thousand restaurant seats have been added there in recent years. A Downtown development corporation, 3CDC, has done a terrific job of remaking Downtown. Hundreds of millions of dollars are going into these projects. I can't be mad. I belong to the city.

CHAPTER TWENTY-SIX

I WON'T BACK DOWN

Tom Petty and the Heartbreakers, 1989

I don't like answering to anyone. That's why I ran away from home. That's why I didn't go with the flow at Winegardner & Hammons and left to start my own restaurant. Only dead fish go with the flow. I couldn't have the creative freedom I wanted and needed if I were working for anyone else. I've spent my entire life living on the edge, from the time I jumped out of the window of my mother's house with my little white suitcase and hopped on that ice cream truck. If you're not living on the edge, you're probably taking up too much room. The trick to living on the edge is not falling off.

When someone becomes very successful, some people will respect him and others will resent him. I realized early on that I couldn't be myself without being controversial. If you are unafraid to speak up and say what you feel is the truth, you are going to have detractors. Very few people generate more publicity in Cincinnati than I do. Most of it is good. Some of it is not so good. I was arrested on the night we opened Jeff Ruby's Tropicana in Newport, Kentucky, because I went after a guy who ran out on a $100 tab. It made head-lines in the papers and was the lead story on local television news. The next night there was a line to get into the restaurant. Everyone wanted me to tell them what had happened. Publicity is like sex: when it's good, it's damn good; when it's not so good, it's still good.

I went national with my feelings about O.J. Simpson after he appeared at my steakhouse in Louisville in 2007, and I threw him out. I also banned my ex-regular, Larry Flynt, after he offered a mur-deress millions to pose for a nude photo in his magazine, *Hustler.* In

2012, I made an even bigger splash with my support of the victims in the Drew Peterson murder trial in Joliet, Illinois—despite the pleadings of my daughter and my lawyer and others not to get involved. I've publicly supported many other controversial causes that may have seemed to some to be none of my business.

God bless Cincinnatians. Most of them know my intentions are good, and it's just me being me. They know I'm spontaneous, emotional, sincere, and dumb. After forty-three years, they know how to take me.

I arrived in Cincinnati from New Jersey in 1970, and I'm still here in 2013. I've outlasted such heroes as Pete Rose, Ken Griffey Jr., Barry Larkin, Johnny Bench, Jerry Springer and other celebrities from back then who have moved on. Former baseball team owner, Marge Schott, threatened to move the Reds out of town, and Mike Brown did the same with his Bengals. Unlike them, I never told the city, "Give me money, or I'm leaving town."

Against the advice of Erik Kamfjord, the man with the MBA whom I looked up to and who spent eleven years teaching me how to be a manager, I decided to take a chance with the Amanda purchase and create The Precinct. Everyone I respected, much more successful men than I, told me it was a mistake to open a restaurant in the city's worst neighborhood during the worst economic times in forty years. I figured, if you ain't got nothing, you ain't got nothing to lose. Six thousand bucks and a used car was everything I had, so it was all I had to lose. Ten months later, Bobby Bare hit the country charts with a song that echoed my motto: "If You Ain't Got Nothin' You Ain't Got Nothin' to Lose." By then, The Precinct was as big as the song.

Developer Gary Wachs once said, "If you take Jeff Ruby out of Cincinnati, you have Dayton." (Now they want a Jeff Ruby's Steakhouse in a $200 million development in Dayton.) I say, if you take Jeff

Ruby out of Cincinnati, you won't have anyone placing controversial, full-page ads in the newspaper, calling for justice. I am emotionally honest, and very few people in today's politically correct society are. Most Americans would rather exercise their right to remain silent than say how they really feel and get their asses fired or sued for speaking out. Every day someone tells me, "You have the balls to say it like it is." It helps that I can afford it.

Johnny Cash once said, "If you know what you want, the tide of popular opinion won't wash you away." Hall and Oates were the number one charting duo of the rock era. One of their hits told kids what I tell them, "Do what you want, be who you are."

Marty Brennaman, the Hall of Fame Reds announcer, has been a close friend of mine since the 1970s. He told a reporter, "Jeff Ruby was spit out of the mouth of New Jersey and landed here. He's as Jersey as Jersey gets."

You can leave New Jersey, but Jersey will never leave you. I didn't want to be what people expected everyone in Cincinnati to be like. As Johnny Cash also said, "You get yourself in trouble when you stop acting like where you grew up."

I hope that every day when I wake up, the mirror is still happy to see me. As Shakespeare, someone I don't usually quote, said, "To thine own self be true." Or, as Sammy Davis Jr. put it in another song, "I've Gotta Be Me."

CHAPTER TWENTY-SEVEN

THE MAN I WANT TO BE

Chris Young, 2009

I wanted to pass on the enormous impact my father figure Jeep Bednarik had on my life. It became my calling. I've been a registered Big Brother to a fourteen-year-old black kid and a fourteen-year-old white kid, both of whom tended to me during my rehab in the hospital after my 1987 accident. I've been a mentor or father figure to countless kids of various races, and a surrogate dad to three brothers who lost their father at a young age. Jeep's role in my life reappeared decades later in the lives that I touched. I call some of these kids "Jeep's grandkids." I had told the boys about Jeep, and they wanted to meet their "grandfather." It was a big day for me when they got to do that.

I went to Jeep in tears when I learned my "father" was not the person I had thought he was for seventeen years, and now kids come to me in tears wanting me to be with them. Those boys who do have fathers often won't go to their dads with their problems. My own kids' friends often called me—rather than their real dads—when they were in jail after a fight. When these boys were being chased by kids from another high school, they phoned "Uncle Jeff" at 2 a.m. Britney, Brandon and Dillon have accepted all of this very well, and they sometimes offer assistance to these kids through their own personal experience with "Pop."

Hamilton County's Department of Human Services officially made Mike Williams my African-American Little Brother. Mike had taken me in a wheelchair to my speech therapist when I was recovering from my head injury in 1987. He was a volunteer at University Hospital, a troubled kid who, at the age of fourteen, had been through thirteen foster parents. He was so nice to all the patients. I went back to the hospital to thank the nurses for everything they had done for me and to visit head-injured patients who were still unable to speak, as I had been for many weeks. My visits meant a lot to those nurses. I noticed newspaper articles about my recovery attached to the walls.

When Mike was seventeen, he called me from Cleveland, where he was in trouble with some guys over a girl. He was scared and wanted to come home, but he had no money. I called Joe Saccone, co-owner of the Hyde Park Grill in Cleveland. Joe had worked for me at Holiday Inn. He picked up Mike where he was in Cleveland, gave him dinner at the Hyde Park Grill, and put him on a Greyhound bus. Joe paid for everything. I met Mike at the bus station and sat in my car and talked to him in front of the Friars Club, where he lived. No wonder people say things about me. I was sitting in a red Mercedes convertible with a black teenager in the iffy Clifton neighborhood at 3 a.m. Sometimes I'm too high-profile for my own good. (Mike is now thirty-nine and in the military.)

Another kid, Chris Webb, was a regular visitor to my University Hospital room, while I was recovering. He brought me the get-well cards and flowers that so many well-wishers started sending after I came out of intensive care. He became infatuated with me, I suppose, because I was a high-profile patient with celebrities from New York to Los Angeles coming to visit me. Chris Webb acted as my personal protector. He, like Mike, was a troubled youth working as a temporary volunteer as part of a rehabilitation program. Chris was living at Altercrest, a boys' home operated by the Catholic Archdiocese of Cincinnati. Rickelle and I decided to pay him a visit. I could never get the name of the place straight, so I just called it "Alcatraz."

We met with the facility's priest and schoolmaster and learned about Chris's past crimes and unfortunate childhood. Chris's biological parents had abused him. When Altercrest's director, Sally Sweeney, told Chris that Jeff Ruby was there to see him, that kid came running out of the dorm like I was Santa Claus at Christmas. It was heartbreaking to see how badly that kid wanted a dad. Rickelle wanted me to rehabilitate this fourteen-year-old kid. Of course, I did. He stayed overnight at our house many times. We certainly were aware that we had our own children to protect, but we took Chris everywhere with our kids, and we saw him behave as a normal, happy child.

One night at about 1 a.m., I got a call from the Dayton, Ohio, police. The cop told me my fifteen-year-old son was riding his bicycle on I-75. That is illegal in Ohio, and the cop was going to take the kid to jail until he told him he was Jeff Ruby's son. He put the kid on the phone. It was Chris Webb. I drove to Dayton and picked up Chris and his bike. At the time, Chris was living with his new foster parents in Dayton.

Years went by and we heard nothing from Chris. One night my daughter, Britney, came screaming up to our bedroom, "Dad, some guy is sleeping in the garage!" I ran downstairs to see a scruffy-looking guy with a beard asleep on his stomach. I turned him over, and it was Chris. I told him, "Son, your past may be a little soiled, but your future is spotless. Go upstairs and take a shower, you're going to work for me." Eventually he became a very good waiter at one of our restaurants.

Most of the boys I've "adopted" have come to me for help, or I happened upon them through circumstance. There was one kid I deliberately sought out, however: Jason Maneol.

"I met Jeff in early January of 1990," Jason told Robert. "I was fourteen and in the burn unit at Shriners Hospital for Children with burns over 80 percent of my body. Sixty percent of the burns were third degree. I was given a 14 percent chance of living. I had lit a fire in the backyard in Atlanta two nights before Christmas because it was extra cold for Georgia, twenty degrees outside. A gas can in the garage caught fire and exploded, and suddenly I was running around literally on fire. The odds of surviving were not in my favor. There had been hesitation about moving me from the hospital in Atlanta to Cincinnati, since I was probably going to die anyway.

"My single mother, who was only twenty-nine, and my younger sister, who was nine, came with me to Cincinnati and stayed at the Ronald McDonald House at the hospital. One afternoon they called a cab and asked the driver to take them to the nicest restaurant around. He took them to The Waterfront, where they met Rickelle at the piano bar. She and Mom hit it off, and Rickelle said, 'You must meet my husband. He's very involved with kids.'"

Later that evening, Rickelle told me about their conversation and suggested that I visit the woman's son in the hospital. "You're so good with kids, Jeff, and this is what you do," she said.

The next day I went to visit Jason.

"He brought me a commemorative plate," Jason remembered. "Pete Rose had signed it 'To Jason, January 23, 1990.' Jeff and I hit it off, and when I got out of the hospital at the end of March it made no sense for us to go back to Georgia. Jeff would take me to basketball games at the University of Cincinnati, and to dinner at The Waterfront. My parents were long divorced, and I'd never had someone around to care about me in that way, from a male perspective. It was a perfect storm. Jeff came at the right time. He told me he loved me and hugged and kissed me like I was his son. I think what he had gone through as a kid gave him that feeling for kids like me. Also, I was a wrestler, which gave us something in common.

"Now I'm thirty-seven and married with kids. As an adult, I've coached wrestling and tried to help other kids the way Jeff helped me. After college I became a landscape gardener for eight years and then got my real estate license. I work for the emergency room at Grady Hospital in Atlanta, where I went first for my burns. I am also a lieutenant in the Emergency Medical Service of Henry County, Georgia, on fire trucks and ambulances."

* * * * *

Rickelle's dad, Richard, was dating a woman who occasionally came with him to our house and brought her fourteen-year-old son, Brad Belletti. His father had been killed in a car crash when Brad was only five. If I was watching a football game, Brad would sit down next to me. If I was lying on the couch watching the game, Brad flopped down on top of me. Clearly, Brad was looking for a dad. Brad knew I was married with kids. I was already a father figure.

I eventually became Brad's "dad." I had no choice. He insisted on it. I have a hard time saying "no." My four dogs always get their way with me in disagreements. I rehire people I have fired. I lose most of my arguments with any kids. And I never won an argument with Rickelle.

Brad made the high school wrestling team and wanted me to go to his matches. Lakota High School was twenty miles from Downtown, but I always took the time, because it was important to him. When his mother had problems with him, she called me to intervene. He was a typical teenager, so she called often. I recall his telling a reporter once that I let him be a kid, and he liked that about me. He said, "Jeff's a big kid himself," and he liked *that* about me too.

One afternoon Brad's mom's call was different. She was crying. "Jeff, Bradley is at Bethesda North," she said. "He tried to commit suicide."

I rushed out of my office on the eighteenth floor of the River Centre Building in Covington, Kentucky, and raced my sports car to Bethesda North across the river in Montgomery, Ohio. I had not seen this coming. When I entered the emergency room, Brad was hooked up to IVs and wearing an oxygen mask. He looked up at me and had only one thing to say, "Are you mad at me?" My instant reply was, "How can I be mad at you? You're alive. I'm happy, Brad."

"Jeff Ruby is the savior of my life," Brad told Robert. "He rescued me when I was on the wrong path, doing drugs and running with the wrong crowd—pretty much by beating the crap out of me. And, at the time, he had enough problems with his own kids. I love him to death.

"When I was fourteen, fifteen and sixteen, he took me to Bengals games and out to dinner. We rode in Carl Lindner's private plane, and Jeff gave me his convertible Mercedes to go to my prom. He'd give me a hundred dollars to buy a Coke and tell me to keep the change. I hung out in his office. Jeff did whatever he wanted to do, whenever he wanted to do it, and often carried a thousand dollars in cash with him.

"I was fifteen when he had his accident, and I rode my bike forty miles to the hospital from our house in Landon. I thought he might be dead. It was one of the worst days of my life. He was alive, but in intensive care, and I wasn't allowed in his room, even though I told them I was his son."

Brad is now forty, living in Oregon, married to his gorgeous Sasha, and working as a caddy at a golf course on the coast. He recently texted me his thoughts on our relationship, some twenty-eight years after I came into his life, in 1985: "I will always need you Jeff," he wrote. "You're my dad as far as I'm concerned. My biological dad would be so thankful and proud of you. I love you."

Coincidentally, I began writing this chapter on Father's Day. The thoughts that my kids put in writing on this day mean so much, especially to someone like me. They really believe there is no better dad, just like your kids feel about you. Our kids feel blessed. What was emotional for me today was receiving text messages from all over America from grown men, some with their own kids, telling me how "blessed" they were to have me as their "father." Some of these men telephoned. The ones who are still kids called to wish me a happy Father's Day.

In 1995, I "adopted" a whole high school football program. Colerain's team had a 13-0 record that season. They were rated fourth in the nation. If they beat Cleveland's St. Ignatius, which was ranked first, Colerain High School would be Ohio State Champions—and the number one team in the nation. But before that game could take place, it was discovered that a third-team player on the Colerain squad was ineligible. The team's record instantly went from 13-0 to 0-13. I saw these kids being interviewed on television about this development, and I felt bad for them. I didn't even know where this school was, but I called their football coach, Kerry Combs, to invite him and his team to The Precinct for dinner to celebrate their great season.

"I had no clue who Jeff Ruby was; I had never been to any of his restaurants," Kerry told Robert. "He said that his own high school football coach had been very important in his life, and he wanted to do something for me and my team. When I told him I had 105 players plus fifteen coaches, he said, 'No problem. Come tomorrow night.'

""We had won the state semi-final 49-0, and it was devastating to all of us to suddenly be left out in the cold. Even before we knew what a big deal The Precinct was, we were happy that someone, a complete stranger, wanted to celebrate our success in such a generous way. Not a single kid on our team had been to a restaurant anything like The Precinct. One of them asked me, 'Is it like Denny's?' After we arrived in three school buses, we found out it wasn't anywhere near like Denny's. When one kid announced that he didn't eat meat, Jeff ordered the staff to bring him a shrimp cocktail. Each shrimp was as big as my fist. It was a once in a lifetime experience, and I will owe him for that for the rest of my life.

"Jeff's an American original. He is incredibly genuine, he's never boring, and he's always got a story. He loves high school football and is still trying to pay back his own high school coach. Some skeptical and suspicious people believe there's some kind of string attached to Jeff's generosity, but although we've become good friends, he's never asked me to do anything—except to speak at his roasts along with the likes of Cris Collinsworth, Mike Piazza and Johnny Bench. But if I needed something from him, I know it would be done.

"He's a brilliant businessman who changed the path of his life a long time ago and is good at helping others do that, too."

The Colerain kids had the time of their lives. You would never have known they had just lost everything they had worked so hard to achieve. Kerry and I became the best of friends, and I've been on the Colerain sidelines ever since. He is now an assistant coach at Ohio State, and I am still "coaching" the Colerain kids with their new head coach, Tom Bolden. When the Colerain team won the state championship in 2004, I bought them dinner at The Precinct.

My first surrogate son, Eddie Powers, came into my life by accident, in 1985. The Waterfront was under construction. I was driving away from the site one afternoon.

"I was twelve years old," Eddie recalled for Robert. "I was walking along the same street, on my way to baseball practice. Jeff was in a red Mercedes sports car, with the top down, sitting at a stoplight. I thought I recognized him. I asked him if he was Jeff Ruby. When he said he was, we started talking. When the light changed, he turned the corner and pulled over. Since baseball was my sport, he called Pete Rose from his car phone and put me on to talk to him. Then Jeff asked if I'd like to have tickets to the Reds game the next day, and he set that up on his car phone right then.

"I didn't have a dad growing up. I still don't know my correct last name. Jeff and I kept seeing each other, at the boat, and at the hamburger joint where everybody who was working on The Waterfront ate their lunch. He met my mother and pretty much became my mentor and big brother, a relationship I tried not to abuse. We went to football and baseball games together, and when I was sixteen and a junior in high school I went to work at The Waterfront. I stayed there until I was twenty-four. Jeff's been a great influence in my life, and I've carried over what he taught me into everything I've done since."

My son Dillon's best friend was an African-American kid, Jordan Bridgett. Because they were the two best running backs at Nagel Middle School, they were put on separate eighth grade teams. When Jordan was seven years old, his dad was murdered, so I spent time with him. Everywhere I went with Dillon, Jordan was right there, sharing the experience. We flew to Detroit and stayed with the Bearcats when they played in the Motor City Bowl. We Christmas-shopped at Neiman-Marcus and ate dinner at Capital Grille. Jordan dined with me at every one of our restaurants–and in every Thai restaurant in every city we went to. I told him that "green stuff" was Japanese guacamole and he would love it. He almost turned white and nearly passed out. It was wasabi—very hot.

His mother, Gaye, told me something Jordan once told her when he was fourteen: "Mom, Mr. Ruby came to my game." Later, he became knowledgeable about food and went to work at The Precinct. Jordan is a food server for us, has a four-year-old son of his own and is doing extremely well. He had the highest grade on a recent food server test.

I wanted to send my son Dillon to Highlands High School in Fort Thomas, Kentucky. He lived in Ohio with his mother, but after what had happened to Brandon I wasn't about to send Dillon to the same high school. If Dillon was going across the Ohio River to high school, Jordan wanted to go there, too, even though it would mean that they would be fighting it out against each other for a starting position as running back at Highlands. Dillon also wanted Jordan to go to the same high school as he did.

No Ohio resident had ever played football for Highlands High School, a nationally recognized football powerhouse. In the town of Fort Thomas, a Kentucky state football championship was as annual as Thanksgiving. I met with head coach, Dale Mueller. I wanted to know if it would be legal for Dillon, who lived in Ohio, to commute to Highlands to play football and attend classes. Dale said he would look into it, even though it would be unprecedented.

If I paid tuition, Dillon could legally live in Cincinnati and attend Highlands and play on the football team. I then told Dale he had himself *two* tailbacks; I paid Jordan Bridgett's tuition, and he came too. Jordan became Highland's first black football player and opened the door for others to follow. One of them, Mike Mitchell, now plays for the Carolina Panthers.

I attended every one of Dillon's football practices. One particular freshman player always came over and stood beside me after his practice was completed and all of his teammates had gone home. Eventually we said "hello" to each other. His name was Jake Urlage. He was the number one running back on the freshman team. His hair made him look like a young Paul McCartney. One night he was triple-dating with two of his buddies. They were going to the movies at Newport on the Levee, where my Tropicana was located. Jake dropped into my restaurant to say hello before the movie started. He said he had seen my red Mercedes convertible out front. When I asked if he wanted some cheesecake, I finally got a chance to sit down and talk to him. His friends hadn't arrived yet. Now that I think about it, he probably came early to see me. I told him I thought it was classy of him to sit in full pads on the steps with his mom in front of all of the other kids before his scrimmage. He explained that he didn't have a father.

He told me his dad had died at the age of thirty-five, when Jake was seven and his brother Nick was five. Their baby brother, Griffin, was just one year old. His mother, Penny, remarried a widower with four kids just one year later. They had no sooner settled in as a family than Jake's stepdad died, also at thirty-five. He died of a heart attack while playing basketball with little Nick. Now his mom had seven kids to raise without a husband, and now seven kids didn't have a father.

I put my hand on Jake's shoulder and said, "I'm sorry." He just said, "It's okay. My mom does a great job. "Nothing more was said of this, and Jake left for the movies. He came back after the show was over, and I had a Coke with him. A few weeks later, Penny called me. She told me Jake was failing in school and asked if I would talk to him about getting his grades up. She thought he would listen to me. "You're all he talks about," she said.

I've been talking to Jake about life's challenges ever since. He began calling me more often than he called his friends, even more than my own kids called me. I began to know Jake's principal, Elgin Emmons, as a result of my relationship with Jake.

Elgin, who has since retired, told Robert, "When I first knew Jake he was sullen, uncooperative and unmotivated. His body language suggested that he was really resentful about being forced to get an education—and just about everything else. He wasn't failing but he was barely eking by. Highlands had only eight hundred students, and 90 percent of them graduated and went on to college or vocational school. Most of them understood that they were academically competitive. Jake was at a serious disadvantage in that environment. He had no skill set for allowing any learning to occur. Jeff saw an opportunity to make a difference with this kid who had lost two fathers, and he poured himself into doing that. He treated Jake, and later Nick, like his own son.

"I'd never encountered anything like it in a long academic career.

Thanks to Jeff, not only did Jake's grades improve dramatically, he developed a more responsible and respectful attitude. He went from never smiling to smiling all the time. It was a huge change. Jeff's strength and skill gave Jake a course in how to live and progress within the culture."

Country music star Lee Greenwood asked me to be his guest at a black-tie fundraiser for NASA being held in Houston. Lee and another country singer, Mark Wills, would be performing. I borrowed a friend's private jet and took Jake and my daughter, Britney. We picked up Lee in Sevierville, Tennessee, and flew to Houston. It impressed me that Jake knew who Lee Greenwood was and wanted to go with us. He was a country music fan, like me. We went shopping at The Galleria in Houston, where I bought Jake a few things, including the first of many tuxedos I would buy for him.

I became, for all practical purposes, Jake's dad after that trip. I called him "Son." Jake called me "Pop." I began drug testing him. I met with his counselors, coach and principal. When Penny told me he wasn't getting the assistance he needed with his ADD, I met with the principal, to get Jake the help. Jake was a handful and very time-consuming. He was a lot like Dillon, and he looked up to Dillon, who was a grade above him at Highlands. Both were good-looking, had ADD, scored more touchdowns than anyone else in their class, and scored with more girls than anyone in their class. Neither of the boys scored well on tests, however, and they wore me out. Plus, I had Brandon, Britney, a turbulent marriage and six high-volume restaurants at the time.

Then I found out I had to raise Jake's little brother Nick. Jake had told Nick he needed "Pop." Holly Collinsworth, Cris's wife, told me to imagine how Nick would feel if I didn't "adopt" him after all I had done for Jake. This year, 2013, I "adopted" Griffin, Jake and Nick's younger brother, who is seventeen and doesn't remember his real father or his stepfather at all.

Jake told Robert, "After we met, and I told him my life story over cheesecake at The Tropicana, Pop never missed one of my freshman football games. And he's been trying to make me a man since day one. He does that by example, in the way he turned his life around, and in the respect he shows for others. My whole family respects him. We see the real Jeff Ruby, one of a kind, who's not afraid to do anything.

"He's one of the greatest guys you'll ever meet. He's confident in himself. He knows what he wants and he takes it. The restaurants speak for themselves He has the biggest heart in Cincinnati. That's why he's the king of Cincinnati."

Nick remembered for Robert, "I was seventeen years old and a junior in high school. I pulled my hamstring playing football. My leg was hurting, and I didn't know what to do about it. My mother said, 'Jake has Mr. Ruby.' I called him, and he drove me in his Ferrari to the Cincinnati Bengals' team doctor. He said I could call him 'Uncle Jeff.' He told me how important it was to learn sports and get good grades, so I could do whatever it was I wanted to do.

"I soon started calling him 'Pop.' When I switched sports, from football to soccer, Pop came to his very first soccer game ever, to watch me play.

"He's somebody who's here for me. I have a good time with him every time we're together. I have a blast. And I always want to make him proud."

Griff said to Robert, "He's an awesome dad, and I'm so proud to be his son and a part of his amazing life."

Sometimes I don't need to "adopt" a young man, because he already has a stable family life, is an excellent student who doesn't get into trouble, and is an athlete at the top of his game. One Friday night in the fall of 2008, I met such a kid, Greg Tabar. He was the quarterback on the Colerain High School football team, and I was watching the game, as usual. Colerain, with a 4-0 record, was the number one team in both the city and the state, and was ranked sixth in the nation.

"After the game, a man wearing a gray suit and carrying a cigar came up to me," Greg told Robert. "He said, 'You played a heck of a game. You should be proud of yourself.' He introduced himself as Jeff Ruby, which meant nothing to me. Little did I know that my life would change that night. He asked me if I and my good friend Nick Preissman, our defensive back who had intercepted a pass and returned it for a "pick six," would like to go to the Bengals-Steelers game on Sunday. I said I'd have to ask and would call him the next day. My parents certainly knew who Jeff Ruby was, 'the man who owns five, five-star restaurants,' and encouraged me to go to the Bengals game with him.

"Jeff's private box, twenty rows back on the twenty-yard line, was lined with pictures of him with celebrities ranging from Aerosmith and President Bush, to Michael Jordan and Margaret Thatcher. The suite had a food bar in the back and a fridge with all types of sodas. The seats in front were like giant, comfortable chairs. It was hard to focus on the game because so many famous people came into the booth, including Bootsy Collins, who had created the "Who dey?" chant for the Bengals.

"As the football season went on, Nick and I grew closer to Jeff, as he insisted we call him. We went to more Bengals games and got to eat at The Precinct. He flew me and Nick on a private jet to the Orange Bowl in Miami, where my brother Mark was playing on the University of Cincinnati team.

"But it wasn't all about that. Jeff was an interesting person, and we became close friends. He became a role model and mentor who taught me lessons I will use throughout my life. He taught me to put others first, ahead of myself, and that you need courage, confidence and pride, but that none of them would be enough if you didn't have passion. I will always look up to him as my role model, try to be successful, and help people in need."

When I show up at high school games where Cincinnati's powerhouse Catholic teams are playing, I'm swarmed by kids asking for photos with me. I don't know the reason for this. I just own restaurants. Besides, I'm Jewish.

Just *days* before Robert Windeler and I finished this chapter, in October of 2013, I visited a young man named Robert Weidner at Children's Hospital. His friend A. J. Moser had tweeted me the night before, "Can we get you to support #RWstrong?" "Who dat?" I tweeted back. A. J. responded and requested my help in three more tweets: "A student at Oak Hills who is fighting leukemia and kicking its ass"; "help spread the word"; "get #RWstrong trending." Robert Weidner is a seventeen-year-old high school junior and athlete in track and swimming who had gone to his doctor thinking he might have mononucleosis, only to find out that he had leukemia. He was rushed to the hospital and scheduled for chemotherapy. I tweeted my concern for his condition to my twelve thousand Twitter followers and asked them to pray for him. I got more than three hundred re-tweets in an hour.

I then decided to pay Robert Weidner a visit in the hospital. I arrived at his bedside with shrimp cocktail, 14-ounce strip steaks, macaroni and cheese, Freddie salads, and carrot cake. I thought it was enough for three days. I stayed for an hour and ate lunch with him.

Robert Weidner then tweeted his four hundred-plus followers:

"*The* Mr. Jeff Ruby, everybody! What a guy! Brought enough food for a week, and the support was crazy. Love you!"

* * * * *

I've been helping, mentoring or "adopting" kids for nearly forty years now, and I'm not going to stop. I understand that people will speculate about my motives. They may comment disapprovingly when they see a kid driving one of my cars. I don't know how many kids who have worked for me have taken my car to their proms. Giving my time to these kids gives me the feeling that *I'm* a kid again. It's a wonderful feeling. My second childhood makes up for the one I didn't have.

As my brother Wayne told Robert, "Jeff's mission is to pay back society for all the good those strangers did, the ones who helped him during his own difficult times growing up, when he felt he didn't have family to help out. They kind of adopted him and helped him, during his troubled period, to be on the right side of the fence."

You can't help someone without helping yourself. All of my "kids" have made me a better man. They made me the man I want to be.

CHAPTER TWENTY-EIGHT

FIND OUT WHO YOUR FRIENDS ARE

Tracy Lawrence, 2006; Duet with Tim McGraw, 2013

Friendship is the medicine of life. However, you're not going to know who your friends really are when the sun is shining on you. As I've found out, you'll learn who they are when a storm hits you, and the only thing you can see is darkness. A true friend will show up holding the umbrella of friendship. A good friend will help you move. A *damned good* friend will help you move a body.

Casey Beathard and Ed Hill wrote the lyrics to a *Billboard* number one country hit that reflect my feelings on the subject:

> "And everybody wants to slap your back
> Wants to shake your hand
> When you're up on top of that mountain
> But then one of those rocks gives way
> Then you slide back down
> Look up and see who's around then.
>> When the water's high
>> When the weather's not so fair
>> When the well runs dry
>> Who's gonna be there?

I tell young kids that, after whom you choose to marry, the most important decisions of your life will be the friends you choose. You'll meet most of your lifelong friends in college, so make sure you go to college. They may help finance your business down the road. When you're a sixteen-year-old kid, you don't give any thought to what I call the college "X" factor: the lifelong friendships you establish there.

Johnny Bench and Pete Rose were the first good friends I met in Cincinnati. Sparky Anderson was my surrogate father—and my friend. Through the three of them, I have met many other players for the Reds, and other local and visiting athletes. But my longest-standing local friendship has been with Marty Brennaman, who came to town in 1974 to be the Reds' announcer, which he still is in 2013. Marty spends a lot of time on the road with the team, but we both still live in Cincinnati, while so many others have come and gone.

Marty told Robert, "Jeff and I met through Sparky Anderson. Jeff was somewhat established in town, while I was the newcomer, but we first crossed paths when neither of us had the proverbial pot to piss in. Soon we had other friends in common, like Johnny Bench, but it's very accurate to say that Jeff and I have lasted longer than the others as friends here in Cincinnati. We do have periods when one of us pisses the other off, but then we always patch it up. I'm usually the one who will call first.

"Back then he was really something as a brawler, and he would fight at the drop of a hat, but I quickly learned that he's a very sensitive person. A lot of people don't know that about him. Friendships are very important to Jeff, and it's important to him to maintain them. He also takes great pride in the kids he's mentored who have turned out well. His own kids have turned out sensationally well, and you have to give credit to him and Rickelle for whatever they did and however they did it.

"The secret of his success as the best restaurateur in town is that he knows his business inside out, and he will go to any extremes to make sure his standards are kept. Even back at Holiday Inn, working for someone else, he was developing really good gathering spots. His success at those hotels begat his later success with his restaurants.

"My biggest mistake was not investing in The Precinct when I had the chance. I've been kicking myself ever since.

"As a person, Jeff hasn't changed all that much in the nearly forty years I've known him. He's essentially the same person I met in 1974. Others will say they notice a difference between the pre- and post-accident Jeff Ruby. But I don't see it, except that he's older and more mature, like most of us."

Thom Brennaman, Marty's son and now a sportscaster himself, came into my life as a boy. We, too, have become friends over the years. Thom told Robert, "In the 1970s it was Reds policy that I was allowed go into the dugout with my father before the game, but not into the press box. I would go sit in the stands, in Sparky Anderson's seats. Jeff would be there, too. Both of us would be sitting by ourselves. He wouldn't have had to talk to me at all, but he did.

"When I was twelve, thirteen and fourteen, we got to know each other pretty well. He was a big strong well-built guy with cuts and scrapes all over him, from fighting in bars. He was also very funny.

"My senior year in high school, Jeff offered me a job at The Precinct, bussing tables, since I wasn't old enough to park cars. I went to a meeting the first day, and sat through a two-hour training seminar. Then I announced that, although I appreciated the job, since I was playing high school soccer on Saturday nights, I couldn't work then. He went at me: 'If you can't work Saturday, our busiest night, you can't work here.' He said it in a fun, cool way, but he wasn't fooling. So I ended up never working for him. If I had been playing *football* on Saturday nights, instead of soccer, he'd have said, 'Come in whenever you can.'

"We moved away shortly after that. I went to college and traveled for my own career as a sports broadcaster, and I didn't see Jeff at all for about fifteen years. But we reconnected, and now I talk to him three or four times a month. He has definitely mellowed a lot since his accident, but I still see signs of the old fiery toughness I remember seeing in him when I was a kid. He's still a hard-working, driven guy who does a lot of charity work where he sees a need. While he's not shy about it, he probably does five times as much that doesn't get any publicity."

My first two partners at The Waterfront were football players Cris Collinsworth and Boomer Esiason. I met both of them at The Precinct during their rookie years with the Cincinnati Bengals in the early 1980s. Boomer led the Bengals to the Super Bowl in 1988 and was the NFL's Player of the Year. Boomer Esiason could not only run an offense, he could run just about any company in America if he learned their playbook. He has every tool a person needs to manage people: intelligence, leadership, and charisma.

In that '88 Super Bowl, we suffered a devastating injury. Tim Krumrie, our all-pro nose tackle, broke his left leg in two places. I was watching the game with Cleveland Browns all-pro cornerback Hanford Dixon. Hanford is a heck of a guy. At half time, I told him I was going to sneak into the Bengals' locker room and see how Krumrie was doing. Hanford told me I would never get in. But I've learned that the way you get into places where you're not allowed, is to act as if you *are* allowed.

I not only got in, I got upset when I saw that Tim was lying on a table and had been just left there without even a television to watch the second half. I ordered stadium personnel to get "my" player a television, and they did. I even had someone bring him a cold beer. The Bengals were ready to take the field for the second half. As they ran past me through the tunnel, Stanford Jennings looked questioningly at me. I said, "Take it back for a TD," and I slapped his rear end real hard. He ran back the kickoff ninety-three yards for a touchdown, the Bengals' first of the game. I'm a frustrated football coach. My sons' high school coaches unfortunately had to put up with that.

The drama of the Super Bowl wasn't over just because the game was. (Cincinnati lost.) Boomer described for Robert what happened the next day.

"After we lost the Super Bowl, my wife, Cheryl, and I wanted to go to Aruba with Jeff and Rickelle, and just get far away from football for six weeks. When Jeff went to pick up our plane tickets at the Delta counter at Miami airport, they weren't there. Delta claimed they'd never seen our reservations, which Jeff's secretary had made. He snapped like I've never seen anyone snap in my life. It was frightening. He knocked over at least twenty-five rope stanchions. Can you imagine how that would have looked if there had been social media and Twitter back then? Cheryl asked me, 'How unstable is this guy? Should we really be traveling with him?'

"Jeff finally got the tickets straightened out, but we couldn't fly to Aruba that day and had to stay overnight in Miami. We agreed that the four of us would go out to dinner that night. When Cheryl and I arrived at Jeff and Rickelle's hotel, I called their room. In my best Esteban Alvarez accent, I said that I was from the Miami Police Department and that I had a warrant for his arrest for disturbing the peace at the airport. Since it was an international airport, it was a federal offense. Mr. Ruby was to come down to the lobby—immediately—or I would come up to his room. I was actually standing outside his room with my finger over the peephole so he couldn't see out, trying to keep from laughing.

"I knocked on the door, and I heard him tell Rickelle, 'Don't let him in. I'm not leaving my room.' I heard her ask him, 'Are we gonna spend our whole vacation in a hotel room?' I knocked even louder." I finally opened the door and saw that it was Boomer—and his idea of a joke. By way of apology for the earlier incident at the airport, Rickelle told Cheryl about my ongoing problems since my accident, which had occurred only six months before.

"He hasn't been right since the head injury, and they say it's going to take a while," she explained.

According to Boomer, my behavior remained bizarre throughout our trip to Aruba: "Every restaurant we went to, he'd order about ten different entrees, in order to sample them all. I put on twenty pounds on that trip."

Boomer described our relationship to Robert. "To truly understand Jeff Ruby, you have to understand the negatives, as well as the complicated positives. I love him to death, and he's one of the top five guys in my life I'd want with me in the foxhole, because he's a tenacious fighter and somebody who is really, really loyal. But it's actually 90 percent love and 10 percent hate. There are times when you just don't want to be around him, or have him ever call you again. There's a lot of smiling and eye-rolling when you're with him, and there's never a dull moment. Jeff's got the ADD thing going on, and a caricature persona he plays to a bit. He dresses like a gangster from the '1940s. He thinks of himself as Bugsy Siegel. He also thinks of himself as Toots Shor, the New York restaurateur who held court with the big names in industry, media, politics and sports. And people do gravitate to Jeff. They somehow find him, and he brings them in.

"He's one of the most unexplainable individuals I've ever met. He's Don Rickles, John Candy, Sammy Davis Jr., Frank Sinatra, and Dean Martin all rolled up into one. He's a good guy, and he's never done anything other than help me anywhere I've ever asked for it. He would always push me to be better on the field. We do like to bust each other's chops, but we do it to motivate each other to become better at what we do.

"There is a tenacity, a competitive nature that makes him survive. He makes fun of Donald Trump, but there's a lot of Donald Trump in Jeff Ruby. There's also the showmanship, and his failing and getting back up, and failing and getting back up again."

"Jeff's a walking contradiction. His compassionate and human side at times can be overwhelming. I've seen him take homeless kids and sick people and give them money, feed them, and then give more money to the food bank. He would be a psychotherapist's dream patient. Actually, he would be an ideal candidate for a psychological think tank. They'd come up with fifty different diagnoses.

"During the NFL strike in 1987, he actually banned my teammates from The Waterfront, even though I was an investor in it. He hated the fact that we were on strike. He said, 'You guys have got to get back to work; this is crap. I don't want you hanging out in my bar, getting in fights.' I had to remind him that it was my bar, too. How in the hell could I walk into the locker room, look my teammates in the face and say, 'Oh yeah, by the way guys, you can't come to my restaurant'—not a good message to send.

"This guy could have a legitimate reality show, and he wouldn't have to act."

* * * * *

Cris Collinsworth was an all-pro receiver for the Bengals. He's an amazing guy, a special guy. That's why he was NBC's choice to replace the popular former Oakland Raiders coach John Madden when Madden retired from broadcasting on *Sunday Night Football*. Cris has won fourteen Emmys. He has provided a good sounding board for me, as has his wonderful wife, Holly, who is smarter than both of us.

Cris met Holly at The Precinct as a result of a promotion I had with The Beach Waterpark. The winner of a bathing suit contest would win a day at The Beach with Cris. Holly just happened to be at The Precinct for dinner with her parents that evening, but she did not enter the contest. I had never seen Holly before, and I thought I knew just about every good-looking girl on both sides of the Ohio River. They either hung out at The Precinct or they worked there.

Cris took one look at Holly and told me he wanted her to be the winner. I told him she hadn't entered the contest, so she couldn't win. "I don't fix these contests," I said. He insisted, however, that *this* girl was the one he would have the date with, and I gave in. The other babes in bikinis were furious. Their tempers were hotter than their bodies. "She wasn't even wearing a bathing suit," one complained. Hell hath no fury like a woman scorned in a bikini contest. I explained that black dresses were what they were now wearing on the beach in L.A.

Cris and Holly never went to The Beach Waterpark. They got married instead. I was honored to be in their wedding. They have four remarkable kids. I, of course, take full credit for all of this. Lots of married couples from that generation first met at either The Precinct or The Waterfront, and I feel very good about that.

Cris told Robert, "Jeff's one of my four or five best friends anywhere, and I love him. Being friends with him, you become a pretty good listener. He likes to talk. If I have the time, I'll just sit there and listen to him venting like crazy about something that's on his mind. Sometimes that patience can backfire on you. If he calls me at home and starts to go on, I usually put him on speaker phone and work on the computer or watch TV and throw in an occasional 'uh -huh.'

"Jeff still thinks of himself as a nose tackle on a football team. A member of his staff in The Precinct kitchen was selling drugs, and Jeff confronted him about it. The guy smarted off, and Jeff hit him, knocked him through the door, down the stairs and out into the street. This guy threatened to sue, and Jeff wrote him a check for twenty-five grand. To this day, Jeff says it's the best $25,000 he ever spent in his whole life. He loved it.

"He's not really a restaurateur. He's really Barnum & Bailey, and he wants to be the show. If you want to feel like a celebrity, go to one of Jeff's places, and you will feel like one. I get calls from him all the time whenever he's with some celebrity he wants me to say hello to. You'd have to pay me a billion dollars to walk up to a movie star sitting in a restaurant. But with Jeff it's 'of course they want to meet me and have their picture taken with me.' Some people like it and some people don't like it, but he's never going to change. He is a natural. He has no fear.

"As for investing in his restaurants, I don't remember having a choice. He's always got something going on, and he just kind of waves his magic wand and you sign up for it. He collects the names of athletes and local business guys to make it sound better. And he was very clever about the financing. Instead of going to banks, he pre-sold food. You'd get $20,000 worth of meals at The Waterfront if you invested $15,000 in cash. Then you'd go in and just sign your name for your meal, as a part owner."

* * * * *

I've made as many good friends through my love of music as I have through my love of sports. Sometimes they've even overlapped. Johnny Bench, who converted me into a country music lover, took me to see the legendary George Jones perform at Bobby Mackey's club in Wilder, Kentucky, in 1980. Bobby, who is a traditional country singer and guitarist himself, opened the club in 1978, and it is still the pre-eminent country music club in Northern Kentucky and greater Cincinnati. I've continued to visit it often over the last thirty-three years, and Bobby and I have become good friends. The night of my sixty-fifth birthday, April 19, 2013, I went to Bobby Mackey's and sang, "Me and Bobby McGee," on stage with Bobby himself playing guitar and singing backup.

Bobby told Robert, coincidentally on the day George Jones died, April 25, 2013, "Jeff's a people person, and as a nightclub owner, I'm always impressed by that. But, more than anything, he really can sing."

Bootsy Collins is a native Cincinnatian, and someone whose music I'd long admired, even before I met him. I knew him for a long time before we opened Bootsy's together, and we've remained fast friends since its closing.

"The timing of our restaurant was a little awkward, with the money thing in 2008; it was goin' downhill and everybody was hurting," Bootsy told Robert. "In another time and place it might have worked, but I wouldn't change a thing about the experience. Jeff and I had always talked about doing something together, and we just kind of clicked, kind of like the odd couple. He's a very motivational guy, and I wasn't on the road at the time. I wanted to put something down in Cincinnati, where I was raised.

"Jeff and I had a blast doing it. The cat is so creative, and he threw himself into the creation of the place, its structure and design. He understood about the colors, and he opened up things in a way he could express some of the things he wanted to do in a music/party restaurant. He gave it everything he had. We both gave it our all. There's definitely no one to blame. It was a very good learning curve and I look forward to getting another opportunity to try it again.

"We had a heck of a good time at Bootsy's, especially on birthdays and holidays. One New Year's Eve, Jeff got up on the bar and sang 'Auld Lang Syne,' and he can croon. Our last Halloween party was incredible. It was a Batman and Catwoman theme, and everybody was dressed in costume. It looked like a scene out of Hollywood.

"I also learned some behind-the-scenes stuff from Jeff, more than I ever knew went on, just watching him talking to the staff. It was an inside look that most people don't get to see. He not only motivated his people to work, he taught them to understand ethics, and to do all of those things his restaurants do so well. He does it like clockwork.

"Jeff is a topnotch guy, but a lot of people don't really understand him. I understand him more, because I understood James Brown, who recorded for King Records, which was based in Cincinnati. James always told me that entertaining is 75 percent business, and only 25 percent music. Jeff is built the same way. Jeff is wired to entertain with his restaurants. That's what's funny to me about him. He loves it. If you were to take it away from him I don't know what he would do. It's a gift he's been given, and he's taken it to the bank."

Nick Lachey is another native Cincinnatian who has done very well in the music business, both with the boy band 98 Degrees and as a solo singer. He graduated from the public School for Creative and Performing Arts in Cincinnati, and went on to Miami University in Oxford, Ohio. Nick and I have also talked about doing a restaurant together.

"We did sit down and discuss the possibility," Nick recalled for Robert. "But it didn't feel right at the time, since I'd moved to Los Angeles and my wife and I had a new baby. As a kid, I wasn't that aware of who Jeff Ruby was. But The Waterfront was a happening spot when I was in high school, and we went there for our after-prom party. In 2001, Britney and I dated briefly, having met at The Waterfront. I'm proud of her accomplishments with the company. She has really put her stamp on it.

"Jeff's been good to me over the years, and we stay in pretty fair contact. I greatly respect what he's built, and his outstanding food. They are a testament to his vision, hard work and discipline. He's also done great things for the city, and been generous with his time and his money. This is not lost on any of us in Cincinnati."

Travis Tritt and I met at Jeff Ruby's Steakhouse in Louisville and we became friends instantly. He's a great guy as well as a great performer.

"My wife and I were going to the Kentucky Derby in 2007, and staying in a hotel right next to Jeff Ruby's restaurant," Travis recalled for Robert. "We'd heard how great a place to eat it was, so I called to make a reservation. Of course they were booked solid. But when Jeff heard it was me calling, he said 'Come on down, we'll get you a table.' While we were eating, Jeff came over to the table and we chatted for a bit and found we had a lot in common in terms of our musical tastes, especially old blues and soul songs, and with the people we knew. That sort of established the beginning of our friendship.

"Our shows have always done particularly well in the Tri-State Ohio, Kentucky and northern Indiana area, so we are there often, and Jeff comes to see us whenever he can. One night in the middle of summer, we did an outdoor concert in Indiana. Jeff called at the last minute and ended up sitting in the front row. After I sang "When Something Is Wrong (With My Baby)," the old Sam and Dave blues song I had recorded with Patti LaBelle, Jeff stood up and gave me a personal standing ovation.

"I get a kick out of him. He's eccentric, a character who at times can be a caricature, and he's on so many different trips. Not a lot of people are that distinctive. And he can be outlandishly funny. He's a real friend, and I respect that he calls them as he sees them. He's a salmon swimming upstream, when he could so easily go with the flow. We share our views on the current political situation, but we view some issues very differently. We probably agree 60 percent of the time, and on the other 40 percent we just agree to disagree, and we don't take it personally.

"Jeff blames me for his being the owner of a big touring coach like the one most of us in country music have. Performing one hundred and twenty shows a year, my bus was my home away from home. When Jeff saw it, he said 'Geez, this is nice.' The next year, at the Derby, he had a touring bus of his own."

Phil Pitzer is a lawyer I've known since Lucy in the Sky days, and we have been friends ever since. He now lives in Los Angeles and has produced a sequel to the classic 1969 movie *Easy Rider.*

"Jeff Ruby is the best promoter I know in the world." Phil told Robert. "So when I acquired the rights to do the sequel, which is called *Easy Rider: The Ride Back*, I knew he could help me find investors--and consult with me on the music for the soundtrack. He said, 'I'm in' right away, and he became a co-executive producer of the movie.

"He and Johnny Bench have small speaking roles in the movie. Bench has done tons of TV, and he knew what to do, but Jeff was new to acting a role in a script. He had the first line in the scene, on a baseball field, but when the director yelled 'action,' Jeff just stood there, waiting for Johnny to speak first. It took two or three more takes to get it right."

Kelly Walker has performed at our restaurants for fourteen years with her group, Kelly Red and the Hammerheads, an eclectic country-rock band. (Think Little Feat, Bonnie Raitt, and the Allman Brothers, but with their own twist.) In early 2011, the house she owned with her husband of twenty-seven years, Kevin Walker, burned down. Five months later, Kevin, a piano player, died suddenly of a heart attack, at the age of forty-seven.

"Jeff rose to the occasion both times, and saved the day," Kelly told Robert. "He also saved my life. When I was growling and screaming 'I'm gonna kill myself,' he grabbed me in a choke hold and calmed me down. He said, 'no matter what happens, I got you.'

"When we had the fire at our house, the building was insured, but the contents were not. Jeff gave a benefit and raised a bunch of money to fill the hole we were in. For my husband's funeral, which was an hour out of Downtown, he took his bus and filled it up with employees. It was a hot summer day, and he went down the line of people waiting to get into the church, handing out bottles of water and food.

"I've never seen kindness like I've seen from that man. He's done so many kind things for so many people. I've never met another human like him, and I don't think I ever will. I can't say enough good things about him.

"Yes, he's eccentric, and I've seen him tear the rear end out of people. He expects excellence. I know that. But he's kept musicians in Cincinnati working for thirty years. He loves music so much, and he's kept live music going here. He doesn't just talk the talk, he walks the walk. All I ever did was play music, so that would have been enough."

Perhaps my best friend I met through the music business is Ben Scotti, the co-founder, with his brother Tony, of Scotti Brothers

Records. Ben, like me, was born in Newark, New Jersey. His family moved to Long Branch when he was a teenager. Ben played in the National Football League, for Washington, Philadelphia, and San Francisco. He and Tony also produced television shows, including *Baywatch*.

"I went to Cincinnati in 1985 to promote the *Rocky IV* soundtrack album, which was on Scotti Brothers Records," Ben recalled to Robert. "It was a monster album that contained a lot of hits, including 'Living in America' and 'Eye of the Tiger.' I asked the concierge at my hotel where I could get a good steak. He sent me to The Precinct. I was by myself, but I'd made a reservation. I was eating and enjoying myself, and I turned to my right to see this fella, a strong lookin' guy. He was lookin' at me. Then he came over to me and said, 'You're Ben Scotti. You played with the pros, and you're Scotti Brothers Records.' He'd seen my name on the reservation list, and knew all about the teams I'd played for, and about the record business. He told me he was from Neptune, New Jersey, and that his high school football coach had been Jeep Bednarik.

"I said I knew Jeep. His brother Chuck and I were teammates on the Philadelphia Eagles, and good friends. That was a coincidence. I liked the guy right away. He had a great personality, and was very outgoing and very kind. He's from Jersey, a rough and ready guy, a man's man and a former ballplayer. We just hit it off.

"Then Jeff told me that the limo driver who had brought me to the restaurant was wanted by the police. I thanked him for telling me, but said my hotel was only a couple of miles away. We said goodnight, and I got in the limo. On the highway, I heard a siren, and a police car pulled us over. The cops put the driver in handcuffs. I'm sitting in the back seat. Who do you think is behind the police car? Jeff Ruby. He said, 'I saved your life, Ben Scotti, and you owe me," and he took me back to the hotel. He said that next time I came to

Cincinnati he wanted me to come to his restaurants, and to let him show me around. That was the beginning for a couple of Jersey guys."

Because the enduring anthem, "Eye of the Tiger," had previously been used in *Rocky III*, been nominated for an Oscar, and won a Grammy for its group, Survivor, it was not a logical candidate to be played again on CHR (contemporary hit radio). But I called the Q102 program director, Jim Fox, and got him to play "Eye of the Tiger" on the air, along with "Living in America." Over the next few years, I managed to get a lot of Scotti Brothers Records songs on Q102. In appreciation, Ben gave me framed platinum albums of each of the songs. Those plaques were lost in our house fire, so Ben replaced them with the smaller platinum cds, since the long-playing records no longer existed.

"I came back to Cincinnati on several occasions, to promote records," Ben told Robert, "and he treated me like a king at The Waterfront." He said Cincinnati was my second home, and it really was. In 1987, our movie company released a small comedy called *He's My Girl*, starring David Hallyday and T. K. Carter. David had a great record with the title song. I wanted to get it played on the big rock station in town, knowing that their play list was very tight. Jeff picked me up at the airport and said he wanted to take me to his house, because his wife and he were having problems, and he wanted me to help him out. I said I didn't even know his wife, had never even met her. I was very uncomfortable, because I didn't know what to do. I was embarrassed. We chatted a bit, and I met the kids. There was definitely something in the air. I talked to Rickelle, and I just said, 'I hope things work out with you and Jeff.'

"The next day, he, she and I had lunch at The Waterfront. It started to rain. I felt bad about things, and I left. The next day, I got a call from the radio station's program director who told me about Jeff's accident the previous night, and that there was no certainty he

292

was going to make it. Being Roman Catholic, I said prayers for him and had a mass said for him. Two weeks later I got a call from the programmer telling me that Jeff had miraculously pulled through.

"I went to see him in the hospital the day before he got out. Jeff had a Scotti Brothers hat on, and was wearing an "Eye of the Tiger" T-shirt. He had a big smile on his face. He knew I was coming in, which is why he wore the hat and shirt. I couldn't believe it—always the promoter. This time I took him home in my limo.

"I still had to get David Hallyday's record on the radio station. I asked Jeff if he could call the program director. He was drowsy, but he did call, and said, 'This is so important to me that you play this record. It's a great record and Ben Scotti is my pal, one of the good guys. Do it for the good guys.' Then he fell asleep. Never in my life had I had someone just come back from the dead and tell a program director, 'this is the most important thing in my life.' I flew back to Los Angeles that night and the next day I got a call from the program director telling me the record was on the air. I've been involved in a lot of record promotions in my life, but this was the most unusual."

At the time, Randy Michaels was the CEO of Clear Channel Communications, the largest owner of radio stations in the country, including Q102. (He later went to Chicago to become CEO of the *Tribune*, WGN, and the Cubs.) Randy was an investor in The Waterfront, and regularly hung out there, especially in our La Boom dance club. He thinks I walk on water, and he gives me more credit than I think I deserve. He told Robert that I played a major role in converting another local radio station, KISS-FM 107.1, from a Top 40 format to a dance music format. My club deejay, Mark McFadden, also became a radio deejay in the process.

"I saw Ben Scotti dance his ass off at LaBoom," Randy remembered. "But Jeff and I actually became buddies in the 1970s, at Lucy in the Sky, which was really the only nightclub and disco in town at the time. All the Reds and all the Bengals went there. Jeff has a touch for attracting talented, quirky people. He always gave his places a cachet that reflected his personality."

* * * * *

Tedd Friedman, my lawyer, is my closest adviser, and he knows me as well as anyone does. He told Robert, "I've lived in Cincinnati my whole life. I was in high school when The Precinct opened, and I knew his product before I knew the man. He still serves the best steak in town, and gives me complete grief because I always order the same thing at all his restaurants: New York strip steak, mac and cheese, and a Freddie Salad. Jeff's big personality is in all of his restaurants. He's a project guy, and never happier or more absorbed than when he's working on a new project to the point of exhaustion. For him it's the equivalent of giving birth.

"So much of what he does is just intuitive. Sometimes he works very hard not to let you know how savvy he is. Jeff is a man of integrity. If he tells you something, he means it.

"I really believe there's no line between his business and personal lives."

I'd have to agree that most of my time is spent working to make Jeff Ruby Culinary Entertainment even better. I consider all of my five hundred employees family. Some of them call me "Jeff." Some call me "Boss." Some call me "Mr. Ruby." (What they call me behind my back is none of my business.) Inevitably, given the amount of time I spend with them, some of them have become friends over the years. Brian Welage, my fulltime "Vice President of Transportation," spends a lot of time with me, especially when he's driving my bus. We often go great distances—to Chicago for antique shopping, to our restaurant in Louisville, or to the Belmont Stakes or the Super Bowl. At times it's just the two of us. We've become friends, and like all friends we disagree sometimes.

"He expects what he delivers, in business or personally," Brian told Robert. "He's hard to read at times when he's yelling at you. So you just sit there quietly and take it. *Then* you respond. I'd never disrespect him in front of anybody, but if I know I'm right I'll stand my ground. He once told me, 'Your attitude's a little too big.' I told him, 'I learned from the best.' He laughed.

"Jeff is a very warm, loving person. He means well and he does well. I do think he cares too much about what other people think of him. He says he doesn't, but he does. It seems odd, coming from him."

Bawe Shinholster is in charge of quality control for all of our restaurants. I interact with him a lot, and expect him to say exactly what he thinks about anything.

Bawe told Robert, "Jeff's vision is pretty clear. Everyone knows he's brilliant, but he's even smarter than he seems. He plays coy at times to see if you will drop your guard, and will say, 'They think I'm crazy.' But he's not as crazy as people think he is. It's so much fun to watch him negotiate. It may seem like polite interrogation, but he's really conducting two meetings at once. His mind is always ticking within the tick. He's a businessman; there's no mistake about that. It's show business, but it is business. When he's looking at a profit-and-loss statement, there's no game. He isn't trying to be funny. He puts on his glasses and takes off his showman coat, and he's like a different person.

"He can be a control freak, and he would be the first to say so himself. But he's also very team-oriented and almost indecisive at times. He often bounces off of too many people, and no one person's opinion is more important than anyone else's. He certainly listens to feedback. He's not a dictator. He's constantly asking for advice and confirmation. That is another pleasant surprise."

* * * * *

Chris Sullivan is a founder and former president and CEO of Outback Steakhouse and OSI Restaurant Partners, which has five restaurant brands, including Roy's and Fleming's Prime Steakhouse. A passionate golfer, he began caddying at the age of twelve, and in 2010 was inducted into the Caddie Hall of Fame as both a caddie and a mentor of caddies.

Chris told Robert, "I first met Jeff at The Precinct, but even earlier, as a student at the University of Kentucky, I'd come to Cincinnati to the bars. A lot of the time Jeff was involved with my favorites. Ever since, I've followed his career as one of the true entrepreneurial successes in our business. We, as the owners of a restaurant group, like to watch the creative local restaurateurs to see what they do and how they do it. He has a real vision for the business, and it is remarkable how he continues to succeed in it, year after year. He's a showman as well as a passionate businessman. Jeff also really takes care of his people in a positive way that causes them to execute his vision very well."

Kevin Plank is the founder, CEO and Chairman of the Board of Under Armour, the wildly successful men's sportswear company.

"We share a love of Jack Daniel's," Kevin told Robert, "and we see each other when he comes to Maryland for the Preakness. During that weekend, I always have a party for two thousand people at my Sagamore Farm, which previously was owned, for seventy years, by Alfred Vanderbilt.

"I enjoy colorful personalities, so I like Jeff as a colorful man in my life. He's the greatest story teller in the world. I love his texts, although I don't always understand what he's talking about, and I feel that there is more to the story than I'm getting. I also respect his moral compass."

Santa Ono is the president of the University of Cincinnati, and a regular guest at our restaurants. He called me one day to ask if we would name a steak after him. We did.

"It's a Kobe steak," Santo told Robert. "As soon as they put it on the menu, I went to Jeff Ruby's to cut into it and try it out to make sure it was up to their standards for other steaks. It was.

"Jeff frequently attends our basketball and football games, and we are very grateful for his support of our sports teams. He's a generous person with a huge heart. He cares a lot about people, education, and college athletics. We are both active on Twitter and enjoy our followers. I also host an internet radio show on the campus station, bearcatsradio.listenlive, and Jeff is a frequent, welcome guest on it. He can easily fill up the whole hour."

* * * * *

People say, "You are what you eat." I say, "You are who you eat *with*." Many of my friends are in their respective Halls of Fame, or they will be. Others are simply the best in their business. How could I not want to be the best at what I do for a living?

My friendships in and out of Cincinnati, for the most part, are with people who are more successful than I am. My relationships with the right people have rubbed off on me. My friends have rubbed me the right way.

CHAPTER TWENTY-NINE

WHERE WERE YOU (WHEN THE WORLD STOPPED TURNING)

Alan Jackson, 2001

I was born in a week in which four of America's worst tragedies later occurred. The Branch Davidian siege led by David Koresh in Waco, Texas; and the Federal Building bombing in Oklahoma City, by Timothy McVeigh, both occurred on my birthday, April 19. The Virginia Tech massacre of thirty students happened on April 16. The Columbine High School tragedy happened one day after my birthday, on April 20.

Tuesday, September 11, 2001, was to have been a special day for me, my family, and my employees. It was the twentieth anniversary of our first restaurant, The Precinct. Our fourth restaurant, Carlo & Johnny, was under construction. I was staying at The Hannaford Suites down the street so I could work on the building "24/7." The motel was named for the famous early twentieth century architect Samuel Hannaford, who designed many of Cincinnati's historic buildings, including the Music Hall and the building that became The Precinct steakhouse. The motel offered breakfast to its residents, and that morning I had a bite to eat and grabbed a cup of coffee, went back to my room and turned on my television.

Like many Americans, I saw the breaking news that a plane had crashed into one of the towers at the World Trade Center at 8:46 a.m. While I recognized how tragic this was, I assumed that a small aircraft had flown off course and hit the tower. When the second airplane struck the South Tower, I knew these were deliberate attacks on our country. I asked the motel's engineer if he thought the towers could structurally sustain the impact of these crashes. Then I remembered that Boomer Esiason and his assistant Tammi Ammeker used some of Cantor-Fitzgerald's office space at the World Trade Center to work on the Boomer Esiason Foundation. (Boomer had used our company's office when he was with the Cincinnati Bengals.)

At the World Trade Center, Cantor-Fitzgerald occupied five floors (101-105) of the North Tower, and Boomer's office was on the 101st floor. I breathed a sigh of relief when Boomer returned my call, from Denver, having just broadcast the Monday night football game there the previous night. All commercial flights were canceled, and he asked if I thought my friend Carl Lindner would let him use his private jet to get home. Boomer had not heard from Tammi in New York, but said he would let me know as soon as he learned something. Later in the day, someone called to tell me that Tammi had survived. She had been in the basement getting coffee when the attack occurred. However, Tammi was the *only* survivor from those five floors. None of Boomer's friends at Cantor-Fitzgerald made it out. All 658 of the firm's employees who were working in that building at the time of the attack perished. Boomer gave the eulogy or spoke at eleven 9/11 funerals. He lost some very close friends.

Boomer recalled for Robert that "only U.S. government aircraft and small private planes were allowed to fly in the days following the tragedy. I found a guy with a King-Air who flew me and eight buddies back from Denver to New York. As we flew over the lower tip of Manhattan, looking over the World Trade Center site, the pilot told us that we were the only airplane flying over New York at the time."

"Where were you when the world stopped turning?" Alan Jackson's lyrics were written from the heart and could not have been delivered better by Sinatra or Cash.

"Did you burst out with pride for the red, white and blue
and the heroes who died just doin' what they do?
Did you look up to heaven for some kind of answer
and look at yourself and what really matters?"

CHAPTER THIRTY

A BETTER CLASS OF LOSERS

Randy Travis, 1991

Three riverboat casinos in southwest Indiana were within driving distance of Cincinnati. Belterra, the only first-class casino of the three, approached me about taking over their upscale restaurant. The land-based portion of the property had been designed by the renowned Las Vegas casino architect, Tony Marnell, who had gained stature after his work at The Bellagio. Jerry Carroll, the developer of Belterra, assured me that the guest rooms were on a par with any on the Las Vegas Strip.

Belterra was almost an hour's drive from Cincinnati, and I had never been there. The casino sat among cornfields near a town called Moscow, but its own site went by three different names, and I am still not sure of the correct mailing address. Belterra was the only one of the three southwest Indiana casinos with a Vegas-style showroom, so I decided to make my first visit when Lee Greenwood was performing there. I knew Lee would appreciate my coming to his show, and we could have breakfast together the next morning.

Lee and I had met at The Waterfront about fifteen years ago, as he told Robert, when Lee was playing in Cincinnati. "Jeff and I both got up to sing; he did a Righteous Brothers song. I liked him right away, and we've been friends since. I have great respect for what he's done with his restaurants, putting his touch on each place. They are kind of New York and kind of West Coast, and they have the flavor of familiarity as well as excellent food.

"He's quite honest, and sometimes that rubs people the

wrong way, but he has a good heart. He can be a little bit intimidating and even abrasive, but he says and thinks the right stuff, in an honest manner."

I guess I wasn't intimidating or abrasive enough in my early dealings with Belterra Casino.

Kirk Hauser, the casino's director of player personnel, knew I was coming to check out Belterra, and he pulled out all the stops. He met me at the hotel entrance under a huge porte-cochere the minute I drove up, and he greeted me like I was important. We all like that. Kirk then took me through the kitchen, like the scene in *Goodfellas*, and up in an elevator to the second-floor VIP room that faces center stage. The room has a bar and buffet, and the seats are cushioned and oversized. I was the only VIP present to whom Kirk offered the privilege of ordering off the steakhouse menu instead of going to the buffet.

Pinnacle Entertainment, Belterra's parent company, wanted a Jeff Ruby's Steakhouse at the casino, to attract a more affluent demographic. They felt that the other two local gaming operations, the Argosy and the Crown Victoria, got the "riff-raff." Neither of those casinos had a three hundred-room hotel tower or a Tom Fazio-designed golf course, as Belterra did. But Pinnacle wanted a further draw to attract what casinos call "whales," those gamblers who bet more per hand and stay longer than mere "high rollers"—a better class of losers. Jeff Ruby was the answer.

Negotiations began and went on for months, between me and Alain Uboldi, the casino's president and general manager. I had great trepidation about the demographic. It didn't seem to be a cultural fit for our kind of restaurant. Every time I went there, I didn't see anyone I could envision at one of our steakhouses. My attorney, Mark Jahnke, was very apprehensive and advised me to decline any offer from Pinnacle. I had never questioned Mark's business acumen or second-guessed his advice.

Yet I finally decided, second thoughts notwithstanding, to "roll the dice" at Belterra. Alain and I agreed on terms at a table in his existing steakhouse. Just to make sure that he, like me, hadn't suffered a head injury and didn't have a short-term memory problem, I put everything in writing and mailed our agreed-upon terms to him the following day. I never heard back from him or from anyone at Pinnacle Entertainment.

Months later, through the grapevine, I heard that Belterra had provided one too many benefits for their whales. The casino had flown in some "mermaids" from Vegas or someplace to entertain the whales in Belterra's plush fifteenth-floor suites. The Indiana Gaming Commission got wind of the caper and imposed a $2.5 million penalty on Belterra. Pinnacle fired its CEO, and Jeff Ruby's Steakhouse was the last thing on their minds.

A year later, Kirk Hauser called me to ask if I would open a Jeff Ruby's at Belterra. A group of Pinnacle executives had recently eaten at our Carlo & Johnny restaurant just north of Cincinnati and were impressed with our operation. I reminded Kirk about how unsatisfactory the previous negotiations had been. I told him I wasn't interested in going through that again. Kirk is a straight-up guy, and he assured me it would be different this time. I told him I would think about it.

My strategy is never to be the pursuer on any deal. If a developer, landlord or gaming company wants me, they will call. If they've never heard of me, I'm out of luck. But if they pursue me, I start with leverage. Every one of our deals has been the result of someone coming to us. They ask me to the prom, and they pay for everything— even my tuxedo. I waited for Pinnacle to call. I had been upset over how they wasted my time and money the last time. Now, if they didn't call, I wouldn't lose any sleep.

When they did call, we began the process all over again–and they began their bullshit all over again. Tedd Friedman, my attorney, says that the most difficult people to deal with in a contract signing are homeowners and gaming companies. For six months with Pinnacle, it was all double-talk and "forgetting" what we had agreed upon. I call it "chasing Casper the Ghost."

My usual style of dealing is to start at the top and work down, at a company, bank, city, or state. Since I wasn't getting anywhere by starting in the middle in Indiana, I flew to Las Vegas to see Pinnacle's chairman and CEO, Dan Lee. I was going to Vegas anyway to see Wayne Newton at the Flamingo, and to book him to open the ill-fated Coconut Grove. Wayne had been at The Waterfront once and got on-stage to sing with my house band after hours. Instead of busting us for late-night noise, the cops asked for his autograph. Wayne even sent me roses the next day.

Dan Lee and I met in his boardroom, with four others in the room, including his attorney and his chief financial officer. On his speakerphone, Dan connected to six other people in six different states. In twenty minutes, the deal was done.

Dan, like me, was a Cornell Hotel School graduate and had been Steve Wynn's chief financial officer. Dan's own CFO suggested that I be required to meet final projections that would be tied to my compensation. Dan rejected that advice. A sharp businessman knows how far to go when someone he respects is on the other side. The results at Belterra exceeded both of our expectations, but Dan had known, better than I, what my restaurant would do for his casino.

Casinos have unique nuances and idiosyncrasies that make

running a restaurant in them quite different from running any other restaurant. They also have unusual casts of characters working for them—some with names out of Hollywood.

Dan and I had been negotiating the renewal of our lease, which was due to expire in six months, when I got a disturbing phone call from our vice-president of operations. He told me that the casino's new food and beverage director, Johnny Flamingo, had just informed Belterra employees that Pinnacle was taking over Jeff Ruby's at the end of our lease.

Meanwhile, the Argosy casino was doing a $350 million makeover called "Hollywood." Its new general manager was a Jersey guy who spent damn near every night at Jeff Ruby's and had become a friend of mine. His name? Tony Rodio (pronounced "rodeo"). Tony, of course, is Italian, and I'm a Jew. That was the actual situation in the movie *Casino,* and now in real life.

Tony wanted me to do a restaurant at his "new" casino. He told the president of Penn National, Argosy's parent company, that Jeff Ruby was the Steven Starr of Cincinnati. I accepted that "accolade," but I refused to look at Tony's project each of the five times he offered it to me.

I have always said, "Never confuse friendship with business," I did feel a certain loyalty to the Belterra player representative who had replaced Kirk when he was transferred. The new player rep's name was Joe Cinderella (you can't make this stuff up), and he and I had a close relationship. Whenever things got hairy at Belterra, Joe always leveled with me.

When I got the unwelcome news that the casino was supposedly taking over my steakhouse, I was sitting in a town car pulling into LaGuardia Airport. I was so upset I asked Viktor, my driver, to

305

pull over. I didn't care if I missed my plane. I immediately called my friend Joe Cinderella. All of a sudden, he came down with lockjaw.

Let me get this straight, I thought to myself. The new guy from Vegas, Johnny Flamingo, wants me out. His competitor, from Jersey, Tony "Rodeo," wants me in. And Joe Cinderella, my supposed friend, claims to know nothin.' This sounded like a sequel to *Casino*.

I called Dan Lee from the car, and he made the problem go away. He also made Johnny Flamingo go away. Who needs a reality show when this kind of stuff is my reality?

CHAPTER THIRTY-ONE

BEAT IT

Michael Jackson, 1983

On June 13, 1994, former pro football star O.J. Simpson murdered his wife, Nicole Brown Simpson, and her friend Ron Goldman, who was at Nicole's condo to return her mother's glasses. After a televised trial lasting 266 days, a Los Angeles criminal court jury found him not guilty on October 3, 1995. In his subsequent 1997 civil trial, a jury determined that he was responsible for both murders. Simpson was ordered to pay the victims' families $33,500,000. He completely ignored the order. He never paid a dime. Instead of paying the fine, O.J. signed autographs, posed for photos, and even received an $850,000 advance for his book, *If I Did It*, in which he supposedly described how he would have done the murders, if he had done them. Nearly all copies of the book were quickly withdrawn from sale.

The sad reality is that many of us will lose a loved one long before they should have been taken from us. A parent suffers no more painful a loss than when his or her child is murdered. Janet Thall, Rickelle's mother, got the telephone call that every parent dreads. Janet lived with us the entire twenty-two years Rickelle and I were married. She was the nanny to our three children, her grandchildren. We were there when the call came.

Deron Thall, Rickelle's younger brother, had been shot and was in an emergency room about thirty miles away. Deron wasn't just my brother-in-law; he looked to me as a dad. He was a good kid who came from a broken home and needed direction. I tried to provide that direction for him, and he loved me. In the wee hours, I drove Janet, Rickelle and her sister, Terri, to the hospital. For hours we prayed, sat, cried, and walked the hallway. Night had turned into day when the doctor came out of the operating room to tell us that they had been unable to save Deron. He was murdered on his twenty-seventh birthday.

I wanted justice for Deron, just as Fred Goldman had wanted it for his son, Ron. I knew the intended victim was Deron's best friend, who was in the car when the shots were fired. I also knew that he knew who had killed Deron. The friend, however, denied knowing who killed his best friend. Before the funeral, I took him outside and privately "encouraged" him to tell me who had murdered Deron. I knew he was scared that it might cost him his life, but I made him an offer he couldn't "confuse." As I gave the eulogy in front of more than one hundred mourners, I used the opportunity to urge him to help Deron's family make sure that the killer didn't get away with murder. I told him that, if that were to happen, it would make their suffering much worse than it already was. I said all of this during my eulogy. Deron's friend bravely did the right thing. The next week, Deron's killer was arrested.

I sat in that Hamilton, Ohio, courtroom every day of Deron's murderer's trial. I listened to his attorney do what some of these won-derful people make millions doing: helping their clients get away with murder. These lawyers, liars for hire, essentially drive the "get-away car." This one put Deron, who now couldn't defend himself, on trial. He claimed his client was aiming at the street, and it was all an accident. (But Deron was sitting in a car when this killer stood outside and fired bullets at him.) The killer was found guilty and sent to prison, but he was paroled after eight years. Deron's life had been valued at eight years.

The image of Fred Goldman's reaction when O.J. Simpson's "not guilty" verdict was read will never leave me. I had an emotional allegiance to him throughout the many agonizing years he endured not only the murder of his son, but the torment the murderer was seemingly set on creating for the families of the victims. I admired the astonishing strength Fred Goldman maintained through those years, even though I would have handled it differently.

As a parent, I could relate to both the Brown and Goldman families. My sons were waiters, just as Ron was. My daughter is married to a former NFL player, just as Nicole was. The murdered Deron and Ron were only weeks apart in age at the times of their killings.

I had known and liked O.J. Simpson. Whenever he came to Cincinnati, he visited one of my restaurants. He was congenial. We sat and had drinks together and took photos together for the restaurants' walls. Most of our wall photos are head shots, or from the waist up, but one shot of O.J. came all the way down just short of his shoes. To this day, it bothers me that the photo didn't capture "them ugly-ass Bruno Maglis," as O.J. called the shoes he claimed he had never worn. Had such a photo been found before the criminal trial, would he have been found guilty? (A picture showing him wearing the Bruno Maglis did turn up before the civil trial.)

Simpson was so nice to me when I made him leave our Louisville restaurant (after the trial) that I almost changed my mind. I even considered shaking his hand when he left.

But I had removed O.J.'s memory from our restaurants' walls after the murders, and I dedicated our new tapas restaurant, Bootsy's, to Ron Goldman's memory. Ron's ambition had been to one day open his own tapas restaurant. Now he had one.

Simpson had patronized one of our places after his two trials, our club at The Waterfront in Covington, Kentucky, when he was on his rap concert tour. That O.J. sighting, however, was before he decided to become a novelist. When that happened, I wrote an editorial to the *Cincinnati Enquirer* hoping that, "Barnes would be Noble enough to keep the book off of their shelves." How could this man be so cold-hearted as to further torture those parents by keeping the story in the headlines and making money off his crimes?

Most murderers find Jesus while they are in prison. For some reason, Jesus likes to visit prisons. Some even start their own churches when they get out. After murdering Nicole, O.J. became a born-again woman-beater, and no one stopped him, not even the woman he was beating. I guess O.J. didn't find Jesus, because he didn't go to prison, not then, anyway. After his not-guilty verdict, he said he was going to spend his time looking for the "real killer." He wasn't looking in the right place for the real killer. He saw the real killer every time he shaved.

O.J. Simpson virtually decapitated the mother of his children and murdered an innocent young man who was just doing what we train our employees to do: "Return the guest's glasses or brief-case yourself if at all possible." O.J. committed the murders, the late Johnny Cochran "drove the getaway car," and District Attorney Gil Garcetti lost the trial before it even started. The trial should never have been held in Los Angeles. *The American Film Institute Desk Reference* wrote, "The O.J. Simpson trial competes with the Oscar ceremonies for media attention." Garcetti wanted that attention. The jury not only saw no evil, heard no evil, and spoke no evil of O.J. Simpson, they smiled at him in the courtroom.

There was more circumstantial evidence to prove guilt in this case than the prosecutors had ever before presented to a jury in a murder trial. O.J.'s blood was found at the crime scene, and the victims' blood was found in O.J.'s Bronco. Those facts, plus the cut on O.J.'s hand, and the mountain of evidence proved beyond any reasonable person's doubt that O.J. Simpson committed those mur-ders. But Cochran was also a fan of the O'Jays, and their hit single

"992 Arguments" was probably the goal he set to attack the state's evidence. He might have exceeded the goal. He clearly disregarded the group's first song to reach number one: "Back Stabbers."

We opened the Jeff Ruby Steakhouse in Louisville in June of 2006. This was our first Kentucky Derby weekend. Jason Johnson, our general manager, had the restaurant sold out six months in advance. We had to turn away the NBC crew, including my friends Bob Costas and Mike Battaglia. Mike is an old friend of mine, and Bob always comes to one of our restaurants when he's in town. Even my pal Kirk Herbstreit wasn't able to get a table with his ESPN guys when they showed up without a reservation. We had a Prince (of Monaco); a Queen (Latifah); a Kid (Rock); a Junior (Soprano); a Dr.(J); a Star (Jones); a GoodFella (Joe Pesci); a producer (Jerry Bruckheimer). We even got a "Kiss" from Gene Simmons. We also had a lot of "normal" people in the restaurant.

I decided to go to the restaurant on Friday night because I knew that Nick Lachey had reservations, and there were a few things I needed to discuss with him. Nick had a table in the Churchill Room, in the rear of the restaurant. There were ten people in his party. I talked to him for a few minutes, made my rounds to most of the tables, and looked for a place to rest my weary legs. The lounge was packed elbow to elbow. The only place to sit was on the stage.

I walked up the steps, onto the right end of the stage, and sat and watched everything from that vantage point. Asked if I would like a drink, I hesitated and then ordered one. Maybe, I thought, *I'll sing with the band*. I occasionally do. I pulled out a cigar and began the lighting process. It was time to relax a bit. The dinner seatings were almost finished. Everyone was having a great time. The bar was packed. People were dancing everywhere. My favorite part of the restaurant business is watching people having fun at my place. That makes me happy.

I'd had five minutes of rest when someone came up to me all giddy and shouting, "O.J.'s here." The guy was so excited that I assumed everyone else was going to be as excited to see O.J. Simpson as he was. O.J. became an even bigger celebrity after he became a double murderer. It would be good for business, I knew: photos, autographs, guests telling their friends they saw O.J. at Jeff Ruby's. I had made up my mind, however, when he wrote the book, that he would never again be allowed at one of our restaurants or nightclubs. I would have to ask him to leave.

Every time I have to make an emotional decision, I take a vote among my brain, my gut, and my heart. Two of the three have to be in agreement before I act. My heart said, 'Do it." My brain never could make up its mind, so it came down to my gut. I looked at my cigar, Arturo Fuente, and my drink, Jack Daniel's, to see if they wanted to vote on this thing. They did, and they both voted yes.

Our restaurant was jam-packed, and as the hottest place in Louisville, we had a star-studded cast of celebrities on Derby week-end. O.J. has a huge ego and a mercurial temper. Kicking him out in front of so many people would be too much for his ego. I antici-pated a knee-jerk, combustible reaction, but I was willing to take my chances with him. If he said one f-word, I was going to throw the first punch. My foremost motivation was to serve O.J. some vigilante jus-tice for Fred Goldman. I took another sip of Jack and another puff of Arturo and just sat there for a minute. My brain was still undecided, but my gut made up its mind, and I jumped off the stage.

"Where's O.J. Simpson?" I asked people in the bar. Nobody knew. Finally a cocktail waitress told me he was in the Churchill Room. I didn't say a word to the two uniformed Louisville cops who were working for us that night. I simply walked right by them and headed to the Churchill Room hellbent on "getting it on" with O.J. Simpson.

O.J. was sitting at the head of the table, but he was all by himself, surrounded by twelve empty chairs. Our manager, Jason, had followed me. He later said he had watched my face as I walked through the restaurant and he could tell something was bothering me. Jason followed me into the Churchill Room.

I looked at O.J. from the other end of the long table and simply told him, "I'm not serving you." He looked dumbfounded and just sat there. Then, Jason told me, I swung my arm up like a baseball umpire does to signal "you're out." I then walked out of the room and waited for him outside the door.

O.J. came out of the room and walked over to me. He remembered me from The Precinct and The Waterfront. He said, "I understand. Is it all right if I get the rest of my group so they know that we have to leave?" I couldn't believe how agreeable he was. "Sure," I said.

O.J.'s girlfriend came up to us. She wasn't as understanding as he had been. The blonde was about half his age and looked like Nicole's twin. "This is a free country," she barked, "and O.J. is allowed to eat at a restaurant."

I said, "If I were you, being blonde and all, I would be less worried about this guy being allowed to eat at a restaurant and more worried about him being allowed to murder me too."

"He was found not guilty," she shouted back.

"He was," I agreed, "but he was found guilty in the civil trial. You wanna bet on the verdict if this thing winds up going best two out of three?"

Howard Stern and Jimmy Kimmel called me on Stern's radio show a week later and asked me, "Where did O.J. Simpson even find

"JEFF RUBY IS ON A ROLL....HE JUST REFUSED TO SERVE THE REDS' BULLPEN."

A cartoon by Jim Borgman that appeared in the Cincinnati Enquirer *shortly after O. J. Simpson visited Jeff Ruby's Steakhouse in Louisville*

twelve people who would want to have dinner with him?"

I said, "It was the jury."

After O.J. told me he had to find the rest of his party, I let him go look for them. It was very crowded, and I did not follow him. Later, as I began walking through the restaurant, people began to stand up and applaud. Before long, nearly everyone in the place was giving *someone* a standing ovation. I looked around to see if O.J. was still there. When I realized the applause was for me, I knew I had made the right decision.

A short time later, Michael Jordan, Charles Oakley, Ray Buchanan, and about thirty other black celebrities walked in. We put them in the Churchill Room. One young black kid was on crutches. "You'd better be careful," I said as I greeted him at the front door. "This place is packed, and it's going to be hard to get around on those crutches. What's your name?"

314

"Chris Paul," he answered. I told him that I knew his college coach. Later he handed me his cell phone. He had called his Wake Forest coach, Skip Prosser, to tell him he was at my restaurant. It was a very considerate gesture, both to me and to his former coach. It was also good to speak to Skip. He and I reminisced for a while. Not long after that conversation Skip died of a heart attack. He was just fifty-six years old. He had the respect of all who knew him.

O.J.'s table of thirteen, twelve of whom never were seated, was now replaced by Michael Jordan's table of thirty-two. Thirty-one of them were African-American. Michael, by the way, is always a gentleman.

Four days later, I received a call from my friend Dave Wagner, anchor for WLWT, Cincinnati's NBC affiliate. He had heard about "the O.J. thing" and wanted an interview. I was smoking a cigar at Straus Tobacconist in Cincinnati when Dave called, so I told him to meet me there. Jim Clark owns my favorite hangout, and I wanted his store to get a little local publicity. Deborah Haas from WCPO, our local ABC affiliate, also interviewed me. The next day, my O.J. eviction story made national television.

The first call I received after the story broke was from Fred Goldman. He told Robert, "I didn't know Jeff Ruby, and I had never eaten at any of his restaurants. But when I heard it on the news, I called him to thank him."

Mission accomplished.

I was out of the office when Fred called, but the minute I heard he had, it made my day, and I wanted to call him back immediately. I was supposed to be doing a live interview with John Gibson for Fox television at the time. Fox was renting studio space from WCET,

Cincinnati's public television station, for $2,500. I never made the live telecast because I was talking to Fred Goldman, which to me was more important than any personal publicity. Later, I did go on Gibson's live radio program to explain that, and to apologize for being a TV no-show.

It never crossed my mind that telling O.J. to leave would make news. When Bill Hemmer of Fox News called me, I asked, "Why is this news?" I've been kicking people out of my places for years. I kicked comedian Sam Kinison out of The Precinct back in the 1980s. I once banned the Cincinnati Bengals from The Waterfront, and two of my closest friends and partners in the restaurant were stars on the team—their all-pro quarterback Boomer Esiason and all-pro receiver Cris Collinsworth. Their teammates got into too many fights in our club.

Bill Hemmer and I go back to when he worked in Cincinnati as a reporter for the local news. He explained, "This is such a big story because you're the only one who's had the balls to kick O.J. Simpson out of a place of business."

I never gave any consideration to how the public would react. I hoped it wouldn't hurt our business, but I wanted justice for Fred Goldman, and I didn't want O.J. Simpson signing autographs and posing for pictures in my restaurant. Earlier that evening, on television, I had seen O.J. at The Oaks, the Friday afternoon Derby preview race at Churchill Downs. He literally walked the red carpet and was by far the most mobbed celebrity for autographs and photos.

Yale Galanter was O.J.'s attorney, and he went on the offensive. He threatened to sue me. The distinguished former federal prosecutor Wendy Murphy told *The Globe,* "Ruby should be honored, not sued. Forget putting Ruby's name on a lawsuit. His face should be on the cover of *Time* magazine's 'Man of the Year' issue." That never happened. But O.J.'s mug shot was on the cover of *Time* right after the acquittal verdict.

Galanter went on national television and claimed that my re-fusal to serve O.J. was racially motivated. Our manager in that room, John Wilson, is an African-American. We served African-Americans all evening long and every night at that restaurant, as we do at all of our restaurants. I also owned a restaurant with an African-American Rock 'N' Roll Hall of Famer. Bootsy Collins was my partner at Bootsy's. He is one of my best friends. Muhammad Ali and his wonderful wife, Lonnie, showed up at the Louisville restaurant for dinner shortly after the O.J. incident. He told Jason that he admired me for what I did. He then drew a mountain on one of our white linen napkins. He told Jason he would finish his artwork when he returned. It was Ali's way of illustrating to me that I have climbed the mountain of life, like he has, and that I was brave for what I did. He chose our restaurant to cater a fundraiser for his Ali Center at his home on Derby Day the following year. He asked me to be a speaker at the event. Don King has also had dinner at our place in Cincinnati and praised me for throwing O.J. out.

When Galanter realized that the race card was a "Joker," he changed tactics and told the media that my kicking O.J. Simpson out was a publicity stunt. I told the media that being O.J. Simpson's lawyer was a publicity stunt. Nobody knew who the hell Yale Galanter was before O.J. became his client. That's when he began showing his face on every TV show he could. He was on the *Nancy Grace Show* almost daily. Nancy and I became friends. She lost her fiancé at the hands of a murderer and is a fierce crusader for the families of murder victims. She came to Cincinnati to speak at The Aronoff Center. When Nancy mentioned to the audience that I was in attendance with my daughter, eighteen hundred women stood up and applauded. I later explained to Nancy how easy it was for me to decide not to serve Simpson at my restaurant. "If a Los Angeles courthouse didn't have to serve O.J. Simpson justice, why should a Louisville steakhouse have to serve him dinner?"

George Maloof, owner of Palms Casino Resort in Las Vegas and the NBA's Sacramento Kings, went on television to announce that he was "taking a page out of Jeff Ruby's book," and banning O.J. Simpson from his hotel and casino. Other casinos followed his lead. (This was before the armed robbery for which Simpson was finally convicted.) The next time I was in Las Vegas, Maloof "comped" me a penthouse suite. O.J. Simpson made me famous.

My telephone rang for days after the incident. Boomer called to ask if he was still banned from The Waterfront. I received a call from someone who said he was the president of the Ohio chapter of the National Association of Serial Killers (NASK). He didn't think it was fair that I wouldn't serve O.J. It turned out to be a joke call from George Pintea, an old friend I hadn't heard from in years.

Our office also received a not-so-funny, threatening call from the Oakland chapter of the Black Panthers, and they were serious.

The entire O.J. Simpson "Dream Team" has been to our restaurants at one time or another since the trial. Maybe it was their way of showing support and feeling "guilty" about "not guilty." The late Johnny Cochran dined at Jeff Ruby's when he was in Cincinnati for a book signing. Robert ("Legal Zoom") Shapiro has been to The Precinct. F. Lee Bailey came to our places both before and after the trial. Barry Scheck came to Jeff Ruby's in Cincinnati. I knew in advance when they were coming, so I stayed away from the restaurants to keep from getting myself in trouble. But, I *thought* about throwing them out, too.

CHAPTER THIRTY-TWO

JOLIET BOUND

Eric Clapton & Wynton Marsalis, 2011

This song, written by an obscure artist named Kansas Joe McCoy, relates to a guy who is about to be arrested in Joliet, Illinois. I headed for Joliet with the best of intentions. Little did I know that I, too, would be arrested in Joliet. The detective who arrested me had the first name of Jeff. The cop who fingerprinted me had the last name of Outlaw.

If ever innocent victims of crime needed an advocate it was in Joliet, Illinois, during the summer of 2012. What made the trial of Drew Peterson for the murder of his third wife, Kathleen Savio Peterson, so far-reaching was the incriminating involvement of two police departments, and that Peterson was a police sergeant who actually got away with *two* murders. Those murders of two women, both married to the same diabolical, wife-beating husband, would not have occurred if those who were trusted and paid to protect those women had done their jobs.

Peterson was a cop in the town of Bolingbrook, Illinois, and he was friendly with the city's mayor. An assistant state attorney–a female, by the way–ignored a written plea for help from the victim, who warned that her husband was going to kill her. Had the police and the district attorney done their jobs, four children would still have their mothers.

Peterson had silenced two women by using corruption and power. As the title of the television movie about the case suggested, he was *Untouchable.* I would have called that movie *Silence of the Corrupt.*

I have often been an advocate for people who have been let down by the justice system, poor people for the most part. What energized me to involve myself in this particular matter was witnessing the most unimaginably bad behavior ever conducted by defense attorneys in a press conference at a murder trial. The deaths of two women had become fodder for a stand-up comedy routine for a trio of Chicago defense attorneys in sunglasses. Those lawyers followed the comical pattern of their client, Drew Peterson, who had been clowning in front of the cameras for the five years since the murder of his third wife, Kathleen. He apparently found her death and the sudden disappearance of his fourth wife hilarious.

After watching that disgraceful press conference on television, and knowing that the victims' loved ones had witnessed that heartless mockery, I decided to express my opinion on behalf of the families, by placing ads in eighteen newspapers in and around Chicago. That decision galvanized supporters of justice in the Greater Chicago community. A couple from Chicago (the Smiths) even drove to The Precinct for dinner, just to show their gratitude and hoping to meet me, which they did. Mary Parks, a friend of Kathleen's, called to thank me after she read a story in the *Chicago Sun-Times*, which had interviewed me about the ad. Mary, who was later a key witness in the trial, also alerted me to the disdain that the judge in the case had for the Illinois state attorney, James Glasgow, who would be prosecuting Peterson.

From Joliet, WJOL radio's Kevin Collins interviewed me over the phone for fifteen minutes. That interview attracted even more support for what I was doing. Chicago's WGN-TV and WGN radio jumped on the story, as did some internet shows that were heard around the world. With help from me, sympathy began to switch to the victim.

Drew Peterson preyed on good-looking young girls from low-income families who were vulnerable, impressionable, starry-eyed and needed a father figure. He was forty-seven and his fourth wife, Stacy, was just sixteen when they began their "love affair." Money can buy sex but it can't buy love. When the girls realized just whom they had married, they stopped loving him. And when you stopped loving Drew Peterson you stopped living. Yet Peterson was truly "Untouchable." Every internal felony indictment against him, including bribery and alleged drug and cash thefts while working undercover, was dropped. He was also involved with a loan shark who was convicted of murdering a cop. Peterson's gorgeous second wife's brakes mysteriously did not work one rainy night, and her car rolled to the bottom of a hill. When she came out of her coma ten days later, she was no longer gorgeous. The murder of his third wife and the inexplicable disappearance of his fourth wife, Stacy, were swept under the filthy rug at the Illinois State Police Department. This was Greater Chicago, the birthplace of police corruption and, just for good measure, the defendant brought in Chicago's preeminent Mafia attorney.

Like many spouse-murderers in America, Peterson had become a celebrity. He had appeared on *Larry King Live* and *The Today Show*, and had even been offered a role in a movie. Joe Hosey wrote a book about the case, *Fatal Vows*. The TV movie, *Untouchable*, in which Rob Lowe played Peterson, was based on Hosey's book.

Peterson's trial was big news nationwide. Curiously, despite the fact that the man on trial was a classic example of a perpetrator of domestic violence, not one women's group used that national stage to support the victims and to raise awareness of this issue. NOW (National Organization for Women) did not attend, nor did the victims of the advocacy group, the National Coalition Against Domestic Violence. Also absent were the Domestic Violence Support Group from Illinois, the Battered Women's Network, and Parents of Murdered Children.

Attorney Jeff Gold, who was covering the trial for CNN's *In Session* and for Fox News, thought it was extraordinary that a restaurateur from Cincinnati, who didn't know anyone involved, became the only advocate to speak up publicly for the victims.

CNN's Beth Karas told me that in her entire legal and court television career, Drew Peterson was the most corrupt cop she had ever seen. She said she couldn't say that on the air, so I made sure I said it for her. Hoda Kotb, a reporter for NBC's *Dateline*, called Peterson "one of the most flamboyant criminals of the past decade." Illinois State Attorney James Glasgow, who was prosecuting Peterson, said he was "a thug who would threaten people because he had a gun and a badge, and no one ever took him on. He's a psychopath. He feels nothing. He can do whatever he wants and not feel any remorse, shame or compassion. That's an extremely dangerous person."

This trial was not televised. It soon became clear to me why: the judge did not want America to get an inside look at Joliet justice. By the time the case was brought to trial, Stephen White, the original judge, had retired. It was then assigned to a judge who had previously run for state attorney and been defeated by Jim Glasgow, the man now responsible for prosecuting Peterson on behalf of the State of Illinois. The two men despised each other. The judge, inexplicably, did not recuse himself.

"He's hated me for thirty years," Jim Glasgow told Robert. "Twice he tried to get me fired. He was so vindictive in the trial that he cut my evidence to the bone. It was unique in the annals of jurisprudence. When Jeff came to Joliet, he provided a nice counter-balance."

I later learned about Peterson attorney Joel Brodsky's reputation for questionable ethics, and Peterson's crimes as a cop. At a blackjack table in Harrah's casino, after I arrived in Joliet, I sat down at a high-limit table, where a former Will County state attorney was the only other player. The old-timer didn't know who I was, or what I was up to. I used the blackjack game as an undercover way to gain valuable information. I was winning and learning simultaneously. As long as I kept winning, I kept learning. The former state attorney told me that when Peterson worked undercover on drug busts he typically stole the drug money. He was charged, but never prosecuted. He became a millionaire on a $42,000 yearly salary.

Jeanine Pirro saw my first ad slamming Peterson's attorneys and asked me to be on her Fox News show. Pirro opened the program with an unflattering commentary about the judge, followed by an interview with two of the defense attorneys. I got to follow that segment, and Pirro couldn't have been more supportive. I asked her a question that was scheduled to be run as an ad, three days later, in twenty Chicago-area newspapers: "Has a *judge* ever been charged with obstruction of justice?" The former Westchester County judge chuckled.

The good news was that the judge was so transparent that anybody who was paying attention could see right through him. When the state had evidentiary or incriminating evidence, he seldom let it in, or allowed their witness to testify. Peterson's record of beating the hell out of his wife was deemed not relevant. It was like watching a referee favor one team to win by penalizing only the other team. This was not a murder trial at all, in my opinion; it was a political trial. Prosecutor Jim Glasgow was up for re-election two months after the verdict would be reached, and the judge wanted Glasgow, his former political opponent, to lose the case and lose the election. Everyone in Will County, including the judge, knew that Glasgow would be defeated if Peterson were to be found not guilty.

Glasgow was in for a helluva fight against the ex-cop's eight attorneys, and I wanted to help him win that fight by going to Joliet. Glasgow's team was already getting the shit kicked out of it, and the defense hadn't even argued *their* case yet. Nobody gave Jim Glasgow and his colleagues much of a chance, even though everyone was certain that Peterson was guilty. It would be O.J. Simpson and Casey Anthony all over again. Justice would not be served to the loved ones of the women who were murdered. If this monster Peterson walked, I thought, we might as well legalize murder.

My three kids, my friends and my wisest advisor and attorney, Tedd Friedman, insisted that this was one mission I must pass on. They were all convinced that I was risking my life. After my appearance on Pirro's national broadcast, I received two life-threatening calls on our corporate office's voicemail. My detractors were convinced that I was merely seeking publicity. Almost nobody else had any idea why the hell I wanted to go to the trial in Joliet.

One exception was Joe Deters, our Hamilton County Prosecutor since 1992. He told Robert, "I've known Jeff since then, when I was first elected. He gets just fascinated by crime stories. He played an important part in our prosecuting the Marcus Feisel case. A four-year-old foster child was murdered by his foster parents, who had staged a fake kidnapping. Jeff publicly offered a ten thousand dollar reward to find the kid, before we knew he was dead. Jeff had a lot to do with putting the heat on the foster parents and getting a conviction.

"I got a kick out of his being ass-deep in the Peterson stuff. Why did he need to be involved? Peterson was such a piece of shit. That was the attraction for Jeff. He believes in justice; it's in his DNA. It's not an act. It's not a hobby. He locks on like a pit bull when he gets a cause; that's just Jeff. He should have been a prosecuting attorney."

Brian Welage, my "Vice President of Transportation," who also "packs heat," was willing to drive me to Joliet in the bus. My 6 foot 2 inch, then-twenty-one-year-old surrogate son, Nick Urlage, would do anything for me, so he came along for the ride.

Someone had to show support for the forgotten families. Sue Doman, the victim Kathleen's sister, told Robert. "Even before Jeff came to Joliet, he reached out to me. He got my phone number somehow, and called to tell me how sorry he was, and not to worry. I had no idea who he was, but it was comforting. He said he would get us a place to stay overnight in Joliet, since we live 110 miles away. That ended up being a suite at Harrah's casino, where Jeff was staying. My husband and I were in financial difficulties as a result of all the motions we had filed in the case. And of course it was a difficult time emotionally. We were really vulnerable. When Jeff arrived in Joliet and we met, I felt surrounded by angels. His being there got us through."

Peterson had an army of Chicago attorneys to support him— and a judge to boot. The Chicago Mafia attorney on the defense team was known as Joe "The Shark." With The Shark circling the water looking for blood, I figured the families needed a lifeguard from the Jersey Shore. The deck was not only stacked against the victims, it was stacked against justice. A murderer had a judge ruling in his favor, and the majority of the *In Session* legal analysts agreed with him. Only Vinnie Politan seemed to be as annoyed as I was.

Although most of the good people of Will County believed that Peterson was guilty, the vast majority, including a city councilman, believed he would be acquitted. I spoke to jurors from another trial in that courtroom and they agreed that the Peterson jury would vote to acquit. I told everyone this wasn't Will County. It was "Won't County." If the judge *won't* let incriminating evidence in, and *won't* let key witnesses testify, a double-murderer won't be found guilty. There was no forensic evidence, no eye-witness, no confession, or proof that he was even at the crime scene. He had a powerful defense team and world-renowned forensic experts. And just to assure "reasonable doubt," the original autopsy declared Kathleen's death an accidental drowning. It was clear that this judge was determined to make it very difficult for the state attorney to secure a guilty verdict. Would this judge rather see a defendant get away with murder than see his political opponent, Jim Glasgow, get re-elected? Yes.

The state attorney Glasgow was the only "class act" in the courtroom, and I wanted to meet him just so I could tell him that. But I never expected to get inside the courtroom.

Another reason I went to Joliet was to discuss my interest in posting a reward for finding the body of Stacy Peterson, the fourth wife, who had been missing for five years. Stacy's disappearance was a murder, and I believed the reward would remind everyone of that. After all, Peterson's lawyers not only joked about her absence, they "cleverly" put her on their witness list. I believed that offering the reward during the murder trial might help both families see that their daughters received justice. I didn't want to offer the reward without the proper approval. But, with the exception of Jim Glasgow, no one would listen to me.

When I finally was able to talk to the lead detective for the Illinois State Police (ISP), he had no interest in the idea of my offering a reward for finding Stacy Peterson's body. He all but tried to talk me out of it. Of course, had the ISP investigated the cop's third wife's "drowning death," the cop's fourth wife would still be alive. The ISP wasn't ever going to find Stacy. They couldn't find fish in Lake Michigan. That's why I put up the reward in the first place. With Peterson behind bars and no longer a threat, and with $100,000 to pocket, amnesia is curable. Someone might fall out of a tree, hit his head on the ground, and suddenly regain his memory.

The naysayers, as expected, said I posted the reward for my own publicity. If I cared what people said, I never would have opened my first restaurant. I'd rather lose some of my business by taking a stand than lose all respect for myself by not taking one.

Tedd Friedman, who had opposed my going to Joliet, told Robert after the trial, "While there was a publicity element to his involvement, and his new Twitter profile was elevated, that was not his underlying motivation. Jeff really feels for the underdog because he *was* the underdog. It's the defining characteristic of his life and why he feels so deeply."

This wasn't the first time I had gotten involved in a legal matter on someone else's behalf. I feel bad for people when they go through a tragedy–whether I know them or not. But when they're "double victimized" because they're underprivileged, poor, or a minority, and the defendant is a celebrity, wealthy, powerful, or has high-powered attorneys, it really upsets me. I've had a penchant for the underdog ever since I was a kid. I was the only Jew in every elementary or high school I ever attended, and I've been a "street fighter" all my life. As Clarence Darrow said, "Lost causes are the only ones worth fighting for."

When Jim Glasgow heard that I was in the courthouse, he sent his deputy chief, Ken Grey, to pull me out of a room where I was listening to the trial. I thought I was in trouble and about to be told to leave the courthouse. (That would come later.) To my surprise, Mr. Grey informed me that Glasgow wanted to meet me so that he could thank me for my support. Grey said Glasgow admired me.

"He's *my* hero," I said. "One of the reasons I came here was to shake his hand."

During my initial conversation with Glasgow, he asked me if I had seen the movie *Ghost*. I asked him why the question.

"You have a ghost at Carlo & Johnny," he replied. Jim Glasgow, as it turned out, knew all about Jeff Ruby. From then on, I would be watching the trial in person.

On my first day in the courtroom, I sat next to Stacy's spokes-person, Pam Bosco. She was virtually the only voice for the victims, since Glasgow, unlike his adversaries, had taken the high road. He brought some gravitas to the proceedings. The humor and "schtick" was provided by Joel Brodsky of the defense team and by Peterson's bizarre behavior before and during the trial. Brodsky made a conscious decision to gain sympathy for Peterson by attracting media attention.

On my second day in the courtroom, I watched attorneys Joe Lopez and Steve Greenberg in action on cross-examination for the defense. Lopez and Greenberg are seasoned attorneys, and so were others on the team, but too many cooks can screw up the soup, and too many lawyers can screw up a defendant. They made more gaffes than Joe Biden at a campaign rally. From the day Brodsky first appeared on Nancy Grace's TV program as Peterson's attorney, I knew he was unqualified and unprofessional. Brodsky then fired Greenberg for a huge mistake that Brodsky himself had made. Greenberg in turn sued Brodsky. Peterson fired Brodsky and rehired Greenberg, then changed his mind, I guess.

Greenberg and Brodsky were suing each other, and Peterson was appealing on grounds of ineffective assistance of counsel.

I was still worried that Peterson, like O.J. Simpson, was going to get away with murder. That was the reason I put those ads in the papers. I wanted the public to know about the injustice going on in that courtroom, and I wanted the victims' families to feel better after seeing those ads. It was also the real reason I was arrested. It was the first time in history anyone had printed evidence in newspaper ads that a jury was prevented from hearing at a murder trial.

I also got to see up close just what Jim Glasgow was up against. The state's star witness had flown in from Germany, and before his witness chair was warm he was told to go back to Germany. The defense convinced the judge that he shouldn't testify after all. Scott Rosetto is a captain in the U.S. Air Force whose testimony would have corroborated Pastor Neil Schori's, and whose credibility would have been bolstered by his not ever having met the pastor.

Stacy had told Rosetto that on the night Kathleen was found dead Stacy woke up in the middle of the night, and her husband was no longer in bed with her. He was in the laundry room grabbing some other woman's clothing from a bag and putting it in the washing machine. He was wearing his black SWAT uniform, which was wet. She was certain that those weren't the "pajamas" he had gone to sleep in that night. Rosetto would also have told the jury that Peterson had told Stacy, "If you say 'this' it will be the perfect crime." "This" was what Drew told Stacy to tell police when they interviewed her about where he was that night. He spent hours working with her on his alibi. The ISP, as a "professional courtesy," gave Peterson the privilege of sitting next to his wife to make sure she didn't forget anything.

Wednesday, August 22, 2012, the day Pastor Neil Schori testified, was the turning point of the trial, and also the day I was told to leave the courtroom and never come back. What set me off was that the judge almost didn't let Stacy Peterson's pastor testify either. Schori was the other witness to whom Stacy had told everything that would be enough to convict Peterson. Now, however, the killer cop was being granted something called "marital privilege." I turned to Beth Karas and said, "It's nice to know there's legal protection called 'marital privilege' that gives someone the privilege to kill his wife. If this guy doesn't testify, it's 'game over.'"

The trial was in recess, so I left for the hallway. Jeanine Pirro and Beth assured me the pastor would indeed testify, but that not all of his testimony would be allowed in. That calmed me down, and I re-entered the courtroom, stood in the aisle and waited for the trial to reconvene. Peterson, who used the recess time to size up female court observers and to wink at blondes who caught his eye, while patting his heart, noticed me. I later learned that he knew who I was and the position I had taken in the trial. Peterson locked in on me and stared at me. If looks could kill, I would have been his third victim. The "stare-down" continued for several minutes. I was face-to-face with one of the two most evil human beings I had ever come into contact with. (O.J. was the other.) I couldn't throw Peterson out because this wasn't a steakhouse, it was a courthouse, so I mouthed, "Fuck you," instead. I repressed the impulse to walk over and punch him in the face.

Peterson became furious and bolted for Brodsky. I didn't think it was any big deal. He hadn't heard me say anything, because I hadn't. He just read my lips. I left the courtroom for the hallway, and after a while a Will County deputy came along and told me to leave the building. I complied. (A cartoonist's illustration depicted the cop physically removing me from inside the courtroom. It was inaccurate, but it looked cool.) I knew the judge would eventually find a way to keep me out, since he found a way to keep everything else out that the state wanted in.

When I got outside, the media wanted interviews. I was also asked to do a long segment on Vinnie Politan's show on CNN. I publicly admitted to what I had done, and I even apologized to the judge. I explained that while what I had done was wrong, I didn't know it was illegal. Court was not in session at the time, and neither the judge nor the jury was in the courtroom at the time.

During the lunch break, Steve Greenberg warned me I could

be in trouble. He gave me the name and number of a lawyer I should hire. A Chicago attorney who was a guest on *In Session* gave me her card, and she told me if I was charged with contempt of court she would represent me pro bono. I knew I was in trouble, not for what I allegedly had "said" *to* Drew Peterson, but for what I had actually said *about* the judge:

That very same day I ran half-page ads in twenty Chicago area newspapers, including *The Joliet Herald-News*. The judge saw them. They read:

"Has A Judge Ever Been Charged With Obstruction Of Justice?"

"America Is Watching!!!

…that justice is not being served for what happened to Ms. Savio in 2004.

…that a judge just might see to it that a prosecutor gets his pay-back for what happened to him in 1992.

…that Drew Peterson is winking at blondes in the courtroom.

Joliet Justice!"

Another ad I got a kick out of said simply, "The trial of Romeo in Joliet."

Over a midnight hot dog at Harrah's with Jeff Gold, he told me the magnitude of my incident with Peterson. It was, according to Gold, the first time anyone had ever confronted the bully. People who liked him talked to him, and people who didn't like him stayed away from him. No one ever said anything negative to Drew Peterson, let alone "fuck you." He was so upset, it flustered him for the remainder of the day, and he did not communicate as usual with his attorneys.

One of the ads that ran in Chicago and Joliet area newspapers

Instead, he kept looking back at where I had been sitting. Brodsky told Gold that I "got under his [Peterson's] skin."

The next night I was arrested, but not for what I had mouthed to Peterson. I was arrested for exercising my First Amendment rights and for being an advocate for Jim Glasgow. Jim reminded me that I had told the media, "This judge would rather see this defendant get away with murder than to see this prosecutor get re-elected."

Like the Blackhawk song goes,
"There I done it.
There I said it.
There you have it.
I don't regret it."

But I wasn't arrested until the next night. It took longer than the judge thought it would for my arrest to be executed. For the first time in his long career as state attorney, Jim Glasgow refused to sign an arrest warrant. Nor would any of the assistant state attorneys comply with the judge's order to have me arrested. The judge was forced to find a special prosecutor to execute the warrant.

On my arrest warrant were scribbled the words "trial participants included," to precede the printed words "shall have no contact with any member of the jury in the case of People vs. Drew Peterson." Tedd Friedman in Cincinnati had a copy of it before I had a chance to read it.

"It was absurd that Jeff got arrested," Jim Glasgow told Robert. "The judge should have had to show cause for contempt of court, and he couldn't."

Joe Lopez came over to talk to me outside the courthouse on lunch break. I told him, "I'm not talking to you, you ratted on me. You had me thrown out of court." He came back with, "I didn't beef you, Jeff." I was busting his chops in Spanish, and we were hugging each other. It was hilarious, and the cameras loved it. Joe actually wore a Jeff Ruby's Steakhouse hat in his interviews.

At a sandwich shop, where I finally found Ms. Bosco, who had been avoiding me about the reward, I learned that I might be rearrested for violating the warrant, by talking to Lopez. I needed to get out of Joliet–fast!

I briskly walked across the street to where our bus was parked, directly in front of the courthouse. I told Brian and Nick to run to the hotel, pack all of our clothes and hurry back to the bus—but without the luggage. When Nick and Brian returned, we drove the bus back to the hotel, where the bellman was waiting with our luggage. We sped off for the Indiana state line. Once we crossed it, they couldn't serve me with a warrant. We hadn't eaten yet, but we couldn't stop until we got to Indiana. The road to hell is paved with good intentions. Our road was heading for the first Kentucky Fried Chicken in Indiana. As my Twitter feed lit up with video of the Lopez-Ruby sidewalk jabber, I told Brian to "step on it." This judge was as fond of me as he was of Glasgow. Our forty-five-foot tour bus was now breaking the law, too, or at least its driver was, but we made it across the line. I never knew I liked Indiana so much, and I never tasted better chicken in my life.

* * * * *

Back in Cincinnati, I got a call from Greenberg, telling me that, according to the judge's people, the judge would drop the charges against me if I didn't run any more ads and stopped talking to the media. I made a call to my sources, who told me that my new pal Greenberg was lying. I was told, "You've got them scared to death. Keep doing what you're doing."

(Greenberg and I nonetheless stayed friends, and his teenage son, Ti, is a big fan. Ti is a student at the University of Indiana. In his Business Presentations class, the professor assigned a paper nominating candidates for a "Courageous Business Award." Ti interviewed me and wrote about me. His paper was declared the winner.)

In the meantime, I kept writing more ads. My daughter Britney intercepted them, and emailed them on to Tedd Friedman, making

334

the ads even more expensive. Getting his unsolicited advice costs money, whether you take it or not. Tedd's a terrific attorney, and he tries to protect me from a lunatic named Jeff Ruby. On his advice, I toned down a few of the ads, and I didn't place some of the others.

The Peterson case went to the jury the same week I was scheduled to be in New York City to meet with three top cable network executives interested in airing reality shows about me. The meetings could not be rescheduled, but I chose to be in Joliet for the verdict with Kathleen's and Stacy's families.

I returned to Joliet on the "Justice Bus" (at my own risk) for closing arguments and the verdict. That week in Joliet seemed like a month. We arrived Sunday, September 2, 2012, the day before closing arguments were to begin. The victims' families and friends spent time in my bus while the jury was deliberating; I realized just how much my involvement had meant to the families. They felt I was their "rock," and during deliberations they leaned on me for strength. They asked for my opinion when the jury asked to review evidence or had questions during deliberation.

Kathleen's brother Mike worried when a juror asked the judge for the definition of the word "unanimous." I said that in my experience jurors' questions weren't worth agonizing over.

"Don't read the tea leaves" I told Mike. "They surprise you every time."

"Thanks, Mr. Ruby. I feel better now," he responded to my somewhat truthful comments. Actually, I thought we might have a hung jury. By then I would have settled for anything except "not guilty."

On Thursday, September 6, 2012, I was in my bus wearing casual clothes and following the trial on my iPhone. The only problem with parking in front of the Will County courthouse was that we had no satellite signal. Brian kept me updated by staying beside *In Session's* field producer, Nancy Leung. Suddenly I saw Charles Pelkie of the state attorney's office running toward the "media center" yelling that the verdict was in.

For me, it was pretty emotional stuff. I ran back to the bedroom of my bus, and changed into a suit I had brought from my hotel room just for the verdict day. I knew I had thirty minutes to put on my most "Mafia suit," I had chosen it to rub it in to Mafia attorney Joe Lopez–after we won.

The bay of TV cameras was longer than the Sunday buffet at the Drake Hotel, and I was on the sidewalk behind them. Suddenly one of the media guys turned to me and said, "Guilty." I said, "Are you sure?" I kept asking every media guy there, "Are you sure?" They all said, "Yes, guilty." I had tears in my eyes and went into a celebration mode like I never had for anything that had happened to me before in my life. All the cameras and everyone outside were focused on me. I was hugging and kissing every woman in Joliet.

When Kathleen's family came outside, I finally got to hug them, and that was something I will never forget. I embraced her dad, stepmom, sisters and brothers, and listened to them give me too much credit for the verdict.

The only "Perry Mason" moment of the Drew Peterson trial came at his sentencing on February 21, 2013, and I was there for that, too. My Joliet attorney was Steve White, who had been the original judge in the case. Steve had negotiated an agreement whereby the charges against me would be dismissed, and I would be permitted in the courtroom for the sentencing if I "behaved" for 120 days, not only in Joliet, but anywhere in America. I had to stay out of trouble wherever I went. I asked for that clause to be limited to a 90-mile radius of

336

Joliet, but my request was denied. So I tried to stay home as much as I could.

Jim Glasgow and me celebrating with cigars after the Drew Peterson sentencing

I joined Kathleen's family in the courtroom. Peterson was sentenced to thirty-eight years in prison. As it turned out, I was the only one not thrown out of the courtroom that day. The "Perry Mason" moment came when Peterson chose to go to the witness chair to read a thirty-five-minute statement over a microphone. At the top of his lungs he screamed, "I did not kill Kathleen."

Kathleen's sister Susan Doman shouted back, "Yes, you did, liar." The judge had her tossed out.

Peterson then said he had paid for the funeral.

Sue's brother Henry said, "No, you didn't, I did." Henry also got a police escort out of his sister's killer's sentencing.

* * * * *

Had I listened to the death threats I received, the advice I was given, and the criticism leveled at me, wife-murderer Drew Peterson just might be a free man today. But I did in this case what I always do. I listened to the person who has to live with his decision—me. I know that person better than anyone else knows him. I was arrested in Joliet for exercising my First Amendment rights. I outdid myself. It was the fifth state I'd been arrested in, but this time it was a good thing. I will never forget my experience in Joliet, Illinois. It was "jail" time well spent.

Drew Peterson is now serving a life sentence, which means that my life is in danger. Illinois has no death penalty. He has nothing to lose by getting revenge on me. As prosecuting attorney Jim Glasgow said to me, "You had a great deal to do with this guilty verdict. What you did resonated everywhere." The other person who said the most meaningful thing was Kathleen Savio Peterson's sister, Sue Doman. She told Robert, "Jeff Ruby was sent by God. And I told him so every day I was with him. And I've thanked God for Jeff every day since."

CHAPTER THIRTY-THREE

NEW YORK, NEW YORK

Frank Sinatra, 1980

As we went to press, a friend of mine made me an offer to take over his restaurant space and turn it into a Jeff Ruby's Steakhouse. The property is on the West Side of New York, near Carnegie Hall. I might just be going home, after more than forty years. Why not? Every New Yorker who has dined at our places has told us there isn't a steakhouse in their city that can touch us. Boomer Esiason and Cris Collinsworth, who both work in New York, have been telling me that for years. New York Yankees All-Star pitcher C.C. Sabathia told *USA Today* that our Precinct was his favorite steakhouse in America.

The Peter Luger steakhouse in Brooklyn has been around for a hundred years, and it used to be good. You see it every so often on The Travel Channel. It ought to be featured on an episode of *Unsolved Mysteries*. There are a dozen better steakhouses in New York City, and everyone knows it. Actually, there are very few good ones in the Big Apple. Ours have higher Zagat ratings than every steakhouse in New York City.

As Frank Sinatra sang out in one of his signature songs, "If I can make it there, I'll make it anywhere. It's up to you, New York, New York."

CHAPTER THIRTY-FOUR

THE LAST SONG

Elton John, 1992

Since I chose to name the chapters of my life with titles of songs or albums, fittingly, this final chapter is called "The Last Song." For me, the emotional kicker is that the song is about a father's love for his son. As a son, that was something I could not relate to, but as a father I very much do. Bernie Taupin's somber lyrics painfully tell of a father who disowned his son when he learned he was gay, but who finally shows his love at his boy's bedside as the boy lies dying of AIDS:

> "I can't believe you love me, I never thought you'd come.
> I guess I misjudged love between a father and his son."

I had five "dads" in all and never attended one funeral.

Elton John ruled rock music for most of the 1970s, while I was working my way up the Holiday Inn ladder and grooving to Earth, Wind & Fire. I had just three goals in life. I wanted to fall in love with and marry a gorgeous girl, have a son, and own my own restaurant. That was it. That was all I needed and I would be happy.

It took me eleven years to get that restaurant, twelve to get that blonde bombshell, and thirteen to get my first son. We had our daughter Britney a few months after we got married, so I went to work immediately and we had Brandon one year later, in the same month—December.

Funny thing about this life of mine, I became better than I

340

wanted to be. And I could've been better sooner if only I had known it was possible for me. I constantly tell kids that the biggest mistake many of them make is that they underestimate themselves. "Don't be afraid to be what you want to be," I tell them.

Having three kids so quickly stunted the growth of my business, but it was more important for me to see them grow than it was to see my company grow. I wanted to be the dad I never had, coaching my boy's youth football team, attending every one of the boys' high school practices and games, going to Britney's games, meeting with their teachers and counselors, dealing with all the conferences and the confrontations. As a kid I was never called into the principal's office. I was forty-nine years old when I was called into my kid's high school principal's office.

"I'm not buying your story," he said, after I had replied to his questions and explained the situation.

"My story is not for sale," I said, and I walked out. I get angry when I tell the truth and the listener does not believe me. I don't lie to anyone. It's too damn much trouble. When you tell the truth it's over with. If you screwed up, you admit it and apologize. End of story!

I make no apologies for who I am, and I don't think most of us need to. Getting involved in Drew Peterson's murder trial in Joliet, Illinois, in 2012 was risky business, and none of my business. I did not have a dog in the fight. I didn't know anyone involved in the case of the murder of Peterson's third wife, Kathleen Peterson, or in the family of his fourth wife, Stacy, he was suspected of murdering and who is still missing. Yet, the two most productive weeks of my life were those I spent at a courthouse in Joliet, Illinois. I had a sense of purpose there. It was rewarded on September 7, 2012, when justice was served to two families, one of which wasn't even directly involved in the Peterson trial. They were two families I had never met, and had not even heard of before the trial. They were people of humble means who couldn't afford to "buy" justice.

As I reflect on my life–my moderate success and achievements–and put it all in perspective, I realize it was always what I did for someone else, rather than for me, that meant the most to me. None of these most satisfying events happened on a football field, on a wrestling mat, at a great university, by owning successful restaurants, at my Hall of Fame induction, or from The Precinct's being featured on the Food Network's "Chef Wanted." They happened because I helped other people.

ACKNOWLEDGEMENTS

We both want to thank, first of all and most of all, Ashley Wartman, Jeff's executive assistant, who has been with the project from the beginning. She transcribed and copy edited Jeff's longhand pages, and kept us both on track for a period of four years, not always an easy task. We also want to thank Cris Collinsworth for his spirited foreword, and Mariel Wood for her help on many aspects of the book. We especially want to thank Rick Dees and Hugh Dodson, who brought us together for this book project.

Jeff would also like to thank Jim Borgman, Joe Hosey, Nate Leopold, Joe Posnanski, Mike Meiners, Ross Van Pelt, Kroger, Joseph Beth Booksellers, the communities of Covington, Louisville, and Cincinnati.

Robert would like to express great appreciation to his interview subjects, who did so much to round out the Jeff Ruby life story: Dusty Baker, Jeep Bednarik, Johnny Bench, Brad Beletti, Susan Brown Gitlin, Mike Cowans, Tad Dowd, Neil Bortz, Marty Brennaman, Thom Brennaman, Marvin Butts, Bootsy Collins, Cris Collinsworth, Kerry Coombs, Joe Deters, Sue Doman, Boomer Esiason, Tedd Friedman, Gary Ginn, Jim Glasgow, Fred Goldman, Lee Greenwood, Bruce Hoffman, Doug Irvin, Erik Kamfjord, Kevin Kline, Danny Knepper, Wayne Kranz, Nick Lachey, Santo Laquatra, Buddy LaRosa, Tommy Lasorda, Bobby Mackey, Tom MacLeod, Jason Maneol, Don McNay, Russ Menkes, Dave Meyers, Randy Michaels, Joe Morgan, Anthony Munoz, Santa Ono, George Pintea, Phil Pitzer, Kevin Plank, Eddie Powers, Len Renary, Betty Sieburg Richter, John Rijos, Brant Rogers, Pete Rose, Marvin Rosenberg, Brandon Ruby, Britney Ruby Miller, Dillon Ruby, Rickelle Ruby, Ben Scotti, Bawe Shinholster, Dave Stevens, Chris

Sullivan, Greg Tabar, Joe Talamo,Travis Tritt, Griffin Urlage, Jake Urlage, Nick Urlage, Mary Anne Valente, Kelly Walker, Brian Welage, and Kate Wenderfer.